The Handbook of Play Therapy and Therapeutic Play

This completely revised and updated second edition provides a comprehensive introduction to using play to communicate with troubled or traumatized children and their families, and to heal emotional damage. The book gives examples of good practice in different settings and situations, including schools, hospitals, residential settings, families and foster carers. The book also includes a consideration of the support needs of workers and carers.

Drawing on psychodynamic, systemic and attachment theory, this book provides an integrated theory base for using play in therapeutic work with children. It emphasizes non-directive approaches to therapeutic play and play therapy, based on supporting the child's developing self within the safe boundaries provided by the setting and the worker's emotional holding and containment. Areas explored include:

- children with disabilities and illnesses
- daily living with abused and traumatized children
- helping troubled families
- difficulties in early years
- children experiencing separation, loss and bereavement
- children moving to new families.

The Handbook of Play Therapy and Therapeutic Play is an invaluable resource for all of those using play therapy with children and will appeal not only to play therapists but also to professionals working in the broader field of therapeutic play. It will be useful whether the readers are at the beginning of their training or are well-established and experienced practitioners and managers.

Linnet McMahon is a retired Lecturer in Social Work at the University of Reading, where she tutored and for some years led the MA in Therapeutic Child Care course. She was a play therapist and supervisor, and now provides training and consultancy in therapeutic work with children.

The Handbook of Play Therapy and Therapeutic Play

Second Edition

Linnet McMahon

LONDON AND NEW YORK

First published 1992
by Routledge
27 Church Road, Hove, East Sussex BN3 2FA

Reprinted 1993, 1995, 1997, 1999, 2000, 2002, 2003, 2005

This edition published 2009
by Routledge
27 Church Road, Hove, East Sussex BN3 2FA

Simultaneously published in the USA and Canada
by Routledge
270 Madison Ave, New York, NY 10016

*Routledge is an imprint of the Taylor & Francis Group, an Informa
business*

© 2009 Linnet McMahon

Typeset in Times by
RefineCatch Limited, Bungay, Suffolk
Printed and bound in Great Britain by
TJ International Ltd, Padstow, Cornwall
Paperback cover design by Aubergine Creative Design; paperback
cover illustration from family work by Roz Smithson

This publication has been produced with paper manufactured to
strict environmental standards and with pulp derived from
sustainable forests.

British Library Cataloguing in Publication Data
A catalogue record for this book is available from the British Library

Library of Congress Cataloging-in-Publication Data
McMahon, Linnet
   The handbook of play therapy and therapeutic play / Linnet
McMahon. – 2nd ed.
      p. ; cm.
   Rev. ed. of: Handbook of play therapy / Linnet McMahon. 1992.
Includes bibliographical references.
   1. Play therapy—Handbooks, manuals, etc. I. McMahon, Linnet.
Handbook of play therapy. II. Title.
   [DNLM: 1. Play therapy—methods. 2. Child. 3. Infant. WS 350.2
M1675h 2009]
RJ505.P6M37 2009
   618.92′891653—dc22
                              2008034283

ISBN: 978-0-415-43941-1 (hbk)
ISBN: 978-0-415-43942-8 (pbk)

For Kendra, Kate and Lily

Contents

Tables and figures

Tables

Figures

Acknowledgements

The second edition of this book owes much to my learning from colleagues and students on the MA in Therapeutic Child Care course at Reading University, particularly Adrian Ward, Teresa Howard, Deborah Best and Paul Cain. I greatly value my learning from Jenny Harrison and Monica Lanyado. I am grateful to the many people who contributed their experience of play in therapeutic work with children to the two editions of this book. I have named them in the text, either alongside their practice example or together at the ends of chapters. I have not been able to trace a number of people, including Julia Prosser and Elaine Howells, who provided material for the first edition which appears again here. I thank them all. I greatly appreciate the help of Steve Farnfield, Nina Rye, Susan Monson, Peta Hemmings, Clare Sheridan, Nicola Phillips, Kate Burke, John Diamond, John Rivers, Jenny Sanders and Jackie Whitelock in providing comments and suggestions on different chapters. I thank Virginia Ryan for her help and encouragement. Any mistakes and misperceptions are, of course, my own.

Permissions

I am most grateful to Pat Crittenden for permission to reproduce a modified version of her Dynamic Maturational Model of attachment. I thank the British Association of Play Therapists for permission to use parts of Nina Rye's articles 'A strange way to make a living' from their newsletter *Play Therapy* (2004, 39 and 2006, 46) and to reproduce parts of Deborah Hutton's article 'Storytelling and its application in on-directive play therapy' (2004, 1, 1: 5–15) and Nina Rye's article 'Filial therapy, parental separation, and school refusal: a case study using an attachment perspective' (2005, 1, 3: 10–17) in the *British Journal of Play Therapy*. Thanks to Barry Bowen for permission to use a modified version of his article 'Externalizing anger' from *Context* (1996, 26, 30–33).

I thank Jessica Kingsley Publishers for permission to reproduce in Chapter 4 Rosemary Lilley's case study from our book, Linnet McMahon and Adrian Ward (eds) (2001: 109–110) *Helping Families in Family Centres:*

Working at Therapeutic Practice. An earlier version of some of the material in Chapter 4 appeared in my article 'Therapeutic play for young children: helping children manage their feelings and behaviour', *Early Years* (1994, 14, 2: 30–33). An earlier version of some of the material in Chapter 9 appeared in my article 'Developing skills in therapeutic communication with emotionally disturbed children and young people', *Journal of Social Work Practice* (1995, 9, 2: 201–216). Both are reprinted by permission of the publisher Taylor and Francis Ltd (http://www.informaworld.com). Similarly, a version of the practice example of 'Nicolas' in Chapter 9 first appeared in Adrian Ward and Linnet McMahon (eds) *Intuition Is Not Enough: Matching Learning with Practice in Therapeutic Child Care*, London: Routledge (1998: 186–188), and is reprinted by permission of the publisher.

Introduction

Thirty spokes share the wheel's hub;
It is the centre hole that makes it useful.
Shape clay into a vessel;
It is the space within that makes it useful.
Therefore profit comes from what is there;
Usefulness from what is not there.

（from the *Tao Te Ching of Lao Tsu* translated by Gia-Fu Feng and
Jane English (1972) Wildwood House, London)

The state of play

Children and their families are living in a time of uncertainty and change
which places great pressures on family life. Child-rearing skills are no longer
passed from generation to generation, although, at a deeper level, ways of
behaving and responding to situations are often transmitted. Past patterns of
bringing up children are often irrelevant today, and some of them were emotionally damaging. Each set of parents must think afresh about how to bring
up their children and many feel at a loss. At the same time the lack of support
as relatives become unavailable is compounded as functioning neighbour-
hoods decline and the support of the welfare state diminishes. The pressures
of high expectations, the changed role of women, poverty and isolation, put
family relationships under stress, and many families break under the strain.
Stress may be increased by illness, disability or bereavement. Parents may
not always be able to understand or respond to their children's unhappiness
without outside help. In some families there is a long legacy of damaging
and abusive relationships and children's emotional needs have been ignored.
Even schools may not feel safe places for children. While society has been
enriched by the presence of different racial and cultural groups this has also
brought tensions and racism, and asylum seekers and refugees bring their
own experiences of trauma. Although there is better recognition of the rights
of children, of valuing difference, and of the need to take account of children's needs and wishes when there are decisions to be made about their

future, there are difficulties in putting this into practice. Social workers, and other professionals too, often have to operate within procedural constraints and limited resources, and without adequate training in communication with children.

While working with children and families in a child development centre many years ago I wanted to learn more about play therapy. I could find little except Axline's inspiring *Dibs – In Search of Self* (1964) and her *Play Therapy* (1989). Yet I knew from experience that children's play is healing and that as a worker with children I was sometimes in a position to help this healing process. The first edition of this book, in 1992, was the result of my search to find out who was using play in work with children and families. Since then, play therapy has become a growing profession in the UK, with a number of professional training courses, a significant literature, and its own professional association, the British Association of Play Therapists.

The emotional development of children is increasingly understood. Attachment theory and research have refined our understanding of Bowlby's ideas about attachment, separation and loss – the underlying themes of human life. Neurophysiology confirms the lasting damage caused by early trauma. Psychodynamic thinking has become more accessible, with Winnicott's and Bion's notions of emotional holding and containment providing a foundation for therapeutic practice, and Kleinian ideas of projection and splitting helping make sense of difficulties in work with a child but also within wider systems of families, networks and organizations. Winnicott's developmental approach to play helps us in matching the form of therapeutic work to the point in a child's life at which emotional distress or trauma took place. In the healing 'potential space' of play the child can find themselves and live with what they find.

Training in therapeutic play and play therapy can enable workers in different settings and with different kinds of initial training to help troubled children and families. The methods of play therapy are particularly suitable because they provide emotional containment of child or parent or carer, supporting and not disempowering them. Play therapy provides a helping relationship through which the players are able to work on finding their own ways to manage their difficulties. Yet without the framework of a just society it may not be possible for the individual to become creative and autonomous. We can usefully think in terms of concentric circles of containment, like Russian dolls, with the outer circle needing to be provided by society and its social institutions and organizations, and inner circles provided by networks of families, schools and professionals, with the child at the heart.

This book is an introduction to play therapy and therapeutic play. I hope it will also be useful to experienced workers who are interested in further developing connections between theory, practice and the use of self in therapeutic work with children. While keeping the emphasis on practice I have tried to provide a theoretical framework for different forms of work.

Chapter 1 is about the place of play in child development. This provides the essential foundation for understanding how play within an emotionally containing relationship can help children work through difficult feelings and develop the capacity to think. However, workers who prefer to start from practice may want to read ahead to an area of work that interests them, returning later to fill in any gaps. Chapter 2 is about the different theories of play therapy and their application in practice, past and present. These range from psychodynamic and non-directive approaches to focused approaches, some of which are highly structured. Some approaches deal with deeply unconscious levels of thought; others work with the child's conscious understanding of events. Practical guidance for workers starting therapeutic play with children is given in Chapter 3, together with a consideration of the process of play therapy. Chapter 4 is about the use of play to help children and their families in the early years, while Chapter 5 examines play in family work with older children as well. The use of play in family work is a thread that runs throughout the book. Chapter 6 investigates the use of play to help children with developmental problems, and children with disabilities or illness, including stays in hospital, and also children for whom emotional and learning disabilities become intertwined. Therapeutic play and play therapy, including group work, to help children suffering separation and loss through bereavement or family breakdown are considered in Chapter 7. Chapter 8 examines play-based psychodynamic approaches in assessment and treatment of children who have experienced continual trauma and loss, including neglect and abuse. Chapter 9 explores therapeutic play in daily living with the most emotionally disturbed and traumatized children. Chapter 10 examines play in work to help children in moving on to new families, whether long-term foster families or adoption. Some recommended reading is listed before the Bibliography.

Many workers have contributed practice examples. Most of these are their own accounts. Others have been told to me informally and written up with the agreement of the worker. Where appropriate, the consent of family or child has been sought. In all cases, names of children and families, and sometimes identifying details, have been changed to preserve confidentiality. For the same reason, in some chapters, names of contributors of practice examples are given at the end of the chapter rather than with the example.

I hope that the book will give prospective workers some idea of what it feels like to be involved in the messy, complex and often confusing process of therapeutic play with children and families, and give them some help in getting their bearings. I hope too that they will be heartened by the courage of children in facing up to their own pain and growing through it within an emotionally containing relationship with their worker or carer. Children will forgive the mistakes we make provided that they have confidence that we are really trying to understand and to see them through a difficult time. Their power to heal themselves through play can be astonishing. On hearing that her worker was going to give a talk, a girl who had survived horrific abuse said, 'Tell them that we play but it's much much more than that.'

Chapter I

The development of play

What is play?

Ask a child what she has been doing and a likely reply is, 'Just playing.' As adults we may well leave it at that, going along with the idea that play is not an important matter compared with the real business of 'work'. Yet I want to argue that play is essential, for children and adults alike, not simply as a means of relaxing but rather as a way of helping us make sense of the world and having some feeling of control over our lives.

As adults, most of us look forward to a chance to unwind, to a 'breathing space', to 'recharge our batteries', to 'sort out our heads'. Yet the activities we choose – whether enjoying music, playing sports, seeing friends, reading the newspaper, having a bath, and so on – tend to feel most satisfying when our inner selves feel reaffirmed in some way, indicating, as some of these metaphors suggest, that a more creative process than just relaxing has been going on. Most of us are familiar with the mental freezing which can accompany pressure, whether self-imposed or from somebody else. If someone is explaining how to use a new computer we can feel more and more muddled, and can't wait for them to go away so that we can 'play' on our own and gradually become more familiar with this new thing. We may find too that if we stop consciously thinking or worrying about a particular question we may be surprised to find an answer popping unexpectedly into our heads; our mind has been left to play, quietly wandering round the problem, and has found a solution. Play frees us from the fear of failure or disastrous consequences so that we are able to be inventive and creative. When we have heard some bad news we can feel mentally numb and want time on our own to 'digest' it, to 'chew it over', to understand what has happened, to become aware of how we feel and to rehearse how we might respond. We tend not to think of this as play, but play can be a serious business too. Maybe later we will want to talk it through, sometimes repeatedly, with someone else: this is like Winnicott's play 'in the presence of someone' and offers an insight into the connection between adult counselling and play therapy.

So we have different kinds of play, some more obviously playful in feeling than others. All are to do with ways in which we consciously or unconsciously process our experiences, integrating them into our inner mental worlds. This brings a renewed feeling of things making sense, which in turn gives us a sense of autonomy, of things being manageable and under our control, at least as far as our own actions and responses are concerned. In the process we change ourselves and our view of the world. We dare to change because our self is not threatened. On the contrary, the process of playing gives the glorious sensation of a stronger sense of self. Play can be deeply satisfying.

As it is with adults, so it is with children. Making sense of the world is an enormous task for young children. But children have less autonomy than adults, and are often less able to find the words to express their thoughts and feelings. So play has a crucial significance for them. They are constantly at risk of being overwhelmed by events or feelings. Then 'solitary play remains an indispensable harbour for the overhauling of shattered emotions after periods of rough going in the social seas'. For example, when my daughter was finding school stressful she would come home in a temper, disappear upstairs to play for an hour and re-emerge feeling much more settled. Like us, when we cannot take in an explanation of how to work something new, children often ignore the instructions (or our directions) that come with toys such as Lego, and play on their own – exploring, trying something, finding it doesn't work, having another go. They are becoming familiar with the materials and making them their own, a creative and ultimately more satisfying process. Children who have had a difficult or distressing time, or who have suffered a painful separation or loss, may use play to help them come to terms with their experience. Unlike adults who can run things over in their minds, children need to externalize their thoughts through play. In pretend play children can safely bash, bury or throw away the people they are angry with or frightened of, or re-enact something that has happened, perhaps changing the outcome. The child brings into his play 'whatever aspect of his ego has been ruffled most . . . To "play it out" is the most natural self-healing method childhood affords' (Erikson 1965: 214–215). By re-enacting and repeating events, often in a symbolic form, and by playing out their own feelings and phantasies, children come to terms with them and achieve a sense of mastery. They can safely express anger and aggression without harming other people, or without it rebounding to harm themselves. As anxiety is relieved and inner harmony restored they become more able to manage real events.

The pleasure and excitement of playing, the intensity and concentration, the freedom to experiment, to explore and to create, to find out how things and people work and what you can do with them, to give the imagination free rein, and to fill the gap between reality and desire, all these derive from the fact that in play the child is in charge. Thus 'play under the control of the player gives to the child his first and the most crucial opportunity to have the courage to think, to talk and perhaps even to *be* himself' (Bruner 1983). Although play can be a serious as well as a joyous activity, the crucial condition is that errors do not have serious consequences. A child's spontaneous play within a familiar setting is a different kind of experience from exploration of an unfamiliar and potentially frightening world. Risks can be taken because the play itself matters more than the results of play. Play can only take place within a safe boundary, providing both a time and a place, so that the child knows where play begins 'and where it ends and the rules change back to everyday life' (Skynner and Cleese 1983: 298). Huizinga (1949: 10–12) puts it more formally:

> All play moves and has its being within a playground marked off beforehand either materially or ideally, deliberately or as a matter of choice . . . All are temporary worlds within the ordinary world, dedicated to the performance of an act apart. Inside the playground an absolute and peculiar order reigns . . . the laws and customs of ordinary life no longer count.

For young children the boundary of their 'playground' is provided by parents or other adults who protect them from intrusion from the outside world. This may involve a special place, usually with familiar features or objects, or a special time, or both. When two or more children are playing together, or an adult is joining in as a player, they will normally indicate to one another that 'This is play'. This may be a look, a 'play face', a laugh, or perhaps a verbal recognition such as 'You *pretend* to be my mummy'. Play is paradoxical in that the interaction between players is real but the message between them is that what they are doing is not real (Bateson 1973). Inside the boundary the player can experiment with changing normal ways of categorizing things, often a source of humour as the child realizes this. Play can be a 'special way of violating fixity' (Bruner 1976: 31). For example, the child with a new baby in the family may take a delight in playing 'mother' whilst the real mother has to play the baby who, like Hansel and Gretel, gets sent off into the forest.

So play is children's means of assimilating the world, making sense of their experience in order to make it part of themselves. Their experience also, of course, involves the opposite process of accommodation, learning to fit in with the demands of reality (Piaget 1951). The importance and excitement of play lie in its ability to link the real world and the inner mental world of the child. In play, children can transform the world according to their desires, especially a situation 'in which the individual finds his self, his body and his social role wanting and trailing'. The child both imagines and practises being in control, 'in an intermediate reality between phantasy and actuality' (Erikson 1965: 204).

Social play with other children may have some of these healing qualities. The presence of others, however, means that play is often closer to the world of reality. Children may be involved in negotiating or coordinating their actions with one another. The demands of social interaction may sometimes inhibit the playing out of individual inner phantasies, unless the phantasies of several players coincide. The satisfaction of shared play may come from the enjoyment and excitement of play which reflects close relationships and mutual recognition. Yet where play involves a pecking order, those players with little power may find social play hurtful and even damaging. To summarize, the essentials for play are:

- *safe boundaries* – the need for the player to feel safe within a physical boundary of time and space, where the rules of everyday life do not apply, and to feel well enough held emotionally, whether or not an adult is actually present
- *autonomy* – the need for the player to feel in control of the play and the direction it takes, whether or not another person is present or playing
- *no serious consequences* – the process of playing matters more than the results; mistakes do not have serious consequences so that risks can be taken.

For many children such healing play takes place in the normal course of events, probably without adults being aware. The opportunity to play may be enough for the child whose life is not overwhelmingly disrupted or distressing, and when there is someone around who holds the child in mind, providing the emotional containment which helps them manage their anxiety. Children who have had too much going on in their lives can benefit from the active involvement in the play process of a concerned, aware and containing adult. This is where therapeutic play or specific play therapy sessions may help. When we are offering play help we need to think carefully about our provision and management of each of the essentials of play. How we provide them varies, depending on our assessment of the child's needs. We will return to these questions. First, we need to understand the pattern of development of play so that we can recognize the developmental level a child has reached if we are to use play appropriately to help. The development of play is linked to aspects of physical, intellectual and, crucially, social and emotional development. Observations of spontaneous play are invaluable in diagnosis and assessment. The rest of the chapter describes children's emotional and play development from birth to adulthood. This is summarized in Tables 1.1 and 1.2 (p. 34 and pp. 35–36).

The beginning of play in the age of illusion

Maternal preoccupation, attunement and containment – 'good enough' mothering

Donald Winnicott, celebrated paediatrician and psychoanalyst, used to advise parents who were fearful of the enormous responsibility of caring for their apparently helpless new baby that a baby is 'a going concern', with an inherent potential to live and develop. Yet he also observed that 'there is no such thing as a baby, only "a baby and someone"' (Winnicott 1964: 88). Psychologist Lynne Murray's film (2000) shows how within an hour of birth the newborn watches and responds to his mother's (and father's) face. In the relationship between baby and mother (usually but not necessarily the biological mother – and there is no reason that mothering should not come from fathers or even be shared by a number of people) lies the foundations of a child's emotional development. The baby's intense feelings of pleasure and pain, of love and anger, are bound up with the mother.

Winnicott's 'good enough' mother initially meets her baby's needs totally. She is able to do this through her *attunement* (Stern 1985) and *maternal preoccupation* in which she 'gives the infant the illusion that there is an external reality that corresponds to the infant's own capacity to create', making actual what the baby is ready to find (Winnicott 1971: 12). The baby sees themself mirrored in their mother's face and builds up a picture of themself from their mother's responses. The baby feels comfortably omnipotent rather than helpless. The mother's gradual and inevitable failure 'to perfectly accommodate herself to her baby's every need enables the infant eventually to relinquish the illusion of unity and omnipotence', to find their own 'edges' and to explore the reality of the outside world. A 'perfect' mother who remained totally adapted to her infant's needs would not allow her baby to start to experience themself as a separate person.

Psychoanalyst Melanie Klein's ideas are helpful in understanding what happens between mother and baby (Klein 1986; Waddell 2000). The baby's first experiences of the world, pleasant or unpleasant, involve the whole body. Mental development requires the infant to sort and separate, or split, these sensory experiences into good and bad feelings. This gives a space in the baby's mind where good feelings can be stored, to form the beginnings of the self. The baby splits off or gets rid of (or *projects*) the bad feelings by putting them into the mother, with a paranoid fear of their being returned, in the process losing touch with that part of the self. Klein called this the *paranoid-schizoid position* and saw it as part of normal development. It remains to a greater or lesser extent an underlying part of everyone's personality; the tendency to blame and hurt others surfaces at times of stress.

The 'good enough' mother attends to her baby's feelings, good and bad, to such an extent that she experiences them as if they were her own. Bion (1962) calls this process of being open to being stirred up emotionally by the baby *reverie*. (Most mothers will recall the compelling anxiety produced by the sound of their baby's crying.) The mother's task is to act as a container, tolerating without being overwhelmed by her baby's feelings, thinking about them and then giving them back in a more bearable form. She digests how the baby is feeling, sometimes consciously but probably more often without being aware of doing so. She becomes a thinker for the baby's thoughts. For example, if her baby cries furiously when being undressed, the mother may touch or pick up her baby, or hold the baby with her voice saying soothingly something like 'You don't like being all bare do you, but you are quite safe and I'll soon have you dressed'. Whether or not she puts it into words like these, the mother conveys her own good feelings and the infant takes in (or *introjects*) 'the feeling of "being contained", of maternal space having been available for their anxieties to be tolerated and thought about' (Copley and Forryan 1987/1997: 241). By receiving more loving than hating feelings the baby begins to bear and manage their own angry and anxious feelings, and no longer has to get rid of them by projecting them into someone else. When this happens the baby internalizes not only the experience of being contained but develops a mind able to hold thoughts.

A literal example of this containing process takes place when a mother is feeding her baby; there are parallels between physical and emotional digestion. The mother matches her pace to the baby's appetite and interest. If she feeds too quickly the baby feels force fed and turns their head away – it's just 'too much to swallow' or 'needs time to digest'. Or maybe there is not enough and the baby is left feeling 'empty'. We use these expressions to describe our feelings too. What we hope for is 'something we can get our teeth into', even 'a feast' of ideas, providing 'food for thought'.

The experience of emotional holding or containment enables the baby in turn to become a container of feelings, able to hold on to them and *think* about them, a process later helped by putting them into words. Stern (1985) describes this process as the child's initial *emergent self* developing into a *core self* (by about six months), and then becoming a more self-aware *subjective self*, which with the development of language becomes a *verbal self* too. This achievement of a verbal subjective self, of '*reflective self-function*', is the key to a child's resilience in adversity (Fonagy *et al.* 1994). Winnicott calls this stage *ego integration*, the development of an integrated self. Such a child has reached the *age of concern*, Klein's *depressive position*. This does not mean that the child is depressed but that they are able to experience pain and sadness, guilt and grief, that is, concern for others and the beginnings of empathy. So from experiences in their first relationships the baby develops an inner working model of the world as trustworthy (Erikson's 1965 'basic trust') and of themselves as loving and worthy of love. This is the *securely attached* child (Bowlby 1988) who, paradoxically, is confident to explore and learn, knowing that there is a secure base to return to if things get out of hand.

Children with damaged attachments

The consequences of impaired emotional containment

We know that babies thrive on sensitive and responsive care and we have seen how they also need someone who will hold them in mind, that is, who is able to think about them as a separate person in their own right, if they in turn are to develop a sense of self and a capacity to think. Sometimes the mother is overwhelmed by the infant's anger or distress. This may happen if she does not have enough good feelings of her own to hold on to, or if she herself is not 'held' by someone else. Old feelings can emerge as if from nowhere, perhaps unexpected anger or despair with a crying baby, or a feeling of being invaded or taken over. Such feelings may spring from deep-seated, even unconscious, childhood memories of fury and grief with a parent's inability to notice how she was feeling or to think about her as a separate individual. Copley and Forryan (1987/1997) offer metaphors for non-containing responses: 'sieve', where the baby's communication goes straight through or the mother is overcome by anxiety; 'teatowel', where the infant's distress is wiped away; 'nappy' or 'sponge', soaking up distress but taking away some of its meaning; 'dustbin', where pain is dumped; or 'brickwall', a lack or mistiming of response, as in the depressed mothers described by Murray and Cooper (1997).

Research based on attachment theory has helped to identify children's responses to different kinds of non-containment. Young children of 18 months have been observed in Ainsworth's 'strange situation' in which they are left briefly with an unfamiliar person and then reunited with their mother. Securely attached children are readily comforted on the parent's return and return to playing and exploring. Others show *insecure or anxious attachment*. The attachment of children who show much distress, with continued crying and clinging, mixed with anger, on mother's return, is described as *anxious/ambivalent or resistant*. Some children initially avoid their parents on return and refuse comfort (although monitoring has shown that their stress levels are high); their attachment is described as *anxious/avoidant*. A third group shows more extreme behaviour such as frozen watchfulness or dissociation, combining attachment seeking and fear of the parent, a *disorganized attachment* (Main and Soloman 1990), where the attachment figure is also the source of danger.

While secure attachment is widespread, most forms of insecure attachment come within the normal range, with avoidant attachment being a common pattern in older European cultures and ambivalent attachment more frequent in societies such as Japan. Disorganized attachment, perhaps better described as an extreme version of anxious attachment (Crittenden 2000), is relatively rare. Its origin lies in the failure of containment in infancy on account of early traumatic neglect, abuse, separation or loss. The uncontained child finds bad feelings unbearable and continues to project them on to other people in order to find relief. The child is stuck in the paranoid-schizoid position, with a diminished sense of self. As Dockar-Drysdale (1968, 1990) describes, the most damaged children remain *unintegrated* or *frozen*, broken off rather than grown away from the mother and unable to form a reciprocal relationship. Their greatest fear is of *annihilation*. They may try to preserve what is left of the self by *annihilating others*, mentally as much as physically, by treating people as objects. Or they may use *adhesive identification* (Copley and Forryan 1987/1997), holding or clinging to an object such as a bright light (as normal babies do); later a television or computer screen may serve the same purpose. Another version is 'delinquent *merger*' with peers or a gang. Or they may use sensuous feelings or body movements (physical activity, sport, sexuality) to hold themselves together against the terror of falling apart. Paradoxically, this includes self-harm such as cutting. Dockar-Drysdale describes two forms of fragile integration. *Archipelago* children have isolated islets of ego functioning which are not linked up into a coherent self. *False-self* children operate with a front which conceals and protects the turmoil and emptiness within. Crittenden's (2000) Dynamic Maturational Model of Attachment (see Figure 1.1) shows the different defensive strategies children develop as they grow older to cope with danger and lack of containment. Where the adult's dangerous or neglectful response is predictable, a child can use thinking, getting care by caretaking the parent or by being compliant (a false self) although in the process they must damp down and eventually get out of touch with their own feelings, which may emerge in later years in anger, depression and self-harm. Thinking is of no help to a child with an unpredictably dangerous caregiver. Instead they get care by an emotional response of angry demands alternated with coy placation, switching from one to the other in response to acute intuitive observation of the caregiver's mood. As they get older they become ever more controlling and omnipotent.

Research using the Adult Attachment Interview (George *et al.* 1985; Fonagy *et al.* 1994) links the child's insecure attachment to the mother's own early attachment, as revealed in her memories of childhood and her present feelings about them. Mothers who dismissed their childhood and reported it in a split-off way often had 'anxious/avoidant' children, while mothers enmeshed or preoccupied with early relationships tended to have 'anxious/ambivalent' children. Mothers with unresolved early traumatic loss or abuse were most likely to have children with disorganized attachments.

Longitudinal research shows how attachment patterns persist over time (Waters *et al.* 2000) unless something significant changes. Research into the development of the baby's brain has confimed the lasting consequences of early neglect and trauma. Not only is the overall growth of neural connections within the brain inhibited, but the production of stress hormones when the child feels uncontained becomes a built-in response to even minor stresses. Thus the child's ability to self-regulate, to manage their emotions, continues to be impaired (Schore 2003; Gerhardt 2004). The aim of much therapeutic work with the most emotionally damaged children is to repair damaged attachments through the process of containment. Such work must take into account both that the child's overall brain development is likely to have been affected and also that the constant triggering of stress hormones in the easily aroused child means that the child's first therapeutic need is for *soothing*.

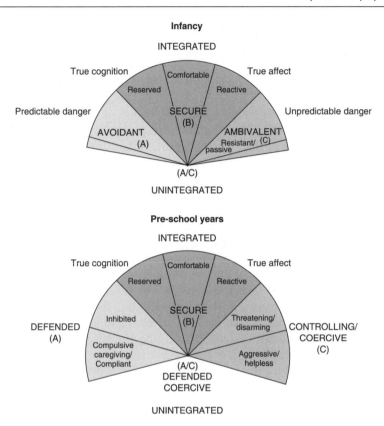

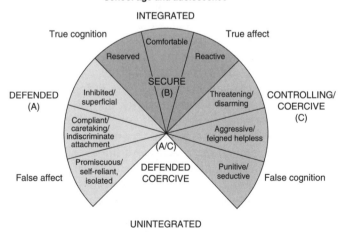

Figure 1.1 A dynamic maturational model of attachment, modified from Pat Crittenden (2000).

The development of play in infancy

The beginning of play is in the safe space between the baby and mother. In their waking hours a baby experiences the distress and pain of hunger and physical discomfort inside or outside their body, the excitement and focused pleasure of feeding, and the relaxed comfort and enjoyment of warmth and physical contact when urgent needs have been satisfied. In this tranquil state the baby responds to the mother's playful talking and touching, exploring and playing with their own or their mother's body. Peller (1964) called this *narcissistic play*. Early experiences are sensual. The infant responds with their whole body to *sound*, such as a rhythmical heartbeat, or being spoken or sung to, to *smell* and *taste*, of mother's milk and her body, to *touching* and *movement*, the warmth of contact-comfort with mother's body, the texture of clothing, the sensation of being carried or rocked and of feeding and eliminating, or of water in the bath, and to *seeing* light and dark, brightness, colour and pattern, faces and movement. Attuned to her baby, the mother imitates, mirroring sounds and facial movements, such as putting out her tongue. The mother watches and waits for her baby's response, which in turn may be a mirroring. She modulates her overtures and responses according to the baby's reaction – continuing while the baby shows pleasure, becoming quieter if the baby indicates she is overstimulated or tired (by turning her head away or showing distress), or actively reaching out to engage a baby who is unresponsive or 'flat' in mood. Thus she keeps in synchrony with her baby in a sort of mutual dance (Brazelton and Cramer 1991; Murray and Andrews 2000).

The mother's play helps her baby discover not only physical but also emotional edges. In turn-taking games such as 'Pat-a-cake' and 'Peep-bo', the mother initially paces the game so that she catches the baby's response and incorporates it, or she leaves spaces where the baby can join in and have a turn. Babies, Winnicott argues, find this play immensely exciting because they are being given the experience of omnipotence or magical control. As the child's imitation becomes more practised, the mother helps the child to take the initiative – for example, hiding her face in 'Peep-bo' – until the play becomes truly reciprocal and part of the child's play repertoire rather than just the mother's. The mother then moves from fitting in with her child's actions to introducing her own ideas to enrich play. Mother and child are playing together but increasingly as separate people rather than as a unity.

Piaget (1951) describes the development of *sensory-motor play*. Babies use their mouths in early exploration, Freud's *oral stage*. They find their hands, then feet, and play with them, finding out how to reach objects, make them move, grasp them and bring them to be further explored by the mouth or both hands. They take delight in repeating a learned action, such as grasping a rattle. In this *practice play* they take 'pleasure in being a cause', becoming more skilful and more familiar with the object. Sometimes play becomes ritualistic as an action is repeated many times with both concentration and delight – for example, peeping through a hole or rolling a ball. At this stage, play concerns only the present, since babies have no words or symbols or even mental images to codify experience. They are using their senses and body to *assimilate* experience, to make it part of themself. Bruner (1966) calls this process *enactive thought*. They are also actively finding out about the real world, a process of *accommodation*. This is possible only as long as the object of exploration is relatively new but not fearful. *Exploratory play* can only take place within safe boundaries. As the objects of play become more familiar, the child moves from asking (not, of course, consciously at this stage) what does this object do, to what can I do with this object.

As the baby develops and becomes more aware of the difference between self, others and the world around, they start to realize that they have a separate existence from mother and are not omnipotent. From about the age of six months they may become fearful if their mother or carer goes out of sight – the beginning of separation anxiety. Play 'under the control of the player', in the safe space between self and mother, is the infant's way of coping with the anxiety that this awareness raises. This is Winnicott's stage of *transitional play*. As phantasies* and imaginings become linked to real people or objects the child achieves their first sense of autonomy and of being in control. Play is a way of bridging the gap between their inner world and the reality of the world outside. Winnicott sees this as the beginning of all creativity. Many children have a soft cloth, ribbon or toy which becomes their soother, comforter, protector and friend. This *transitional object* has its own vitality of warmth, movement, texture and smell which must never be changed except by the child, and which can survive excited loving and mutilation as well as affection and cuddling. Because it is something both inside and outside the child, the transitional object supports the child 'engaged in the perpetual human task of keeping inner and outer reality separate yet interrelated' (Winnicott 1971: 2). It is used as a symbolic means of managing the anxiety of separation, from the brief separation of going to sleep to the longer one of being looked after by someone else. It should thus be clear how important it is for children, of any age, who are moving between places or entering substitute care to keep with them belongings which have such symbolic value. The integrated child who creates their own transitional object has made the first step in symbolic play.

The play needs of unintegrated children with damaged attachments

A child who received 'good enough' mothering in infancy but who later experiences separation, loss or other trauma which creates mental distress

---

* Throughout the text the word 'phantasy' refers to unconscious processes of the mind as distinct from 'fantasy' which is a more conscious wish, day-dream or imagining.

(whether expressed internally in depression or externally in difficult behaviour) may make good use of symbolic communication through play in the presence of an understanding, supportive and informed adult, whether therapist or other worker. This is certainly the case for a securely attached child but also applies to a child with a more anxious (ambivalent or avoidant) attachment where the child's inner working model of the world has developed some kernel of belief in being loved and being worthy of love. Children who, for whatever reason, lacked the experience of being emotionally held in the first year of life are left unintegrated, with damaged attachment. They have not had the safe space in which to play and therefore lack capacity for symbolic play, and so cannot make use of this in therapy. Their play needs are more fundamental. They require *primary experience*.

A crucial part of primary experience involves provision of missed sensory experiences. They can also provide the soothing which, as we have seen, hyper-aroused children need. These children need blankets, cushions, bean-bags and 'nesting material', small enclosed spaces such as cardboard boxes to curl up in, soft toys and teddy bears. Dockar-Drysdale (1968: 141) also recommended sand, water, bubble-blowing and finger-painting materials, glove puppets, storybooks to read aloud, a mirror, warm milk, and a large jar of coloured sweets. Prescott and Jones's (1975) 'softness index' assesses the sensual-tactile responsiveness of a child's environment. The softer the environ-ment, the more it includes materials such as water, paint, dough, clay or mud, sand which children can be in, earth to dig, grass, laps, swings, rockers, soft furniture and rugs, animals which can be held. Cooking and eating – playing with food (eating jelly with fingers), thinking about the associations of smells, listening to and making rhythms and music, singing and being sung to, exploring colours and textures, painting and drawing, all can help to put children of all ages in touch with their senses so that they feel more really alive (Oaklander 1978). This may be provided by their mother (or attachment figure) with appropriate support. If the mother is to contain her child she herself must be contained. Failing this, the child needs a total therapeutic environment which replicates the process of emotional containment.

Unintegrated children are not ready to play and share with other children. They need to play within the safety of a containing relationship. They need the equivalent of the *reciprocal play and turn-taking* games of infancy. For older children these might be action songs, rhymes or finger plays involving body movement or contact. This can include all sorts of play, provided that the adult takes part and supports, rather than drowns, any initiation from the child. The adult needs the skills of the attuned mother of an infant, modulat-ing her response to match the child's, and on occasion 'reaching out' to engage a distant, depressed or detached child (Alvarez 1992). The adult must be able to survive repeated annihilation by the child and to continue to act as a container, holding and thinking about the child's feelings before eventually starting to return them in a more bearable form which focuses on hopeful aspects. This emphasis on hope is vital as the child is likely to perceive any reflection of painful feelings as persecutory. As the child's self start to grow, the adult provides the transitional space in which the child can find themself through play. Dockar-Drysdale (1990) summarizes the processes which must be gone through in order to reach ego integration: experience, realization, symbolization and conceptualization. Children can only benefit from good experiences if they can feel that they have really happened to them, if they have a way of remembering and storing the good thing inside them, at first symbolically but eventually as a conscious intellectual process of putting it into words so that it can be communicated. However, there are no short cuts. The first, most prolonged and most difficult aspect of any therapeutic help is to continue to provide the good experience in the face of continued attacks on it from the child who is well defended against the terrifying possibility of any change which involves getting in touch with their agonizing emotions.

Play in the age of concern and autonomy

Developments in children's thinking and understanding

Towards the end of their first year children with enough good experience no longer need always to project and get rid of their bad feelings. They have been contained and so are becoming containers themselves, able to think about their feelings and experiences. Becoming an integrated and separate person means that they are able to experience feelings of anxiety and sadness, of grief and guilt.

Children's awareness of having a separate existence from the mother is inevitably linked to desperate anxiety about losing her. Powerful *attachment* feelings and *separation anxiety* increase from the age of about six months and remain acute, usually until at least the age of three. This anxiety is reduced by familiar surroundings and people. Children often have secondary attachment figures, such as fathers, grandparents, older siblings or childminders, who can provide the security they need to explore and play. In situations of overwhelming anxiety, only the primary attachment figure, the mother, will do. The work of Bowlby (1969, 1982, 1973, 1980) and the Robertsons (1970, 1976, 1989) has been crucial to our understanding of the processes of attachment. They have also shown how to prevent or mitigate the emotional damage caused by separation and loss, as children move through the stages of response, from healthy *protest* to grieving *despair*, and unhealthy *detachment*, with eventually some form of *reorganization* if all goes well. While a child's attachment needs remain strong into and beyond their second year, the mother's bonding to her child tends to be less intense, often because of return to work or the birth of a new baby. This 'dethronement' affects many children profoundly. Those who cope best emotionally often have fathers who 'take on' the older child (Dunn and Kendrick 1982) or secondary attachment figures such as a childminder or nursery keyworker.

Children's ability to cope with the unfamiliar is helped by their growing intellectual capacities. They become able to hold images in the mind. This *ikonic thought* is a means of remembering the mother in her absence. It also enables the child to make use of delayed imitation in play. This and the development of language prepare the way for symbolic thought and play. Piaget (1951) describes the child's thought at this stage as *egocentric* and *pre-conceptual* or pre-operational. As Donaldson (1978) has shown, it is not that children cannot think logically but rather that they do not yet have enough information about the world; therefore they go by the evidence of what they perceive and experience. Their sense of time is developing but is still weak. They do not know that other people see things from a different point of view, quite literally as well as emotionally. So they assume that they are the cause of others' behaviour. Fraiberg (1959) calls this egocentrism *magical thinking*. One consequence is that children blame themselves for their trauma and loss.

In their second and third years most children learn to control the bodily function of elimination, Freud's *anal stage*. Erikson saw this in the broader context of children learning to hold on and let go, as they struggle with the conflicting needs of dependence and independence. Where this is successful the child establishes a sense of *autonomy* which gives the beginnings of self-control and willpower. Failure results in a sense of *shame* and *self-doubt*. Play continues in the safe space between child and attachment figure. Children only feel free to play when they feel secure and contained in a familiar world. The quality of their play, seen in their ability to relax and become absorbed, their concentration and curiosity, and their development of play themes, indicates how far they have achieved a sense of autonomy.

Development of toddler play

Sensory and physical play

Sensory play becomes linked to *physical play* as children continue to use the whole of their bodies in experiencing the world: warmth and cold, water in a bath or pool, the squelch of mud, sand trickling through fingers and toes, shuffling through fallen leaves, the wonder of paint and fingerpaint, the smell of food, of grass, of tarmac and petrol in a hot street, hard ground, soft beds and clothes, wind and rain, music and singing, picture books and stories. As children learn to walk, run, jump and climb, they take great pleasure in practising these new skills. Mastery of the physical environment is a source of particular satisfaction when children's small physical size makes them incompetent in a world of giants. Children in their second year often play at building towers and knocking them down. Erikson sees this as children's expression of mastery of space, at an age when they have only recently learned to stand upright without wobbling. The triumph lies in the child controlling the destruction. If anyone else should destroy the tower the child may be upset, the vulnerable tower then representing the child (Erikson 1965: 212).

Exploratory and social play

Exploratory and *manipulative play* continue. The play themes of one- and two-year-olds concern attachment and autonomy, separation and individuation – for example, putting objects into containers and, like Eeyore, taking them out again. Brenda Crowe (1980) describes further play themes of up/down, push/pull, fill/empty, hide/seek, do/undo, look/show. Children often talk aloud as they play, Piaget's *monologue*. (In play therapy the worker may do this for the child.) Children also play with language, delighting in the sounds of words and new combinations.

Social play develops from turn-taking games with mother to active games such as 'Hide and Seek', often involving ambush, which again is a reflection of the separation–individuation process (Hoxter 1977). Many children enjoy rough-and-tumble play with fathers or older siblings (Cohen 1987). Outside the family, children play alongside rather than with others of a similar age. In this parallel play the children may appear to be playing together but the origin of each child's play is in their own phantasy. 'Other children seemingly drawn into play are really puppets. Their response is not ploughed back into the play, it falls by the wayside' (Peller 1964: 180). Children talk out loud as they play but it is a *collective monologue*, each talking about their own actions. They may be aware of what other children are doing or saying, and contact may occur through play with the same toy, but it is to their mothers that children turn when they want the other child to do something.

Symbolic or pretend play

The most important development in children's play at this stage, supported by developing language skills, is *symbolic* or *pretend play*. We have seen how the transitional object is the child's first real creation. It is a symbolic object, existing in the real world but with properties given to it from the child's inner world. It may directly stand for the mother and give comfort in her absence. It may also be the child's way of becoming the mother, internalizing her – as a child tells their special teddy what to do (Skynner and Cleese 1983). This internalization also eases separation anxiety. From this beginning, symbolic play develops in a recognizable pattern. Ages given are based on Sheridan *et al.* (2007).

From infancy, children have used *imitation* in reciprocal play with the mother. They elaborate this play, for example, as they copy domestic tasks. These imitations are assimilated and remembered, becoming internal images.

Early pretend play is often *remembered imitation* of familiar domestic situations. At about 15 months, children show definition by use, or *enactive naming*, of a familiar object – for example, putting an empty cup to their lips. Around 18 months, *self-pretend play* occurs. The child performs an action such as pretending to drink or sleep. Then comes *doll pretend*, as children carry round a doll or teddy bear (held the right way up rather than by one leg, Christopher Robin fashion, as they have before), which they feed or put to bed. As teddy 'comes to life' they may make teddy feed itself.

Children start to take the roles of others, progressing from actions to simple roles and then situations. For example, a child may pretend to drive using actions, later going on to play 'I'm Mum driving the car'. This stage of *role play* is sometimes called *decentred symbolic pretend* because the child becomes less egocentric. This is followed by *sequence pretend*. The child develops pretend situations, such as 'I'm Mum driving the car to go shopping'. Pretend sequences become longer and more elaborate. By three years, children may be playing out a complex sequence – for example, undressing teddy, bathing it and putting it to bed. In this spontaneous play the child is usually playing alone, although perhaps making frequent reference to an attachment figure.

Children take pleasure in joining in with pretend and 'silly' games initiated by parents or older siblings. These games can create excitement and fear as well as laughter – for example, in games of chase such as Valentine's (1956) game of 'Roaring Lions' with his infant son. They can involve flights of fancy, or role incongruities, as in Cohen's (1987) description of his one-year-old daughter's laughter when her mother sucked her dummy. A 'play face' often introduces social or *shared pretend* (Garvey 1977), in mutual recognition of pretending.

The imaginative or 'as if' quality of play develops in parallel. Pretend using real objects is followed by pretending with toy objects, usually child-sized. This is followed by the use of miniature toys, such as doll's house people and animals. Pretend play without props, such as offering an invisible pretend meal, involves a still greater degree of symbolism. At the highest level is the use of symbolic objects which bear little resemblance to the real thing – for example, pretending to telephone using an ice-cream scoop. The use of several symbolic objects in a complex play sequence indicates a high level of symbolic play.

Through symbolic play, children in the *age of concern* are working at making sense of the world they live in, understanding how it works and their own place in it, and so increasing their confidence and autonomy. 'Play is the infantile form of the human ability to deal with experience by creating model situations and to master reality by experiment and planning' (Erikson 1965: 214). Children also use play to help them cope with difficult situations where they have experienced fear, anxiety or anger. For most children their own play experience is sufficient to provide self-healing.

A famous illustration of this self-healing is Freud's account of an 18-month-old boy who had a wooden reel tied to his cot with a string. When in his cot he constantly repeated a game of throwing out the reel, murmuring 'O-o-o-oh' and then hauling it back again with a delighted 'Da'. Freud noted that this game coincided with the mother being out of the house all day. He interpreted the game as the child's compulsion to re-enact painful experience (which would now be called separation anxiety), with the difference that the child became master of the situation by controlling the reel's reappearance. (Freud's account is quoted in Erikson 1965: 208–9.) Erikson noted that while this game had a specific meaning for this child, about coping with loss, for most children a reel on a string may simply symbolize an animal on a lead, but for children reaching the stage of autonomy it may signify a new mastery of holding on and letting go. A mother's account of how her rising three-year-old dealt with his father's necessary absence from home for two nights a week shows similar use of play:

> He was angry and confused about his father's departure. He wept when he left and refused to speak to him on his return. He came to terms with this by doing jigsaws almost exclusively for a month. It seemed to me that he was ordering a world in play that he could not cope with in reality. This was confirmed six months later when his sister developed chicken pox and required more attention. The jigsaws came out again, his favourite on both occasions being a complicated 50-piece one. The intensity and consistency with which he played suggested to me that it was a coping strategy.

Children who need play help

Children whose lives have been affected by experiences of separation and loss such as bereavement or parental absence at this stage of their development may benefit from play help. They can find it difficult to cope with grief and anxiety, even if their attachment has been within the normal range. They may suffer play disruption, unable to play because of strong emotions of anger or anxiety, or because they lack the security of a familiar environment or the containment provided by the mother or other attachment figure, particularly likely if the parents themselves are experiencing stress. A new baby, illness, physical or learning disability in a sibling or other member of the family may involve, as a matter of necessity, some lessening of parental support, for which children (at this stage of magical thinking) are likely to blame themselves. Others may be suffering emotional neglect or abuse, or other trauma, and the painful feelings of shame and doubt which result from failure to achieve a sense of autonomy. In play children can re-enact events and play out their inner feelings in symbolic form in the presence of a safe adult, often a parent supported by a professional worker. At this stage, children are quite unconscious of the symbolism in their play and their use of it to make sense of their experience and to cope with anxiety, so the adult needs to respond within the metaphor of play. The sense of mastery which symbolic play provides, within the containment offered by the adult, helps the child to restore inner harmony so they are better prepared to cope with the complicated relationships of the next stage.

Play in the Oedipal stage

Development of children's thinking and understanding

With the child's growing sense of autonomy and identity comes a need to understand roles and relationships in the family and their link to the roles of the world beyond. The child at this *genital stage*, normally between the ages of three and five, may be struggling with the strong feelings of the *Oedipus complex* in which the boundaries between the generations are made clear. Feelings of love and desire for the parent of the opposite sex, and thus of rivalry with the parent of the same sex, become transmuted into a socially acceptable identification with the parent of the same sex. Children become interested in sexual differences and aware of the maleness or femaleness of their bodies. Boys take the additional psychological step of transferring from attachment to mother to identification with father. Children learn that future sexual attachments must be made outside the family, giving the impetus to grow up and develop a wider network of relationships. They are unconsciously absorbing the values of their families and of others in their immediate world. Their *racial* and *cultural identity* is already being determined. Milner's finding (1983) that both black and white three-year-old children chose for preference white dolls and white friends indicates the powerful influence of family and a racist society on children's identity and self-image at a very young age. Since Milner's study, countervailing pride in black identity may have helped provide black children with a positive identity. However, as long as elements of racism persist in society we can never afford to ignore their effects.

  Children at this Oedipal stage are intellectually curious and continually ask questions, about how things work, why people feel as they do, reflecting their growing understanding of space and time as they ask what happens in other times and places and about other people that they know. Their curiosity starts from their own experience of reality. One thoughtful three-year-old's questions to her mother included: Why can't boys wear dresses? What makes the wind blow? Why do men have nipples, they don't feed babies? Where will you sit when I'm driving the car? Why do we have to die? When we have counted to a hundred is that the end? Why can't I see myself grow? Why do firemen kill people in fires? It is hardly surprising that a young child makes a wrong inference based on incomplete information, believing firemen kill people. They are still at Piaget's stage of *intuitive thought* and go by the evidence of what they see and experience A child asked, for example, *why* Mrs Smith is John's mother 'just knows'. A child who goes into foster care may not 'know' that their original home and parent still exist. Magical egocentric thinking is still strong. Children think that they are the cause of other people's behaviour or of events which affect them, believing, for instance, that father left home because they were naughty. Social worker Madge Bray worked with a child who thought he was in care because he 'pinched the biscuits' the morning his mother went into hospital.

When children feel that their sexual and intellectual curiosity is accepted and valued by their family they develop a sense of *initiative* (Erikson 1965), a feeling of direction and purpose. The world is their oyster. If they meet with constant discouragement and disapproval they develop instead a sense of worthlessness and *guilt*, a conscience which can become a crippling burden, especially when fuelled by mistaken interpretations of events. A secure attachment confers both confidence and the ability to think. This includes thinking about other people thinking – realising that their thoughts may be different from yours. This 'theory of mind' has been found to be significantly more developed in securely attached five-year-olds (Fonagy 1996).

Development of play in the Oedipal stage

Sensory, physical and exploratory play

Play in the age of initiative continues and develops many earlier themes. *Sensory* and *creative play* use natural materials such as sand and water, mud and clay, and painting, singing and music, words and sounds. *Physical play* involves exercising new skills, as children become able to run, climb, hop, dance, swim, ride a trike, and throw, kick and catch a ball. Physical play is often incorporated into energetic social pretend play and informal games. In *exploratory play* children investigate and make use of objects and solve play problems. Through their play, children build up their knowledge of the physical world, developing concepts of space, time and number, conservation of quantity and volume, of cause and effect, increasing their sense of confidence and mastery. Erikson noted that body identity and sexual differences are reflected in play constructions. Boys tended to build towers and to make models involving much activity; girls created quieter scenes, typically an enclosure with an entrance. He recognized too that children's choice of play material depended on what is available in the child's culture as well as on the skills a child has developed.

Symbolic or pretend play

In *pretend play*, new themes emerge concerned with the roles which people play outside as well as inside the family. These themes occur in solitary play and in social play with parents, siblings and other children outside the family, nowadays often of a similar age. Peller (1964: 180) writes:

> In oedipal play, the fantasy may be social in its origin (several children putting their heads together). It is usually social by way of content, dealing with several people in various roles, and the execution may be either solitary (e.g. a child plays alone with dolls or toy soldiers) or social (several children playing together). However, contact between co-players is loose. It can be lost, and the players may never know the difference.

The symbolism in pretend play becomes elaborated in the child's development of a complex imaginary theme. A theme may be sustained, but children often change themes rapidly as their thoughts go off at a tangent as they play. For example, a child says she is mum bathing baby, holding a doll in a box full of imaginary water and using a brick for soap. Moments later the box is a table and the brick is food for her family. By playing the roles of others, children not only start to understand how others may feel but also can acquire a better idea of themselves and their own role and identity in the family. In both solitary and shared pretend play, children can safely express their feelings and anxieties. Some children have imaginary friends who are important as companions or scapegoats to represent their split-off bad selves as the age of guilt dawns.

Piaget (1951) came surprisingly close to psychoanalytic thinking in his models of play. In his *compensatory play* the child plays at doing things normally forbidden, or pretends that something has happened that has not really occurred. Such play may be a cathartic neutralization of fear or anger, or it may be a wish fulfilment. For example, a child jealous of the baby may hit their doll, or, in role reversal, play at being the baby. In *liquidating compensatory play*, children facing difficult or unpleasant situations may relive and come to accept them. The child who is ill or injured may play that their doll is suffering. In *anticipatory play*, children play out fears of the consequences of refusing to do what is expected of them. The child constantly told to be careful may have dolls that 'forgot' and come to harm.

Erikson (1976: 69) asked a number of four- and five-year-old children to make something with blocks and toys. From observing their play he concluded that the themes presented in these play constructions may be the repetitive

> working through of a traumatic experience: but they may also express a playful renewal. If they seem to be governed by some need to

communicate, or even to confess they certainly also seem to serve the joy of self-expression . . . If they seem dedicated to the exercise of growing faculties they also seem to serve the mastery of a complex life situation. As I would not settle for any one of these explanations alone, I would not wish to do without any of them.

These different possibilities warn the observer that although a child's play may be a direct imitation of something that has happened, this is far from always being the case. For example, if the child is playing the role of the mother and smacking the doll baby, it does not necessarily follow that the child's own mother does this. It is equally likely that the child playing mother is putting in their own immature response as to how to cope with a fractious baby. Another strong possibility is that the child is expressing their own anger and jealousy of a younger sibling.

Children at this stage are often struggling with the difficulty of separating fantasy from reality. Television, video and stories in books may be experienced as real events. Sometimes too the stories which children invent, or their imaginary companions, take on a mistaken reality. Even then the content of children's fantasies reflects their own experience or their feelings. 'Children cannot fantasize about events which lie completely outside of their experience' (Pithers 1990a: 20). For example, although young children have sexual feelings they cannot enact sexual behaviour in play unless they have either seen or experienced it, whether directly or on a video, photograph or other medium. The detail of the child's enactment or description will often indicate which is more likely.

Fantasy and reality are rarely blurred in every part of a child's mind, even at this young age. For example, a child with an imaginary companion, who feels quite real to the child, is as likely as any other child to be able to give an accurate description of what members of the family did this morning. However, because adults are such powerful figures, under-fives may sometimes agree with a suggestion an adult makes, although they are usually able to resist suggestions which go completely against their experience. On the other hand, they have not learned to 'hedge' and are likely to answer an open question with the truth as they perceive it.

Social pretend play

Dramatic play with other children develops at this stage. At first it is *associative play* (Isaacs 1933), with each child involved in its own imaginative theme and engaged in collective monologue, although there may be a play object in common which results in some joint activity. The beginnings of coordination are illustrated in Brenda Crowe's famous account of two children from different social backgrounds playing in a home corner at playgroup. The boy announces, 'I'm making the stoo for dinner' and the girl responds, 'All right, while you do that I'll just pop to Harrods for the canapés' (Crowe 1983: 109). Dressing-up transforms the self, without necessarily being followed by role play enactment. Some children demand to wear a particular hat or cape, perhaps as a sort of magic talisman to keep them safe in stressful situations such as playgroup and nursery.

Cooperative pretend play usually begins with *domestic themes*, such as meals, shopping, going to bed and being ill, in which the players take different roles, such as mother, father and baby. Packing, going on a trip or holiday, repairing and telephoning are common, and Garvey (1977) also noted that *treating* and *healing* was a constantly recurring theme. Play is assimilative as children make sense of the events in their lives. For example, two boys who had moved house spent all morning shifting the contents of the home corner across the room. Children often construct dens with any available materials, disappearing inside to pretend or giggle together. Both boys and girls become involved in domestic play, and either may play the familiar mothering roles. Playing the 'worker' role may be harder, because less known, demonstrated by the boy who, announcing he was going to work, went out of the door and looked nonplussed as he wondered what to do next.

Roles are less differentiated in informal games of running and chasing or hiding, although there may be a leader and followers. These games are mostly played by boys and often have symbolic themes such as monsters, cowboys and Indians, Batman, Superman, Power Rangers, or whatever is the current fashion. The underlying game is the same, a mutual phantasy, often to do with *averting threat* – for example, killing the monster or putting out a fire. It may be to do with the need for feelings of autonomy and control at an age when boys are establishing gender role identification but lack power in their own families.

Children who need play help in pre-school years

Because of the still limited language skills of pre-school children, observation of play is valuable in indicating how the child feels about self and others. When the adult needs to tell the child something, for example, about what is going to happen, play methods of communication help them understand more fully than hearing the words alone. Play also helps the adult grasp how much the child has really understood. Children who have suffered emotional damage during the Oedipal stage, rather than earlier, may be able to make good use of the provision of a therapeutic play situation, using symbolic play to express and communicate their feelings to an adult able to think about the meaning of their play. As at earlier stages, play for child and parent together, in pairs or in groups, can help to repair damaged relationships and give parents increased confidence and skills in 'containing' their child. Older children who experienced damage at the Oedipal stage may benefit from help which allows them to go back to playing out the symbolic themes of these years. The adult will carry some transference from the child's parents which may be used to help the child to come to a more satisfactory resolution of the developmental tasks of this age.

Play in middle childhood – the age of industry

The development of children's thinking and understanding

Freud described the years between five or six and adolescence as the *latency period*. Gender roles and family relationships have settled into established patterns. Strong drives are relatively dormant. Children's developmental task is to make their way in the world outside the family, specifically in the domain of school and the peer group. This is Erikson's *age of industry* in which children learn the skills of their culture. If they are made to feel inadequate compared with other children, they may develop feelings of *inferiority*, which in turn affect the development of skills. Social play with peers may contribute to these feelings as well as the degree of success in school work or experience in the home and neighbourhood. Adults other than parents may be greatly admired and their opinion of the child may affect self-esteem. Children's racial and cultural identity may be decisively affected. Children learn how others perceive the colour of their skin, the background of their parents, the language or accent they use. Maximé (1986) views the child's *racial identity* as a separate aspect of personal identity. She uses Melanie Klein's object relations theory to understand the black child's difficulty in establishing a satisfactory self-identity in a white majority culture. Black children may introject society's negative images of blackness and use projective identification to 'be' white. They need help in achieving a positive black identity.

Intellectual and linguistic skills at this stage include literacy. Understanding and expression may appear quite sophisticated, clouding the fact that concepts underlying language may not be understood in adult ways. Insofar as the world is familiar and what they are doing makes sense to them, children will be using *concrete operational thought*, understanding cause and effect through their observations of the world. They are rarely capable of abstract thinking. Intuitive thinking will persist where cause and effect cannot be clearly understood, and children's egocentricity will mean that they perceive themselves as the cause of events. For example, they may blame themselves for the death of a parent or the break-up of a separating family. They can be reassured by simple concrete explanations of the reasons for events. For example, adopted children can understand that their birth parents were 'too busy', 'very ill', 'died', 'did not have enough money' or 'had too many children' (Brodzinsky *et al.* 1984).

Around the age of eight many children start to be aware of the complexities of relationships and need more rounded explanations. They begin to see that relationships are not absolute but conditional. They also begin to understand the possible feelings and emotions of other people. If situations and feelings can change then they can also be reversed. (Piaget noted that appreciation of reversibility marked a child's transition from intuitive to concrete thought.) Children who have suffered loss need to enter the process of 'adaptive grieving' (Brodzinsky *et al.* 1984). Their understanding remains related to concrete events and situations. It is not until the approach of adolescence that abstract concepts can be fully grasped.

Development of play in middle childhood

Sensory, physical and exploratory play

Sensory and *creative play* become closer to the creative arts and music. *Exploratory play* comes under stronger social influence with girls and boys diverging in their interests, which focus on the technical and technological skills required in post-industrial society. Computers, constructional games and hobbies such as model-making or cooking take children closer to adult occupations. *Physical play* involves the enjoyment and practice of new skills, from hopscotch, skateboarding, bike and horseriding, to dancing, gym and football.

Solitary and social pretend play, and games with rules

Socio-dramatic play increases in sophistication with the growth of social skills, which allow cooperation and the coordination of roles. Close rapport between players is essential. Each child stays within its allotted role and supports others in their roles. Games may involve more realistic detail than formerly as well as flights of imagination (Garvey 1977). Building camps, adventure games or secret societies go alongside more domestic games of weddings, schools and hospitals. Earlier themes of hiding and seeking, chasing and ambushing, continue with the addition of a new theme, the hunter and the hunted (Hoxter 1977), of the good guys versus the bad. Games may be very elaborate and continued from day to day, although play is still spontaneous and may take off in unplanned directions. Often the planning and preparation for a game take all the time and the intended game may not happen. For example, planning parts and costumes, or puppets, for a show become the real play, rather than the final enactment which may be cursory or non-existent.

While group pretend play may be very satisfying to a child, there is also the possibility of frustration and conflict, of exercising power and feeling oppressed, which arises out of the social nature of play. There is another danger. With older children the boundaries around play that keep it safe are more easily breached; the adult presence may be distant or missing. Group play can lose its space between phantasy and the real world and become, as in

Golding's (1954) *Lord of the Flies*, both a group phantasy, often with scape-goats, and an awful reality.

Games with rules become common at this stage, chasing games such as tag, singing and ring games such as 'In and Out the Dusty Bluebells', counting and hiding games, skipping games, marbles, and numerous card and board games. Piaget thought that from the age of seven games with rules largely replace imaginative games, although others, such as Opie and Opie (1969), have noted that both continue side by side or in combination. Some rules are handed down and given, others are spontaneous. This kind of play fits in with the child's need to learn and practise the rules of social life outside the immediate family in order eventually to become a full member of society. Peller (1964) asserts that the emphasis on belonging to the group and on fairness, the strict rules, and the urge to replay or start again, which typify *post-Oedipal play*, are children's way of coping with their anxiety as they doubt their abilities for the first time. It remains play as long as it is an end in itself and players are bound only by the need to cooperate for the success of the game. Once replaced by an element of compulsion or the need to win it ceases to be play, as many a schoolchild who loathes sports would agree.

Solitary play survives and continues, providing a haven for purely assimila-tive play. Children may play complex imaginative games with dolls and ani-mals. Small world play with miniatures, such as doll's houses, animals, Lego, play people, cars, spaceships, and numerous other vehicles and machines, bricks, blocks and construction materials, can become very elaborate and sustained from day to day. In this play where children are directors of all that happens in these small worlds, inner calm may be restored after, in Erikson's phrase, 'periods of rough going in the social seas'. Books and stories, computer games and television are means of respite for many children. They also provide a way into pretend worlds. These can help children to make sense of their real situations and to try out different solutions in safety. Through identification with powerful children in stories their sense of autonomy and competence can be restored. Yet in today's safety conscious world where more children lack opportunities for play with other children there is a risk that some children may become lost in their fantasies without an adequate bridge to the real world.

Children who need play help in middle childhood

While most children find solitary play sufficient for self-healing, those whose lives are severely disrupted may need the help of an adult presence as they play. Their play may have stopped, or become 'stuck', repetitive and defensive, covering up rather than dealing with painful feelings. The therapeutic adult provides containment, a space where the child's feelings can be borne and thought about. As at earlier stages the adult may be enabling symbolic play, helping the process of self-healing. Children whose intellectual and language skills are sufficient to the task may be able to think about the feelings they have expressed symbolically, and put them into words. This stage of conceptualization enables a conscious retrospective reflection on their experience. However, if children's experience of damage and deprivation goes back over many years they may need at first to go back to much earlier stages of play help.

Play may be especially helpful to children with language difficulties and delays or with other mental or physical disabilities which restrict their ability to talk about their feelings and experiences. Play may simply be used to ease communication with children. Clare Winnicott (1964) observed that children more easily become relaxed and spontaneous when both they and the adult are concentrating on a 'third object'.

The growth of social skills and the social influence of the peer group make therapeutic group work possible at this stage. The support of peers who have had similar experiences helps children feel less alone or stigmatized. Carefully planned play and drama activities and games can help children become relaxed and spontaneous, able to explore difficult emotions together. These groups anchor play firmly to reality. Yet unconscious processes occur which group leaders need to recognize and use.

Play in adolescence – the age of identity

The strong emotions of early childhood surface again in adolescence. The ways in which earlier developmental tasks were dealt with is reflected in behaviour. Issues of trust, attachment and separation, containment and non-containment, autonomy and shame and doubt, initiative and guilt, all re-emerge in the adolescent's developmental task of establishing a sense of *identity*. Failure to achieve this results in *role confusion* (Erikson 1965). Intellectually adolescents are more like adults, with a developing ability for abstract or disembedded thought. Even so, much everyday thought continues to be rooted in concrete explanations of events.

Play continues but is expressed in more adult forms, in the creative arts, sports and physical activity, in intellectual curiosity, within new sexual relationships and in peer group social activity. Because of their need to demonstrate to themselves and their peers that they have become members of the adult world, adolescents often strongly reject what they perceive as more childish forms of play which threaten to return them to a stage which they are struggling to leave behind. Playful fantasies and daydreaming may take emotional energy. Deeper feelings are often more accessible through counselling and talking therapies than through play. Art therapy, however, can be very helpful. Sometimes the use of structured games can open and ease communication between the young person and adult. Playful methods in group work, such as drama therapy, may be very powerful.

Play may be a route to help young people with immature minds who find themselves inhabiting strange physically maturing bodies. They include adolescents with learning difficulties or mental disabilities or illnesses, or language disorders. They may be children so emotionally damaged earlier in life that regression to previous stages is needed to help them rebuild their sense of self.

The play needs of adults

Many adults believe that play is childish and would agree with Piaget that play fades away towards the end of childhood, to be replaced by real work and recreation. Yet adults have play needs beyond recreation from work. We do well to recognize this and to understand that play is not just a filling in of time before real work and learning begin but an essential element of growing and being fully human. As we have seen, play is spontaneous and creative, free from the inhibition produced by fear of failure.

Many aspects of children's play can be seen in adult creativity. *Sensory play* is reflected in art and music, in caring for pets, and in sensual and sexual touching and loving. As parents we can share again many of the sensual delights of childhood. I remember making blissful drippy sandcastles on a warm beach with my husband and small daughters, only to realize that the children were doing something else and my husband and I were playing contentedly together. Playing and laughing with our children satisfied our own play needs as well as theirs.

Physical play becomes translated into sporting and physical activities. *Imaginative* and *pretend play* become daydreaming and thinking, creative writing and arts. *Exploratory play* may become thinking and playing with ideas in science and technology. The great physicist, Richard Feynman (1985: 173–178), tells of his mental freezing when appointed to a post where he felt results were expected. It was only on hearing that it was the university which took all the risks that he became able to play with ideas again, starting from a moment watching the university crest wobbling on a spinning plate:

> I used to do whatever I felt like doing – it didn't have to do with whether it was important for the development of nuclear physics, but whether it was interesting and amusing to play with . . . So I got this new attitude. Now that I am burned out . . . I'm going to *play* with physics, whenever I want to, without worrying about any importance whatsoever . . . just doing it for the fun of it. And before I knew it . . . I was 'playing' – working really – and with the same old problem that I loved so much . . . It was effortless. It was easy to play with these things. It was like uncorking a bottle. There was no importance to what I was doing, but ultimately there was. The diagrams and the whole business that I got the Nobel prize for came from that piddling around with the wobbling plate.

As Brenda Crowe (1983) observed: 'At any age play is not so much what we do as how we feel about what we are doing; play is not even always a doing. Play is a feeling.' Parents who can play are happier, and their children benefit from this too. Those least able to recognize the play needs of their children are often those whose needs were never adequately met in their own childhood. They have learned to bury feelings of pain and loss, constructing elaborate defences to deny to themselves and others that they have been hurt. In the process they cut themselves off from others, preventing further hurt but diminishing their ability to give to their own children the care and the love they themselves had so sorely lacked. Then play may be used irresponsibly, in the interest of the adults and not their children, as in teasing or 'Now I'm going to get you' games (Nover 1985). Parents may play with their children as if they were sibling rivals or as other 'ghosts in the nursery' (Fraiberg 1980). In order to change parents need their own holding environment, whether provided by family or friends or by professional help. Play can help parents to find the spontaneous child within and to use it to meet their own and their children's needs.

Conclusion – who needs play help?

All children need play but not all children need play therapy. Most children do not need extra help in dealing with the ups and downs in their lives. Their own spontaneous play combined with the containment of 'good enough' parenting is sufficient to enable them 'to weather small storms'. Yet some children have too much happening in their lives, separations, losses, abuse, repeated disruptions, changes of family membership and abode, changes of caretakers and attachment figures, illness, disability and stays in hospital. Such events can be too great to cope with unaided. Some children, while anxious and angry, can cope adequately if they have an opportunity to share their feelings with an understanding adult who can help them to make sense of what has happened and clear up the frequent misapprehension that the child was to blame. Play can be a good way of helping these conversations along, with the expression of feelings in symbolic play providing healing. Children who have suffered a profound but isolated upheaval in their lives may respond quickly to therapeutic play, speeding the process of recovery which might otherwise take a long time and interfere with other aspects of development. Troubled children who can benefit particularly from play approaches and play therapy are those who find communication through words difficult, whether because they are very young, or have language difficulties, or have developmental delays and learning disabilities, or who choose not to speak.

Other children, often those experiencing continual deprivation or abuse, or very profound loss or trauma, need more help in exploring and communicating their strong feelings, which have possibly been long repressed or expressed inappropriately. Children whose infancy did not provide 'good enough' mothering remain unintegrated unless they receive emotional containment and primary experience, of which play forms a part. Severely damaged children may initially not be able to play at all, remaining either withdrawn or chaotic. For them a longer experience of play therapy may be helpful, usually combined with other forms of help.

In making decisions about what sort of help a child needs, the worker's observation skills are crucial in adding to the knowledge gained from the child's history. Through observation of the child's play, alone with the worker, or with an attachment figure, or with peers, we can begin to assess the child's state of attachment and emotional containment, and to establish the child's levels of development. The least damaged children will play spontaneously at a developmental level appropriate to their age while those more damaged are likely to be playing at a much earlier stage of development or may have missed out certain types of play experiences. It is important to notice whether the child can use symbolic play. Accuracy in assessment depends on the worker's knowledge of how children of a given age, community and culture usually play (see Tables 1.1 and 1.2). From the child's use of recurring themes in play, workers can learn which aspects of life are causing the child most difficulty. From the intensity of the emotion expressed in play it becomes possible to identify areas of acute distress. Some children may play defensively at first, hiding rather than revealing their true feelings. Others may suffer from play disruption. The extent of disruption and the play events which lead up to it may give the worker insight into areas of difficulty.

This discussion has focused on play in children's development. The next chapter explores different approaches to using play therapeutically.

Table 1.1 Stages in child development

Approx. age	Freud	Erikson	Peller	Klein	Winnicott	Dockar-Drysdale	Bruner	Piaget
0–12 months	Oral	Basic trust vs mistrust	Narcissistic (child by self, includes mother)	Paranoid-schizoid	Age of illusion (maternal preoccupation)	Primary experience	Enactive thought	Sensory–motor
1 and 2 years	Anal	Autonomy vs shame and doubt	Pre-Oedipal (child with mother)	Depressive	Transitional experience Ego integration Age of concern	Secondary experience	Ikonic thought	Pre-conceptual thought
3 and 4 years	Phallic	Initiative vs guilt	Oedipal (child with parents)			(symbolization)	Symbolic thought	Intuitive thought (Fraiberg's magical thinking)
5–12 years	Latency	Industry vs inferiority	Post-Oedipal (child with others)			(conceptualization)		Concrete operational thought
Over 12 years	Genital	Identity vs role confusion						Abstract thought

Table 1.2 The development of play

Approx. age	Sensory play/creative	Physical play	Exploratory play	Social play	Symbolic play
0–12 months	Using whole body and all senses – smelling, feeling, tasting, watching and listening.	Sensory-motor play.	Own and mother's body. Pleasure at 'being a cause' – What is this object? What can I do with this object?	Baby and mother turn-taking games – Peep-bo, Pat-a-cake. Imitation of mother's actions and sounds.	
	Using senses to experience world.	Practice play. Manipulative play, repetitive and ritual play.		Solitary play.	Transitional object. First sounds with meaning.
1 and 2 years	Play with food and own waste products. Play with sounds and words. Using all senses.	Large muscle play – walking, climbing. Small muscle skills – building, fitting together.	Exploring physical world, in/out, push/pull, hide/seek up/down.	Child and mother – hide and seek. Child and father – rough and tumble. Child and siblings – solitary play, and watching parallel play with peers.	Enactive naming, imitative play, self-pretend, doll pretend, role play, and situation or sequence pretend.
3 and 4 years	Sand, water, playdough, painting, words, stories and music, singing.	Running, jumping, tricycle riding, dancing, ball skills, drawing and cutting.	Problem-solving, construction and puzzles.	Associative play or cooperative parallel play. Cooperative play – domestic themes and chase games. Cooperation, competition.	Solitary elaborated symbolic play: complex and sustained themes increasing symbolism in use of objects in pretend, imaginary companions, dressing-up, 'talismans'. Cooperative socio-dramatic play: actions and roles coordinated (weddings, schools, camps, shows, hunter and hunted, continued from day to day). Elaborate solitary 'small world' play, books, stories and television.

(Continued Overleaf)

Table 1.2 Continued

Approx. age	Sensory play/creative	Physical play	Exploratory play	Social play	Symbolic play
5–12 years	Creative art, music, books and stories, and pets.	Games with rules, gym and sports, bike riding, writing construction.	Making things using domestic, technical and scientific skills, computer games.	Elaborate social organization. Formal games with rules.	
Over 12 years and adults	Creative arts, music, writing and books, sex and loving, cooking and eating, children and pets.	Sports and games, hobbies and skills.	Science and technology.		Playing with ideas, thinking, daydreaming, writing and role playing in living.

Chapter 2

Approaches to therapeutic play

Communication through play

A 'third thing'

Many people working with children can recall a time when they have sat opposite a child and tried to find out how they were feeling. The adult, as uncomfortable as the child, resorts to questions:

'How are you getting on at school?'
   'All right.'
   'What's your favourite subject?'
   'Football.'
   'How do you feel about your dad being away?'
   'Don't know.'
   'How are things at home?'
   'All right.'
   'How do you get on with Mum and Paul?'
   'All right.'

Communication has not even started. Clare Winnicott (1964, in Kanter 2004: 189) explains how to bridge the communication gap:

> We spend a good deal of time creating the conditions which make communication possible. We try to establish between ourselves and the children a neutral area in which communication is indirect. In other words we participate in shared experiences, about which both we and the children feel something *about something else*, a third thing, which unites us, but which at the same time keeps us safely apart because it does not involve direct exchange between us.

The 'third thing' may be an outing or journey, a pet, a hobby or interest, but equally it may be a toy or game, or simply play. An informal shared play experience is not threatening and takes out the strain of communication, enabling the worker to build a relationship with a child which is 'personal but yet structured'. The ultimate aim of communication is to help children to sort out the muddle in their lives 'so that things add up and make some sort of sense', preventing and relieving some of their distress. It is concerned with linking real events and people in children's lives with their feelings about them. Clare Winnicott continues (1964: 46–57):

> We have to be able to reach them and respond to them at any given moment and be willing to follow them as best we can. Of course we shall not always understand what is going on or what they are trying to convey to us, and often this does not matter. What matters most is that we respond in a way which conveys our *willingness to try to understand*. And it must be obvious that we really are trying all the time. This in itself can provide a therapeutic experience . . . Having reached the child we try to look at his world with him, and to help him sort out his feelings about it, to face the painful things and discover the good things. Then we try to consolidate the positive things in the child and in his world, and to help him make the most of his life.

This idea of things adding up and making sense is akin to Fonagy's idea of the need for the child to develop a 'coherent narrative' of their experiences, with a reflective self-function which will give them a secure enough sense of self for managing adverse experience, a capacity for resilience (Fonagy *et al.* 1994; Fonagy 2001). Children with a secure enough attachment but in some present distress may be ready to do this, but for the most severely deprived and traumatized children this may only be possible towards the latter part of their therapeutic experience as they develop a more integrated sense of self. Reflective capacity grows out of the child's experience of being held in mind by someone, the process of containment described in Chapter 1. This good experience leads to the capacity to symbolize experience, giving the child some distance from raw emotion, another step towards making it communicable and manageable. Eventually experience can be conceptualized, as the child develops the capacity to contain and think about it, and to communicate it to others.

Focused play in 'direct work' with children

There is a long tradition of direct work in social work with children which draws on the use of a 'third thing' on which both worker and child can focus, reducing the anxiety of a face-to-face interview and easing communication (Aldgate and Simmonds 1988; Aldgate *et al.* 2005; Luckock and Lefevre 2008). Play techniques enable worker and child to get to know one another, to help uncover a child's feelings and to permit their expression. Donald

Winnicott used his famous 'squiggle' technique as a way of equalizing power and quickly establishing communication between child and adult on the level of unconscious processes. He would draw a random squiggle and ask the child to turn it into something, in turn asking the child to draw a squiggle which he would then complete.

Some workers use non-directive play as their way of opening communication with a child but move to using more focused methods. Others make use of focused or directive techniques from the outset when they judge that the child can cope with them, and some older children may prefer, at least initially, not to be in a playroom which they see as for younger children. Other workers use both approaches within a session ('a time for you to play as you choose and a time for me to choose what we do'). The methods chosen depend on the worker's skills and resources as well as on the child's age and developmental stage. They also depend on the aims of work and on the time available. In carrying out an assessment for the court, workers often use focused techniques, preferably following a time of non-directive play. Story stem assessments (Hodges *et al.* 2003) which combine focused and non-directive play are increasingly used (see Chapter 8). Focused approaches are useful too when children are not so much in need of deep therapy as of help to clarify what is happening in their lives, and where there is a clear task on which worker and child are engaged, such as preparation for family placement.

Responding to the child's communication

The worker's role, once they have made clear why they are there, is to respond to the child's communication. Clare Winnicott warns against going ahead of children and verbalizing or interpreting feelings before children have shown that they are ready to think about them. She reassures us that children work things out in their own way. We need to wait alongside the child. It is important to accept painful feelings rather than avoid them, meeting and surviving the hostility of an angry child (whether expressed overtly or by passive indifference). A brief acknowledgment of a painful or frightening experience may touch deeply and there is no need to 'wallow' in feelings. Later we can help the child to put their feelings into words. Timing in choice of a technique must be matched to the child's readiness to make use of it. It is vital to be flexible and responsive. The risk of many directive approaches is that they may take control, and therefore a sense of recognition and empowerment, away from the child, who then responds in a defended way. A rejected reflection may not be wrong. If a child is surprised and overcome by feelings, they may retreat to avoid pain. We need to bear in mind the basic principles of healing play, that the child is in control of their play, in a situation that is safe and contained, within which they create something new. Some focused techniques or very structured approaches may not meet these criteria. Others may be incorporated into a child's playing in a relation-ship with an attuned and sensitive adult, who may introduce an idea as their contribution to supporting play or reaching out to the child. This takes considerable skill and self-awareness if the child's spontaneity and initiative is to be supported rather than drowned. A worker who is too anxious about a technique they plan to use is not likely to be either playful or attuned. Focused methods are helpful in saving time as well as making sure that vital areas of assessment are covered. Yet they risk rushing children into painful confrontations which they are not ready to handle. Their use needs a trained and sensitive worker who can judge when a technique might help a particular child, bearing in mind the child's developmental level, and be ready to abandon it if the child's response indicates.

Views of families and schools, past and present

Ecomaps or mind maps, picture genograms or illustrated family trees, perhaps a family tree with roots and branches, representing past and present families, or with leaves which represent faces of family members, a 'life snake' of early life experiences and feelings, picture flow charts and time drawings are widely used to help the child tell their story (Figures 2.1–2.3). Ecomaps of 'all the people in your life whom you love and who love you' provide clues as to whether an important attachment figure exists for the child, although we need to remain attentive as to whether the child 'is avoiding, or even, faking intim-acy' (Farnfield 1997). In picture flow charts of 'places I have lived' and 'schools I have been to' the child can be asked for each place 'Was this a sad house/school or a happy one?' These help in checking the accuracy of hypotheses based on observations of play and drawing: 'A seven-year-old boy who was having school attendance problems built the school and insisted on having an area "where we hang our bags up". He labelled all the parts of the building as "happy" or "OK" except for this area which was "unhappy". In pushing this further it became obvious that he was being bullied in the cloak-room area. This had not previously been known' (Farnfield 1997). Card and board games are often invented by the worker to meet a particular need. There are also numerous games with rules, playful tasks and play situations which have been devised to help children to make sense of their past, present and future (Carroll 1998; Ryan and Walker 2007; Redgrave 2000). They tend to concentrate on children's difficulties in the real world rather than inner conflicts, although they may help children to distinguish between reality and phantasy.

A child can be asked draw or paint their own family, or some aspect of their life, the worker observing who is included or left out, the order in which people are drawn, their relative size and the child's position, often nearest to the preferred parent or adult. It can be important to know the names the child gives to family members (especially where there is

Figure 2.1 Family tree or genogram.

more than one possible 'dad') and their feelings about each (Bannister and Print 1988). They may be invited to draw 'the time you spend with Mum and Dad' or 'the presents you would give your family'; or they may draw 'the best/worst thing about Dad/Mum is'. Magic pens can draw 'secrets'. Part-completed pictures, such as *The Anti-Colouring Book* ('My nicest dream', 'My worst nightmare', or 'Look through the keyhole and see what upsets me most', Striker and Kimmel 1978), *Moving Pictures* (Alton and Firmin 1987) and *Talking Pictures* (King 1988), are a useful stimulus, as are flash cards with faces or feelings ('Does mum have a sad or happy face? What makes mum angry?'), trigger cards ('I like my . . ., I feel like

Figure 2.2 Ecomap.

crying when . . ., I wish . . .'), or home-made games such as snakes and ladders with sad and happy caterpillars. Social worker John Diaper used *Talking Pictures* with a six-year-old boy who felt left out in his rather chaotic family:

Figure 2.3 Time drawing/picture flow chart.

They revealed Sean's wish for his mother's approval. His *Faces* were sad 'when my mum tells me off' and happy 'when my mum don't tell me off'. He drew *My Favourite Food*, sausages and three baked beans, 'because my mum only give me three'. He drew a shark, 'because it eats everything up'. *My Secret Island* has 'no more people, just me'. For *Who I Would Like to Visit Me in Hospital*, he liked the idea of being 'poorly' and drew himself with a sad face. The only person he wanted to visit him was his grandad, with whom he was due to spend the weekend. He was quite firm that his mum and dad would not come. Similarly, in his drawing of *The People I Would Get to Hold the Rope for Me*, to stop him falling down a cliff, he drew only myself. When prompted he said 'Mum and Dad would let me fall', and added 'They like me but they don't want me.'

Some tasks may have a playful or symbolic element, for example, fantasy journeys to the moon or on a magic carpet ('Who is coming with you?'), or imagining being at a holiday centre and allocating family members to houses. A child's first reaction to sand is often to build a castle; using play people, a child may be invited to place themselves in the castle with other people they would choose, while others are not allowed across the moat. We might invite a child to choose five objects and then to use them in the sand to tell a story, or ask them to draw a house (symbolizing the mother), a person (the father) and a tree (the child) (Sluckin 1989). Computer-based interactive games and activities are increasingly available, for example *In My Shoes* (Calam *et al.* 2006). The worker stays with a reflective response, encouraging without pressure. Any questions need to be open, not leading, for example 'I wonder who lives here?' or 'Who would you like to live here?'

It is important not to jump to conclusions. A court prefers verbal evidence; play and drawing are a catalyst, a means towards this end. Later we can check back with the child. A four-year-old drew a happy face for contact visits seeing mum and a sad face for when it was time to go, confirming 'I want to be with my mummy.' Preparing a child for a court appearance can help lessen anxiety, although of course, what the child might say cannot be rehearsed. However, it is possible to use role play with puppets and dolls, or use drawings or models, or stories such as Bray's *Suzie and the Wise Hedgehog Go to Court* (1989) to explain what a court is for and what happens there. Sometimes a child may be helped to write or say something for the court. It is made clear to the child that it is the court that makes decisions, the worker only promising to tell the court what the child wants. Contact with child, a visit or a letter, after the court case shows that the worker still has the child in mind and can explain simply the court's decision.

Symbolic communication with dolls and puppets

Play people, puppets or dolls can create the emotional distance which makes it possible for the child to 'tell' their story. If they are like the child, perhaps a bit worn, the child can identify with them. An anxious child can also be helped to relax if the worker has a puppet or teddy that keeps making mistakes. Families can be cut out from paper, or made with plastic stick-ons or modelling materials. A child might be asked to select dolls to represent family members, to put everybody to bed and then show us a particular school or weekend day. This draws on a child's episodic memory which may give us a clearer insight than their more tidied up semantic memory. Asking the child to put the furniture in the doll's house 'as near as possible to how it is at home' can give some idea of the sense of order or confusion in the home.

A child may be encouraged to talk to the figures or puppets they are playing with or drawing, or write letters to them. Violet Oaklander (1978) suggests many other fantasy and projective techniques. For example, children might be asked to draw their family as symbols or animals, to go on a fantasy journey, perhaps in a guided fantasy, and draw their room or the place they get to, to create their own world, or a particular feeling, on paper, just using shapes, lines, curves and colours, or to draw themselves as a rosebush or a boat in a storm. The worker may, if it feels right, direct the child's awareness to the content or the process of play, saying, for example, 'You like to do that slowly', 'You are burying the tiger', 'This plane is all alone', or even 'You sound angry'. If a pattern is repeated, the child might be asked about their life, 'Do you like things tidy at home?', helping children own their feelings and projections. Children may be asked to repeat a situation or exaggerate an action, such as a fire engine doing lots of rescuing, and asked 'Does that remind you of anything in your life?' The child with the fire engine replied that since his dad had been away his mother expected him to do everything! Children are often asked to speak as the people, animals or objects in their fantasy or drawing, for example, 'What might that snake say about itself?', 'What would the fire engine say to the truck if it could talk?', or 'Do you ever feel like that monkey?' (Oaklander 1978: 162). Older children might be asked to choose a toy in the room and then to imagine that they are it, describing how they are used, what they do and what they look like, and what they want to do.

Social work consultant Madge Bray (1988, 1991), whose sensitive training on suspected sexual abuse inspired numerous workers, used a special toy box. A wise hedgehog puppet understands a lot and has a badge which says 'I listen to children'. A big bear puppet or a strong and friendly lion represents benign power, a strong person who would hear the child and look after them, 'so we'll tell him shall we?'. If a child picked up a little sheep which baas, she might say, 'It's a very sad sheep. You can hear him crying. I wonder where it is hurting.' Or with a tiny battery-powered trembling rabbit, 'This is a very frightened rabbit; you feel him shaking and trembling. I wonder why?' A musical doll has a head which goes round and round. 'This little girl has so many muddles in her head. Do you know anyone like that? Maybe we could draw a picture of the muddles.' She finds that the child may start to tell her about her 'doll', or draw a picture of her muddles, 'the mummy's telling the daddy off, 'cos the little girl was naughty' (Bray 1991). A rabbit puppet is not very clever so he just has to listen more times than other people, 'so can you tell him again please'. Using a soft toy or puppet, she would tell a story of the wise owl who looks in the windows, and asks what he sees. A child's fearful reaction such as 'Don't look in there' (the bedroom) is noted and respected; the adult takes the attitude that 'If it's important you'll find a way to tell me and I'll find a way to understand.'

Work may simply be focused through provision of specific play materials while play remains non-directive. Jewett (1984) suggests an open-mouthed dinosaur, a van with sliding doors that can take people and furniture, a hulk-like figure and a police car, to help children to play out angry feelings and replay their experience of loss and separation. We may notice how a child sets out farm animal families, where fences are placed and which gates are closed or left open (Waterhouse 1987).

Workers' responses vary according to their training and background. Some deal solely with the child's conscious feelings and views expressed through play. Others recognize less conscious feelings in the child's symbolic play and may choose to convey this recognition to the child, usually working within the symbolism, saying, for example, 'This boy doll looks as if he's very cross with the big brother doll', avoiding the direct interpretation of 'Perhaps you are feeling very angry with your big brother'. Such an approach can be effective, especially with younger children. Going at the child's pace makes the therapy more bearable to the child at any age.

Expressing feelings or managing thoughts – symbolism or cognitive behavioural approaches?

Some children need help in expressing their feelings. These are often the more defended avoidantly attached children who bottle things up inside. The core anxiety of the child with an avoidant attachment is abandonment. The child feels an underlying sadness, anger and emptiness, although on the surface they appear to manage by avoiding contact and intimacy. This fear of contact may find expression in the worker's feeling of being bored, angry and rejected, a useful communication of the (transference) feelings which the worker needs to contain. The therapeutic aim is to help the child with intimacy (Holmes 1996). Sometimes directive symbolic approaches may help the child to express feelings. A water play technique changes a bowl of water into 'good stuff' using food colouring, as the child suggests things which feels good, like cuddling, attention and love. Different members of the family are represented by labelled glasses. The only rules are that the more 'good stuff' someone has, the happier that person is. Whenever a person gives out 'good stuff' to someone else, the person gets the same amount back from the jug. It is then possible to act out situations. Here is John Diaper's 'Sean' again:

Sean took exceptionally well to water play with 'good stuff'. Only twice did he fill up his glass with 'good stuff' from his mother. He usually poured most of his mother's water into either his brother's or his father's glass. He frequently filled up his mother's glass from his own, showing that he kept on giving her love and affection but felt he got little back. He felt he got a fairer share of his mother's attention when his father was there too. He showed that he got love and attention from his father, although not enough, but had more when his mother was not included. His baby brother received 'good stuff' from everyone but gave none out. His teacher, myself, and one or two others were seen as giving 'good stuff'. Unless preventive action was taken to help his parents give him the love and attention he craved, I thought Sean would eventually become enmeshed in either the care system or the delinquency system or both, a prediction which sadly proved to be only too accurate.

These and other focused techniques, such as candle ceremonies for grief work, and planned anger work, need workers who are prepared and able to contain the strong feelings aroused (Redgrave 1987; Owen and Curtis 1988; Cipolla *et al.* 1992; Jewett 1994).

Some children are already prone to venting their feelings on all and sundry, whether in the form of anger or in sexually harmful behaviour. They express their feelings all too easily in actions but lack the thinking which, in Melvin Rose's words, 'turn thoughtless acts into actless thoughts'. The core anxiety of children with an ambivalent controlling attachment is enmeshment or impingement, because blurred boundaries have made them unable to digest experience and fearful of separation. Instead they blame, cajole, threaten or coerce, leaving the worker feeling smothered, taken over and unable to think, as they themselves are. The therapeutic aim is individuation, the development of a separate self which involves being able to think (Holmes 1996). The worker needs to provide clear boundaries and to resist being drawn into a collusive power struggle. The child's thinking process is helped by the worker naming feelings as they are expressed in play. However, some simple cognitive behavioural strategies of the 'stop-think-do kind turned into a game can help a child to think about the effects of their actions on others and better manage their behaviour. For the most damaged and damaging children, this needs to be provided within a physically and emotionally containing setting, as they move from depending on external controls to developing internal controls (Redl and Wineman 1952).

Group work

Structured or focused play techniques are often used in group work when it seems likely that children will benefit from sharing difficult experiences, perhaps of separation or loss, with one another and find that they are not alone. Playful tasks and games to help children feel relaxed and comfortable in a group are used initially, followed by specific games to deal with areas which are causing difficulties for the children. Because there is often little spontaneous play the therapeutic value more often comes from the recognition and communication of feelings rather than directly from the play experience itself. The use of play, however, brings a lightness of touch, a playfulness, which fosters open communication. Some group work, on the other hand, may take a cognitive behavioural approach. Games such as traffic lights involving 'stop (red) – think (amber) – do (green)' can help with this. Other games can involve making choices between, for example, 'getting up when mum calls me' and 'missing school'.

The provision of primary experience

Children who have experienced severe deprivation and trauma in their earliest years are at the extreme end of the attachment continuum, with 'disorganized' attachment. These unintegrated children have even more chaotic behaviour. Continuing trauma and loss mean that their core anxiety is annihilation, against which they have little defence, although for some a compliant false self or taking care of others may cover up their terrifying emptiness. They leave workers feeling helpless and wiped out, as they themselves feel. These children cannot change unless their whole environment changes. They need to go back to the point of breakdown (Winnicott 1965) and receive a version of the mother–infant relationship if they are to develop an integrated sense of self. Such methods work at profoundly unconscious levels. Play will be a significant part of this experience but it will also involve other aspects of nurture and boundary management.

Nurture and sensory play

Where children have suffered nurturing deprivation they often withdraw or isolate themselves, submerging their self to accommodate adult expectations (Thom 1984). Their senses may be dulled by the many traumas that have been suffered, so that they do not know what they feel or how to express feeling. 'Development of the senses – of the "contact function" – looking, talking, touching, listening, moving, smelling and tasting has therefore become an important part of work with children and a significant part of the development of the sense of self' (Aldgate and Simmonds 1988: 14). For example, a child who cannot tell hot from cold does not think of taking their sweater off on a hot day. Sensory work (Oaklander 1978) can 'unfreeze' them, helping the child become aware of their body and their contact with the world. Work might start by asking about the kinds of textures they like and dislike touching, expanding their vocabulary of 'feeling' words. Each session can concentrate on using a different sense – touch, sight, sound, smell and taste. Sensory integration theory and practice (Ayres 1985; Bundy *et al.* 2002) offer further possibilities, including the different effects of light and firm touch.

Sensory experiences can be provided in non-directive play in activities such as water and sand play, clay and playdough, outdoor experiences, painting, finger and foot painting, cookery, junk modelling, sounds, music and singing (Crowe 1974; Redgrave 1987). Baby play (with a basket of baby items for the child to explore and use if they wish, or in a 'home corner') may allow for regressive play. These activities can fill gaps in experience for older children too, although they may need to be provided in an acceptable form, perhaps as puppets rather than dolls, cookery rather than dough play, without any pressure to make an acceptable end product. In new families or therapeutic residential care, attention to the child's needs for nurture can be met through the events of daily living, in the way food, play, bedtimes and bathtimes are provided (Tomlinson 2004; see also Chapter 9). Nurture groups in schools (Boxall 2002) can offer a responsive 'soft' environment (Prescott and Jones 1975) with singing, music, stories and other kinds of sensory play. Children in hospital or other stressful environments may be calmed by listening to soothing sounds and music, such as birdsong or 'womb music' tapes, watching moving patterns of coloured light, receiving gentle massage, or lying in a 'soft play' ball pool or on a transparent waterbed with lights playing through it. This works at a pre-verbal level by helping children get in touch, literally, with themselves.

Relationship play to promote attachment

Understanding of attachment theory and neurophysiology in infancy has led to a number of different approaches which have in common the aim of improving the relationship between child and parent or carer, leading to a more secure attachment for the child. Group-based parenting programmes such as Webster Stratton's *The Incredible Years* use ideas similar to the *ParentChild Game* (Forehand and McMahon 1981), with parents being taught how to attune to their child and respond (and join in) contingently and empathically in play. Other parts of the programme help parents provide boundaries and remain in control of the overall situation within which their child can play. Filial play therapy uses a similar approach, modelling and explaining to parents how to provide child-centred non-directive special playtimes, supporting them in doing so, with the aim of an improved attachment which is eventually generalized to other aspects of daily life. Structure is provided by the time, place and play materials as well as the parental presence but play is directed by the child, with the parent attending to and reflecting the child's feelings as well as their actions.

Theraplay (Jernberg and Booth 1999) also aims to encourage attachment but has a different method. No toys are used; instead parents take control from the start by initiating playful games and interactions. Group-based relationship play (see Chapter 4) similarly uses a programme of interactive songs and games with parents and children. The emphasis in theraplay is on providing a version of a good infant experience, providing nurture as well as an attuned and playful relationship in which the child feels safe and their curiosity is encouraged. Parents are explicitly guided to improve their pattern of interaction. Games are modified versions of parent–baby play. Eye contact, physical movement, touching and singing, and appreciating the child's appearance (hair, face, clothes, and so on) are integral to the activities. Because theraplay replicates missed emotional experiences it is used, as is filial play therapy, with foster and adoptive carers to help them build a relationship and become secure attachment figures for a child (Hughes 2000; Burnell and Archer 2003; Cairns 2006). Theraplay demands the complex skill of reaching out (sometimes literally) to the child to pull them into a closer relationship, while at the same time being attuned, playful and responsive.

Because these approaches share the aim of promoting attachment between child and parent or carer, they limit the need for attachment to be part of the child and worker therapeutic relationship. This means that the child is not faced with the pain of letting go, which is inevitably the case in the child–therapist relationship. However, while no one would want a child to experience unnecessary pain, a well-managed ending of a therapeutic relationship, which may involve attachment, can also be a point of growth.

Non-directive play therapy

Axline's principles of non-directive play therapy

Perhaps most people who become interested in play therapy were initially inspired by reading Virginia Axline's *Dibs – In Search of Self*, a moving account of how she enabled a disturbed and withdrawn boy to heal himself and to reveal his incredible intellectual gifts. Her non-directive approach is based on the belief that children contain within themselves both the ability to solve their own problems and the 'growth impulse that makes mature behaviour more satisfying than immature behaviour'. Axline (1964a: 57–58) writes:

The therapeutic value of this kind of psychotherapy is based upon the child experiencing himself as a capable, responsible person in a relationship that tries to communicate to him two basic truths: that no one ever really knows as much about any human being's inner world as does the individual himself; and that responsible freedom grows and develops from inside the person.

Axline equipped her playroom with a wide variety of play materials, including sand, water, paint and drawing materials, fingerpaint, a doll's house and family, miniature cars and people, a feeding bottle and an inflatable rubber figure. Within this protected setting the child was free to choose what to do. The relationship between child and therapist was the key. Axline, who worked in the United States, was influenced by Carl Rogers's (1951) non-directive approach to counselling. She used his technique of active reflective listening, based on the principles of empathy, warmth, acceptance and genuineness (described in Truax and Carkhuff 1967), but also using the child's play as a means of communication to the therapist (Dorfman 1951). She saw the therapist's task as recognizing the feelings which the child is expressing in speech and play and reflecting these back so that the child can get some insight into how they are. There is no attempt to direct play or to hurry the child. The only limits are those necessary to keep the therapy anchored to the real world and to make the child aware of their responsibilities to the therapy. Axline (1989) sets out eight principles for non-directive play therapy:

1   *The therapist must develop a warm, friendly relationship with the child, in which good rapport is established as soon as possible.* She explains to a new child that they may play with any of the things in the playroom or use them in any way they wish. She does not suggest anything particular that the child might do. If the child sits in silence, the therapist accepts it and sits quietly too.
2   *The therapist accepts the child exactly as they are.* The therapist must be neutral. Praise and encouragement are as inappropriate as criticism and disapproval, since both imply judgment. If the child does a beautiful painting she will not praise it because it is the child's opinion that matters, not hers.
3   *The therapist establishes a feeling of permissiveness in the relationship so that the child feels free to express their feelings completely.* The child needs to feel free – for instance, to 'beat up the mother doll or bury the baby in the sand, or lie down on the floor and drink from a nursing bottle . . . without shame or guilt' (Axline 1964b: 264). For example, she went into the playroom with Oscar who had reluctantly left his mother. He screamed, 'Don't shut the door.' She replied, 'You don't want me to shut the door. You're afraid to stay with me if we shut the door. Very well – we'll leave the door open and you can close it when you feel like it' (Axline 1964b: 98–99).

4   *The therapist is alert to recognize the feelings the child is expressing and reflects those feelings back in such a manner that they gain insight into their behaviour.* Oscar looked round the room and said, 'I'll bust up everything in here!' Axline responded, 'You're feeling tough now.' She warns against falling into the trap of responding to the *contents* of his words by saying, 'You can play with the toys any way you want to but you can't bust them up.'

5   *The therapist maintains a deep respect for the child's ability to solve his own problems if given an opportunity to do so. The responsibility to make choices and to institute changes is the child's.*

6   *The therapist does not attempt to direct the child's actions or conversation in any manner. The child leads the way; the therapist follows.* If the child needs or asks for help in play, she is given only the limited amount needed at the time.

7   *The therapist does not attempt to hurry the therapy along. It is a gradual process and recognized as such by the therapist.* Axline (1964b: 262–263) illustrates this in her description of a six-year-old's play with a doll family and sand tray:

> He took the boy doll out of the house and said to the therapist: 'She is sending the boy out where the quicksand is . . . He cries and tells his mother that he is afraid but she makes him go anyway. And see. He is sinking down and down and down into the quicksand.' The boy, showing much fear and anxiety, buries the doll in the sand. This child is certainly dramatizing his fear and his feeling of insecurity and lack of understanding . . . If she follows the child she will say: 'The boy is being sent out of the house and he is afraid . . . He tells his mother he is afraid, but she makes him go out anyway and he gets buried in the sand.' If she had said, 'You are afraid and your mother doesn't pay any attention to your fears and that scares you still more', she is getting ahead of the child and interpreting . . . Perhaps the interpretation is correct, but there is a danger of thrusting something at the child before he is ready for it.

8   *The therapist establishes only those limitations that are necessary to anchor the therapy to the world of reality and to make the child aware of his responsibility in the relationship.* The notion of the child's responsibility underlies Axline's expectation of the child taking the initiative and choosing how to use time in the playroom. As in all play, freedom is possible only because of the safe limits of the situation. The boundaries consist of time, one hour, usually weekly, and space, the playroom and materials within it. Children are not permitted to hurt themselves or the therapist, and some limits may be placed on the destruction of materials. These limits are not laid down at the outset but explained as the need arises. The child is also helped to understand that the playroom hour is

only part of their life and that the real world imposes other constraints and limits to which they must adapt, whatever they feel.

For example, Axline (1964b: 448–449) told Dibs he had only three minutes more before it was time to go home:

> Dibs suddenly stood up. 'No!' he shouted. 'Dibs no go out of here. Dibs no go home. Not never!'
>
> 'I know you don't want to go, Dibs. But you and I only have one hour every week to spend together here in the playroom. And when that hour is over, no matter how you feel about it, no matter how I feel about it, no matter how anybody feels about it, it is over for that day and we both leave the playroom.'
>
> 'Cannot paint another picture?' Dibs asked me, tears streaming down his face.
>
> 'Not today,' I told him.
>
> He sat down muttering, 'No go home. No want to go home. No *feel* like going home.'
>
> 'I know how you *feel*,' I told him.

Non-directive play therapy based on Axline's principles can be effective in reaching buried feelings and bringing them into consciousness where they can be dealt with. However, as the example of doll play in the sand shows, the therapist does not make direct interpretations of play but stays within the symbolism expressed in play, until the child is ready to move on. Since therapy goes at the child's pace and direction it is unlikely to distress a child by uncovering unmanageable feelings which neither child nor perhaps worker are ready to handle. The worker, however, needs to be alert to areas the child may be avoiding. Non-directive play therapy is invaluable in assessment when the worker has limited information as to how the child is feeling and what the problem is for the child. Therapy is a gradual process and there may be few workers who have time to offer it. It provides, however, great hope of recovery to many disturbed children.

The growth of non-directive play therapy

Children's Hours

Rachel Pinney, who had worked with Margaret Lowenfeld, taught a simplified version of Axline's non-directive reflective listening, which could be safely used by inexperienced workers. An attentive adult described aloud the child's actions (or inactivity) in play, a sort of running commentary or 'recapping'. For example, 'You're looking around – looking in the box – you've found a lion.' Closer to Axline, feelings as well as actions might be recapped: 'You're kicking that chair over – you're really angry', or 'You're crying – you're really hurting.' Or the adult might sit quietly mirroring the body language of a silent child. Pinney (1990: 4) believed that 'children, whatever their circumstances, benefit from having a time and space in which to play out their thought and feelings with an attentive adult who receives all that is said and done without passing judgment'. Her approach was influential in England in the 1980s, when interest in applying Axline's ideas was growing, and a number of workers introduced Children's Hours or 'special times', including for children with disabilities (Cockerill 1992).

Developments in non-directive play therapy

Professional training in play therapy became established in the UK from the 1990s, leading to a more rigorous application and development of Axline's and Rogers' basic principles (Wilson and Ryan 2005). The aim 'is to bring children to a level of emotional and social functioning on a par with their developmental stage, so that usual developmental progress is resumed' (Wilson and Ryan 2005: 4). The relationship between child and therapist is at the heart of the work of non-directive play therapy. Unconditional positive regard or non-possessive warmth means the therapist has real concern for the child but retains a capacity to think about the child's communication and is not drawn into unhelpful collusion or 'rescue'. At the same time the therapist must be genuine and authentic, real and congruent in their relationship with the child. This implies a sophisticated and aware use of self, which is why personal therapy is part of a play therapist's training. Accurate empathy, the ability to be in touch with the child's feelings, together with active reflective listening of those feelings as expressed in words or play, means that the child can feel understood.

There is much attention to the preparation which is needed for a child to have a reliable and predictable one-to-one play therapy session with a therapist, over a planned period, for a given time, in a playroom with carefully chosen play material. Within this framework the child is enabled to play freely, to choose what they do and how they play, and to involve the therapist in play or not as they wish, hence the term non-directive. However, the framework around play provides the necessary clear and safe boundaries and careful thought is given to the therapeutic use of limits (Landreth 2002). The planning for play therapy involves working with the child's parents or carers, as well as with any network of professional agencies involved, to ensure that the work is sustained, supported and reviewed.

Play, especially pretend or symbolic play, is used as the means of communication because of its assimilative and organizing function in a child's development. The themes of the child's play are observed and examined for their symbolic meaning, as well as what they reveal about the child's emotional developmental stage, but this will not be interpreted back to the child except through the reflection of feelings expressed in play. This reflection goes deeper than simply mirroring the child's words or actions; it aims to provide the child with a version of their expressed emotions which helps them feel understood and enables them in due course to understand themselves better. At the same time the reflection stays within the metaphor of play. 'The assumption is that given the opportunity to express themselves freely, children will reach solutions and resolve their own difficulties themselves, using play experiences and their therapists to do so' (Wilson and Ryan 2005: 2).

Other child-centred creative therapies – story making, art, music, dance and drama

While maintaining the child-centred focus of non-directive play therapy, some other approaches place different emphases on aspects of the work. Some play therapists emphasize a narrative approach or story making, sometimes writing down for the child the imaginative story the child has constructed in play (Cattanach 1997), or using books and stories, which might match their feelings (Bettelheim 1976; Rustin and Rustin 1988; Gersie 1990, 1991; Dwivedi 1997) and give hope for the future. These approaches fit well with attachment theory's notion of the child's need for a coherent narrative which becomes an integrated part of their inner world, helping the child feel that their experience makes some kind of sense. However, they require a child who has achieved a capacity for symbolization which the least emotionally integrated children may yet lack. Art and music therapies provide forms of communication through the specific materials available. While this may be at a symbolic level they can also reach much earlier bodily states of sensory experience, providing a version of the good experience of infancy (Case and Dalley 1990). Dance and dramatherapy work at a similar level of embodying feelings (Chodorow 1991; Jennings 1992, 1999), as well as going on to work at symbolic levels in role play enactments.

These creative approaches are exemplified in art therapist Ann Gillespie's account of work with Sonia, an 11-year-old black child trying to cope with life in a foster family after a childhood of uncertainty and violence. From a beginning of inertia and hopelessness, with Sonia's only burst of energy going into drawing a sad little black dog (herself?), her relationship with the therapist grew as 'Sonia drew and talked about countless cradles, babies and mothers', including babies who looked 'too old' (herself again). Much of their communication was unspoken, operating through the medium of drawing, painting and modelling, 'entrusted as I am with elements of her that are so deep and hurtful that they have to be hidden in fairy tale pictures and thick crude paint'. Gillespie (Jefferies and Gillespie 1981: 14) continues:

> After she discovered I had conferred with her family, she drew a
> fortified castle, warning me to keep our special relationship defended

from outsiders. Twin-towered it stands, surrounded by its moat, door securely barred, alone in a large hilly countryside. Outside stand two riderless horses, one brown, one white (like us), saddled and waiting until we are able to continue our journey.

Therapy helped Sonia to cope with deep levels of emotional pain, freeing her to benefit from relationships offered by her foster parents and her social worker.

Creative arts therapies are often acceptable to older children (and adults) who feel too grown-up to play but may not be able to cope with talking therapies. Sometimes group work may be a rich and stimulating creative and social experience, a means of sharing and acknowledging one another's creative impulses and feelings through art, dance and drama. It makes use of techniques such as mime, masks, improvization, puppetry, myths and stories, movement and dance, combining therapy with ritual and theatre. Therapists expect to nurture and be fed by their own creative art process. The underpinning theory of many of the creative arts therapies is psychodynamic, an approach we now discuss.

Psychoanalytic child psychotherapy

Psychoanalysts in the Freudian tradition developed the theory and practice of psychoanalytic work with children. Anna Freud and Melanie Klein were influenced by the pioneering analytic work with children of Hug Hellmuth in Vienna. Donald Winnicott, Erik Erikson and Margaret Lowenfeld contributed in their own very different ways. Recent years have seen marked changes in emphasis in child psychotherapy towards the significance of the child–therapist relationship and the emotional containment provided within that relationship.

Anna Freud's child psychoanalysis

Anna Freud worked with her father Sigmund Freud in Vienna and moved with him to London where she founded the Hampstead War Nurseries, later to become the Anna Freud Centre for the Psychoanalytic Study and Treatment of Children. Before starting therapy she aimed to create a loving and caring relationship with the child so that the child would like her and feel dependent on her. Play was one of the main ways of achieving this. Also by observing play she was better able to understand the child's problem. Unlike Melanie Klein who thought that all play was symbolic, Anna Freud believed that it could be a replaying of real events or even pure exploration. For instance, a child who looks in her therapist's handbag is not necessarily looking to see if her mother's womb is holding another baby. After initial assessment she used play methods less than 'free association', asking children to 'see pictures', tell stories, draw, or describe their dreams.

Anna Freud saw playing in therapy as a means of permitting children to talk about conscious feelings and thoughts and to act out unconscious conflicts and phantasies. Interpretation to the child of the symbolism of their play might follow, but only if it was suggested by a good deal of material. The positive tie created earlier helped the child 'face up to the often very painful revelation of repressed material' (Freud 1936, 1965). The immature self of the child used the analyst as a model for identification. Anna Freud's analytic work was often with latency age children, those who had developed strong psychological defences and therefore resistances to therapy. She always kept sight of the child's real world and worked only slowly down from reality and conscious feelings towards deeper levels of the child's unconscious. She did not think a quick, deep interpretation could be lastingly therapeutic.

Melanie Klein's psychoanalytic play therapy

Melanie Klein started her psychoanalytic work in Berlin and, like Anna Freud, moved to London as the Second World War loomed. She believed that children's play could be used as the equivalent of free association in adult psychoanalysis, revealing unconscious anxieties and phantasies. Play was the means for communication of children's unconscious. She concluded that it was possible to work with very young children; many of her patients were under five years old and some were as young as two. Klein thought it was important to analyse the child's transference – that is, the child's feelings towards the therapist which had their origin in the earlier mother–child experiences. Anna Freud, in contrast, felt that transference was less significant since children were still developing their relationship to their parents. Parents were still real and present as love objects, which also meant work with the parents could directly benefit the child. In contrast to Anna Freud, Melanie Klein made profound interpretations to children of the unconscious meanings of their play from the outset. If the child strongly rejected her interpretation she felt that this indicated it was correct. Her view was that when a child accepted an interpretation their anxiety and guilt would lessen, enabling the symbolic exploration of feelings, free of the fear of damaging real people. Her interpretations often involved sexual meanings which she did not hesitate to offer to the child. It is perhaps this which led many people to reject her ideas, although with today's awareness of some children's sexual experience a reappraisal may be due.

Klein's most significant contributions have been her explanation of the origin of the child's emotions in 'object relations', tracing them back to infancy (see Chapter 1), and her specific use of play in therapy. She was possibly the first therapist to use a carefully planned playroom. Her materials included a large number and variety of miniature toys with many human figures, drawing, painting and cutting out materials, and water. Each child's materials were kept in their own special drawer. Children directed their own play. If they gave the therapist a part in role play she would play the part allotted, whether in playing shops, doctor and patient, schools and so on, or mother and child play. Klein (in Mitchell 1986: 41) comments:

> In such games the child frequently takes the part of the adult, thereby not only expressing his wish to reverse the roles but also demonstrating how he feels that his parents or other people in authority behave towards him – or *should* behave. Sometimes he gives vent to his aggressiveness and resentment by being, in the role of parent, sadistic towards the child, represented by the analyst.

The therapist neither encourages nor disapproves of expressions of aggression but interprets their meaning to the child. Klein (1937) stressed the importance of working with the child's negative transference (such as anger expressed towards her but originating in the child's experience of a parent) as well as the child's good feelings towards her, so that the child could not continue to split people (or parts of people) into being all good and others all bad. They could then bring together in their own mind a sense of there being both good and bad aspects of the self which could be tolerated and thought about.

Margaret Lowenfeld's make-a-world technique

At her Institute of Child Psychology in London, where the first child psychotherapy training was established, Margaret Lowenfeld (1979) encouraged children to construct a series of miniature worlds in a sand tray, choosing from the enormous collection of miniature world material, stored in tiny drawers, which consisted of figures of people, soldiers, wild, domestic and farm animals, houses, cars, boats, fences, trees and so on. She would tell children to use pictures in their heads to construct their world. When completed she asked the child to explain it to her. She considered that the therapist's role was to encourage and help, and that this was more useful than making interpretations, which she used only sparingly. In accord with her Jungian view (Jung 1964), Lowenfeld saw the child's expression through symbolic play as all important. Her own understanding of the child's play still largely used sexual symbolism. She noted some recurring themes in children's worlds, such as a dam holding back water (feelings) to be eventually released. A child often built a volcano, representing internal turmoil, at the point where it had stopped getting rid of its bad feelings by projection. Lowenfeld also asked children, usually at the start and end of work, to make a design or picture with a set of wooden mosaics (www.lowenfeld.org). She would record it carefully and think about its symbolic meaning but, as in her sand tray work, would make no interpretation to the child.

The make-a-world technique using sand play has been borrowed and adapted by play therapists and 'bare foot therapists' for a wide variety of children who have some capacity for symbolic play (Kalff 1980; Newsom 1992). Elizabeth Newson describes the worker's role as quietly watchful, perhaps with some reflection or 'recapping', avoiding praise such as 'That's nice'. When the child has finished they are asked if they want to tell you about their world, and after two sessions may also be asked if they are in their world. Children often use a symbol, sometimes a particular animal, to represent themselves. No interpretation is offered. Newson suggests following a make-a-world session with a playroom time in which the worker is actively involved in role playing under the direction of the child. She considers that this dual version of play therapy offers the child an alternative language to look at their predicaments, creating something which makes sense to them.

Erik Erikson – play as therapy

Erik Erikson (1965: 215), a child psychoanalyst who started as a teacher in Anna Freud's school in Vienna before going to the United States, recognized the healing power of play:

> Modern play therapy is based on the observation that a child made insecure by a secret hate or fear of the natural protectors of his play in family and neighbourhood seems able to use the protective sanction of an understanding adult to regain some play peace. Grandmothers and favourite aunts may have played that role in the past; its professional elaboration of today is the play therapist. The most obvious condition is that the child has the toys and adult for himself, and that sibling rivalry, parental nagging, or any kind of sudden interruption does not disturb the unfolding of his play intentions.

In his own work Erikson used quite deep interpretations – for example, a child who built a rectangle of inward-facing dominoes was helped by the interpretation that it was his coffin. However, he recognized that the level and timing of interpretation was crucial. He noticed that when a child experienced overwhelming emotion, such as excitement or anxiety, it could disrupt their play. This might happen suddenly or slowly inhibit play. He explained that the process is similar to 'resistance' to transference in adult therapy, occurring when painful repressed material is getting too near the surface. The therapist's task is to try to understand the meaning of the play which led up to disruption. The therapist may interpret this to the child, trying to put their experience into words to increase their insight.

Significantly, Erikson recognized that play therapy does not take place in a vacuum but that social context is crucial. A child's identity ultimately depends on finding a reflection within the child's own culture. Play therapy could only be successful where there were social and cultural reinforcements, both in the family and beyond. This could be denied, for example, to a black child in a white culture.

Donald Winnicott – play in the potential space

The work of Donald Winnicott, a paediatrician and psychoanalyst, gives us a theory of play highly relevant to play therapy. In infancy it is the mother (or attachment figure) who reliably provides the 'potential space' within which the child is protected from impingement from the external world and so feels free to play (see Chapter 1). This 'being alone in the presence of someone', that is, being in the mind of someone while playing on their own, is about the child developing the capacity to be alone. Winnicott observed that the pre-occupation of a child playing is akin to adult concentration. In play, children use objects from the real world in service of some aspect of their inner world, and this precarious interplay makes play an exciting and creative experience. It is this bringing together in play of aspects of the child's internal world of feelings and phantasies (the 'me') with the reality of the external world of objects and people (the 'not me') that is so powerful, because in the 'transitional space' something new is created, which feels intensely real. Play is about 'being honest with oneself'. 'Playing facilitates growth and therefore health ... It is good to remember always that playing is itself a therapy' (Winnicott 1971: 41, 50).

Similarly, 'psychotherapy takes place in the overlap of two areas of playing, that of the patient and that of the therapist. The corollary of this is that where playing is not possible then the work done by the therapist is directed towards bringing the patient from a state of not being able to play into a state of being able to play' (Winnicott 1971: 38). Although Winnicott thought that useful interpretation could take place as long as play was mutual, illustrated in his case examples in *Playing and Reality* (1971) and *The Piggle* (1980), he believed that fundamental psychotherapy could take place without it. 'The significant moment is that when the child surprises himself or herself. It is not the moment of my clever interpretation that is significant' (Winnicott 1971: 51). In this he differed from Melanie Klein, observing that she was only interested in the content of play as a way of receiving communication from the child and that she had not recognized the value of the child 'playing'. Winnicott makes 'a plea to every therapist to allow for the patient's capacity to play, that is, to be creative. The patient's creativity can be only too easily stolen by a therapist who knows too much and does not hide his knowing' (Winnicott 1971: 57). This was as true for work with adults, he felt, as for children. The art is to be present but without making demands. 'It is in playing and only in playing that the individual child or adult is able to be creative and to use the whole personality, and it is only in being creative that the individual discovers the self' (Winnicott 1971: 54).

Winnicott's (1965) other significant contribution has been in his notion of the facilitating environment. He emphasized how crucial to the baby's mental development was a 'good enough' mother's 'holding', both physical and emotional, of her child. This gives the child a reliable and predictable experience of being held in mind and cared for, allowing the development of an integrated self instead of the unheld child's fear of 'falling to pieces'. The mother (or other attachment figure) can only do this if she in turn is protected from impingement by someone who holds her in mind and looks after her (Winnicott, writing in the 1960s, saw this as the father). This notion of circles of holding or containment is directly relevant to the provision of therapeutic child care and play therapy, and directs us not only to look at how families provide a holding environment but also how networks and organizations do (or fail to) do so.

Developments in child psychotherapy

Containment and inner mental space

There have been significant developments in both the theory and practice of child psychotherapy (Daws and Boston 1977; Boston and Szur 1983; Szur and Miller 1991; Lanyado and Horne 1999, 2006). Work is now rarely with neurotic children from well-off families and more often with severely deprived and traumatized children in poorer circumstances, and with autistic, psychotic and learning disabled children once considered not amenable to psychotherapy. The medium for child psychotherapy remains play. Changes in theory and technique have meant more emphasis on working on the child's experience in the present rather than on interpreting their past. With this has come attention to the relationship between child and therapist as the key factor in facilitating change. This fits well with object relations theory, in broad terms, the relationship between people or parts of people, which, while owing much to Melanie Klein's theory of infant mental development, has been taken further in theories of 'a holding environment' and 'containment' (Copley and Forryan 1987/1997; Waddell 1998), drawing on ideas of Winnicott and Bion, as well as on research in child development and attachment. Like the 'good enough' mother, the therapist provides emotional holding or containment of the child, providing an inner mental space in which she attends to and reflects on the child's communication This has much in common with maternal preoccupation and 'reverie', as Monica Lanyado (1991: 32) explains:

> Our patients need first and foremost to feel securely held by the kind of mind they come into contact with when they are with us, and by the external therapeutic environment we provide . . . The children that we see also know whether or not we are genuinely engaged with them, without

us saying anything. They can feel it, through the non-verbal communication system which they still rely on so strongly even well on in childhood, and they can see it by looking at our faces.

Within the session the therapist must receive and tolerate a child's terrible stories and bizarre behaviour, together with the emotional pain they convey, without being overwhelmed by the onslaught. Lanyado (1991: 34) gives the example of a chaotic abused boy who felt almost literally 'bad' inside, spewing out revolting sadistic phantasies in play. She had 'a profound experience of a filthy chaotic baby who desperately needed cleaning up', but first she faced the enormity of the essential task of containing his feelings. Only when there was a potential relationship in which all was not chaos could the child start to take in (introject) a healthier experience. Lanyado insists that this process 'does *not* mean that it is wise to encourage purely cathartic experience'. A therapist constantly protecting herself from attack cannot think. Firm boundaries make possible the therapist's essential task of keeping a space in her mind to think, and 'it is this thinking about the feelings which is therapeutic', not simply their expression:

> We, as therapists, have to be similarly always prepared to be surprised by the direction in which a child's associations, fantasies and play take us. This is effectively the result of what we mean by a non-directive approach. We need to be prepared at times to observe and receive vast quantities of therapeutic material, hold them (often paradoxically) in our minds and not feel unduly disturbed by this ... With this in mind, all interventions that we make in a session – insightful comments, linking statements, reflections, interpretations and so on – need to be regarded as working hypotheses and presented to the child as such, for our joint consideration.
>
> (Lanyado 1991: 35)

Firm boundaries around sessions mean that the child has a reliable experience, for some children their first good experience of containment. The therapist's ending of sessions or unavailability during breaks also gives an opportunity for children to express their anger with someone who matters to them and to find that the therapist is not destroyed nor that they are rejected.

Child psychotherapists share a belief that 'play has meaning, and even play of the most meaningless kind has meaning' (Alvarez 1992: 165). The child's communication may be received through the symbolism of the child's play. A boy playing a cops and robbers chase game who changed the robber's van into a refuse collection lorry 'may have portrayed an underlying hope that the worker would be able to collect together and hold some of his conflict' (Copley and Forryan 1987/1997: 231). The child's communication may also be received through becoming aware of the transference – which may be the child's own feelings about themselves (for example, chaos, mess, badness) or about a significant figure in their life (anger and grief for a lost parent) projected into the therapist. There is now much attention to use of the counter-transference, the feelings which being with the child arouse in the therapist, to help in becoming aware of what the child is feeling, especially when this is otherwise unclear. For example, a child who makes their therapist feel bored or sleepy may be projecting their own feelings of depression, anger and despair. One who pointedly ignores them may make them feel useless and helpless, and this may reflect how the child is feeling. This diagnostic counter-transference is distinguished from the personal countertransference which consists of the therapist's feelings in the present which arise out of their own life experience. Confusingly these may at times coincide, which is why super-vision is so essential in helping sort out what belongs where.

Hunter (1993: 214–217) explains that children in care have often had insufficient reflection back to themselves of their thoughts and feelings and are barely aware that they have them. She gives the example of a 'rather blank' 14-year-old boy whose sessions elicited in her 'a mind-numbing absence of thought'. Peter repeatedly played a story with small dolls of a minded baby in a pram. On inspiration she asked what the story might be called, to which he replied, 'Minding the baby'. When she asked what the baby was feeling he replied, 'with a ghost of a shrug, "nothing"'. She responded, 'Oh I think I see. The baby's minded but he's in no one's mind. He's not taken out of his pram, he doesn't really understand the parents' absence or what they are doing. No one seems to think of him. He's minded but in a very thoughtless way. It's a mind-less mind maybe.' Then Peter whispered near the baby, 'He wants to get out of the pram.' Hunter explains: 'The role of a therapist is firstly one of reflection, and then of amplification. These children are discovering or clarifying for the first time that the "whisperings" of their imagination are their own wishes in a world where they have long ago learned passivity.'

Although interpretation of play continues to form a major part of current psychotherapy, a more cautious approach means that its timing and level becomes important, and it may consist of reflections or linking statements rather than a deep interpretation in terms of the child's life. It may stay within the metaphor of play, as in the previous example. Perhaps one of the reasons for the overall change in emphasis has been the development of work with severely deprived children whose internal worlds are fragmented and chaotic. These children cannot make use of interpretation until they have had a version of the initial good experience they did not receive in infancy.

'Essentially, we are talking about a non-directive play experience which is safely contained by the presence of the therapist.' In the same way as the baby only feels free to explore and to complete a play experience if they have an attachment figure physically and emotionally available as a safe base to return to, so the disturbed child 'can often only have this creative play experience in which they can begin to discover who they are, in the presence of the therapist' (Lanyado 1991: 38, 2004).

Creating a therapeutic environment in families and organizations

Systems thinking and defences against anxiety

An indication of how much or little room a child actually has for growth within their present living environment is given by the degree of difficulty in establishing an overall therapeutic or facilitating environment within which therapy sessions can place. Unsatisfactory relationships within a family, between families and professionals, or within the professional network, risk sabotaging therapy, as does a parent's envy of growth in their child. Sabotage of the mental space of therapy through missed sessions, unhelpful messages and early termination is a constant risk. 'This space is frequently extremely difficult to set up in the first place and months of painstaking work may need to be done with all the adults in the child's life before there is any point in the therapist seeing the child' (Lanyado 1991: 35). There are times when it is more appropriate to work with all the adults involved in order to create a more secure and sensitive living environment for the child. Some play approaches involve the family in play, as Chapter 5 discusses. A related concern is confidentiality, working out what information needs to stay within the session to help the child make the most use of the mental space available and how much it is helpful to the child to have known by other people.

Systems thinking offers a way to work with some of the difficulties. It sees any family, group or organization as a system of interconnected parts. Therefore change in any one part of the system will affect other parts. Because a system tries to maintain a state of balance which keeps it intact then any attempt to change it by pushing all the parts at once will meet with in-built resistance, while a 'nudge' to one small part may set in motion much greater change in the system as a whole (Ward 2007: 161). Systems thinking helps look at the overall pattern of relationships in a unit to understand what is happening. Family therapy is based on a well-established tradition of systems thinking (for example, Byng-Hall 1995). It has the virtue of replacing blaming an individual with an understanding of the pattern and history of relationships in the family, and between the family and the wider society in which they find themselves, which has led up to the action. Poverty, social class, racism, attitudes to gender, sexual orientation or disability or other forms of difference, may all play a part.

Understanding what happens in organizations and networks, thinking about the unconscious processes at work (Obholzer and Roberts 1994; Hinshelwood and Skogstad 2000), is similarly useful: for example, in understanding how a child's disturbance may be projected not only into their immediate worker but can be mirrored in the disturbed functioning of the whole organization, unless there is a space where it can be thought about and understood. Menzies-Lyth (1988) explained how workers in daily contact with children's mental pain and distress develop mental defences against feeling it themselves. These defences interfere with their task of helping by giving attention to routine or domestic tasks without regard to how a particular child is feeling at any one time. Menzies-Lyth observed the effect of these defences against anxiety in the care of children in hospital and they are commonly found in day care and nursery care of young children (McMahon 1994), settings where the primary task is rarely seen in terms of supporting children emotionally. Winnicott's notion of a 'holding environment' and how it can be provided and supported is directly relevant here, above all in the idea of circles of containment. This is a task of management and leadership. It involves the provision of mental spaces at all levels within any organization or network where the impact of the work on the workers can be digested, thought about and understood. With this emotional containment workers and therapists can make themselves available to bear and think about the children's communication of unbearable feelings and find ways of managing it together (Couper 2000). Supervision, both individual and group, provides a mental space for thought. Mattinson's (1975) 'reflection process' may reveal the way in which difficulties in the worker's relationship with a child are mirrored in the relationship in supervision, where it can be made sense of (Hawkins and Shoet 2006). A similar reflection process may be operating in the organization or network, and needs the spaces where it too can be understood.

An integrated theory for play therapy and therapeutic play

This chapter has shown that although there are differing approaches to using therapeutic play in work with children, they have some things in common. They share a belief in the importance of a child's imaginative life and in the value of play, especially symbolic play, as children's natural means of expressing, communicating and coping with unconscious feelings. The healing power of spontaneous creative play occurs when the child 'surprises himself or herself'. The therapist or worker provides the play setting within safe boundaries, 'the potential space', which makes this healing play possible, offering the child a 'containing' relationship, providing an inner mental space in which the child's anxieties can be borne and thought about, and in due course handed back to the child in a more bearable form. Attunement, reflection and the use of self are the worker's most powerful tools. How this is provided depends on the child's developmental level.

Holding and containment in infancy and in therapy – a matching process

The underpinning theory for play therapy lies in the vast and growing body of theory and research in child development, especially its emphasis on the importance of the first relationships in infancy in providing the basis for a child's emotional health and an integrated sense of self (see Chapter 1). Attachment theory and research play a crucial role in linking psychoanalytical ideas of mental development to child development research. Attachment theory (Bowlby 1988; Holmes 1996; Main *et al.* 1985; Crittenden 2000) emphasizes the child's need for a 'secure base' from which they can explore and play, and so develop an 'inner working model' of the world as providing care and of themselves as worthy of care. Attachment research (Fonagy *et al.* 1994; Fonagy 2001) supports the notion that being held securely in mind enables the child to develop a 'reflective self-function'. This is akin to Winnicott's (1965) idea of ego integration, reached through the 'good enough' mother's preoccupation with her baby which enables her to provide sensitive and responsive care that is both reliable and predictable – a 'holding environment', so that the baby feels emotionally as well as physically held. This in turn has a parallel in Bion's notion of 'reverie' and 'containment' and Stern's (1985) 'attunement' as a mother responds to her infant's non-verbal communication, if necessary reaching out to engage a baby who has become out of touch, and then leaving space for their response. Out of this playful 'conversation' the child develops a sense of a separate self, and with it the capacity to play and to explore the world of people and things, which is the beginning of independent thinking and creativity. They become a 'container' of experience, able to connect feeling and thinking.

Play therapy and therapeutic play aim to provide a version of such an emotionally containing relationship within which the emotionally troubled or damaged child can find themselves and repair emotional damage through play. Play is the primary medium of communication, although all behaviour has meaning and can be seen as a communication. The work of the therapist is in providing the holding environment, including at times quite clear boundaries, within which the child feels secure, the attunement, 'reverie' or inner mental space in which to think about the feelings which the child is communicating, and the essential warmth, acceptance and empathy, avoiding collusive rescue, placating or retaliation. All these require the use of self to tolerate and think about the sometimes painful feelings the child arouses in them, to recognize their origin in the child's projection (or getting rid) of unbearable feelings. In due course the worker passes them back to the child in a more bearable form. This will rarely be a direct interpretation to the child, but more often a naming of some the feelings expressed indirectly through the symbolism of play.

Such emotional containment is not a distanced intellectual process. It is about being real in the relationship with the child. A creative response can create 'moments of meeting', significant for change. Use of self requires reflection on our own background and experience, both in broad social terms as well as in specific early relationships, in order to understand how they affect us in the present. This is a task for personal therapy or an experiential group, or both, depending on the mode of practice. Supervision, individually or in a group, continues this important process.

Therapeutic play in the 'potential space'

What form therapy takes depends on the child's existing capacity to contain experience, which in turn depends both on the child's previous experience, especially in infancy, and on the nature of current attachment and containing relationships in the child's life. Children who have experienced an emotionally secure enough start in life will have developed a capacity for play and with it some degree of emotional integration or 'reflective self-function', even when subsequent relationship difficulties, separations, losses or trauma cause distress. Children with anxious attachments may also be able to make use of play therapy, although ambivalently attached controlling children often need particularly clear and firm boundaries, while more avoidantly attached defended children may need a measure of 'reaching out' from the worker (Alvarez 1992; Holmes 1996). Play therapy provides the child with a 'potential space' in which to play 'in the presence of someone', using toys and other materials within a physically and emotionally safe boundary. Play under the child's control, supporting their autonomy, allows the child to make a bridge between the inner world of their phantasies and imaginings and the real external world, creating something new. Play often takes a symbolic form, giving the child some distance from the distressing experience. It gives the child a way of making the real world and their connection to it better understood and above all more manageable and less overwhelming or frightening (Erikson 1965; Winnicott 1971). Healing occurs both through the child playing out their experiences in play and through an emotionally containing relationship with the therapist.

Children who experienced unsatisfactory parenting and fearful attachments from the first year of life, and who have continual experience of traumatic loss or abuse, have not had the opportunity to develop an integrated self and remain fragmented and unable to think at any satisfactory level. Developing the capacity to play 'alone in the presence of someone' (that is, where they feel 'held' in the worker's mind) is very pertinent to working with very deprived children who cannot tolerate their own company for more than a few minutes and have to find someone else to bear (through projective identification) the difficulty they experience in being with themselves. The nurturing and containment of a therapeutic environment for daily living is an essential part of the work, giving them the good experience they had missed.

The worker may contribute to this by using one or another form of relationship play to promote the child's attachment to parent or carer (whether in the child's birth family or in a new family). When this is not yet possible, the worker may become an attachment figure by providing a version of a good first relationship and an opportunity for repair or growth through play. Therapy may involve bringing the child from a state of not being able to play to a state of being able to play, to tolerate being 'alone' in the presence of the worker, and so to think. The key features are a therapeutic relationship which attends to the meaning of the child's communication, and in due course to the symbolism or metaphor of play as the child reaches this stage. This work with the most damaged children makes great demands on the worker to reach and engage with the chaotic inner world of the child, and to provide emotional holding and containment (Lanyado 1991; Waddell 1998) which is likely to be constantly challenged and attacked. Understanding of unconscious processes of projection, transference, and countertransference can help the worker to understand and withstand the angry and painful feelings involved in the work. The task is to survive the child's hating, to stay with feelings of anxiety, uncertainty and not knowing, keeping hope alive so that the child may in time come to have hope themselves and risk the frightening demands of growth. Eventually the child may become able to connect feeling and thinking and to construct a coherent narrative of their life (Fonagy 2001).

Values, systems thinking and unconscious processes in families, networks and organizations

Therapeutic work always takes place within the context of a particular society, with its social institutions and policies, as well as legal constraints. This context needs to be understood, including the influence of power, prejudice, dependency and difference, often operating through subtle forms of oppression such as institutional racism, and their link to age, gender and sexuality, social class, race and culture, poverty and deprivation, illness and disability, and so on. Workers need to reflect on personal and professional values in all the complexity of their application (Banks 2000). Alongside developing anti-oppressive practice and valuing difference are questions of moral philosophy such as when should we respect a child's privacy or keep confidentiality, what is consent, should we always be truthful. Attending to the voice of the child raises complex questions about what is the child's voice; what a child says they want may not be the same as what they communicate in other ways.

Systems theory is needed as a basis for understanding and working with the child within the social, family, professional and organizational systems. Specifically this consists of basic understanding of family systems and the rationale for family work and therapy (there is an extensive literature, e.g. Byng-Hall 1995) and understanding of working in organizations as systems, including unconscious processes at work (Obholzer and Roberts 1994;

Hinshelwood and Skogstad 2000). All work involves attending to relation-ships with the families and carers of children, and sometimes they may directly be helped to take over the task of providing containing play. There may be a whole network of family and professionals involved in the care and education of the more severely damaged and deprived children. While a play therapist may be working one to one with a child, there is also a need to acknowledge the therapeutic work taking place through 'the work of the day' with other carers such as foster parents, residential care staff, as well as school and family, that is, working with the whole system. Ideas of 'holding environments' or 'circles of containment' for carers and staff help in finding ways of providing mental spaces where workers can reflect on feelings aroused in the work and find support in managing them in ways which fur-ther the task (Ward and McMahon 1998; Hardwick and Woodhead 1999).

Conclusion

I hope that I have given a sense of how integrating theory, research and practice can underpin the task of therapeutic play with distressed or dis-turbed children so that, within an emotionally containing relationship, they can have a creative play experience in which they can connect thinking and feeling, begin to discover who they are and make sense of their lives, out of which can grow hope for the future.

Chapter 3

The process of therapeutic play and play therapy

Workers may use therapeutic play in different ways, according to their perceptions of a child's needs and the demands or constraints of the context in which they work. At the simplest level, play is used to facilitate communication between child and adult about matters of which the child is aware but which are hard to discuss, either because the subject is painful or embarrassing or because the child lacks the ability to use other forms of expression. All workers who need to communicate with children from time to time can helpfully use play in this way. Yet play usually reveals much deeper meanings of which the child may be unaware. If play takes place in the area of illusion between the child's inner reality and the outside world, helping the child to mediate between the two, and is spontaneous, exciting and capable of surprising the child with its own discoveries, then its potential power is immense.

The context of therapeutic play and play therapy

Since the early 1990s professional training for play therapy in the UK has become well established. Other workers who use play in therapy arrive at their knowledge through their own professional training or in post-qualifying training and continuing professional development. The work of most play therapists and creative arts therapists, as in child psychotherapy, is focused on the therapy session. They may avoid seeing the child in other contexts so as not to confuse the relationship. They can then remain a subjective figure to the child, concerned above all with the child's inner world. However, they will work closely with others in the child's world, including both family and professional networks. The social worker, in contrast, has a role in relation to the child in the real world, as well as roles in relation to other members of the child's real world. This gives the social worker the opportunity of being able to act as a bridge between the outside world and the child's feelings, as Clare Winnicott (1964) describes. Difficulties may arise from conflict with other aspects of their role, such as work with parents, statutory obligations, assessments and reports to the court. Their role is as an objective part of the child's reality, although they may reach the child's inner world too. Court officers and guardians may use play in making assessments for the courts, while play therapists can provide therapy as well as assessment. Social workers tend to use focused methods of assessment and therapeutic play, although social work therapy teams staffed by trained play therapists are reclaiming the therapeutic role.

There is a long tradition of using play in child and family mental health services, exemplified by psychiatric social worker Prestage's (1972) account of her work with Kim. Even stronger has been the influence of systems based family therapy, leading to an emphasis on family work. Workers (who have a professional background in occupational therapy, nursing or social work) in child mental health, as elsewhere, are likely to be working with aspects of the child's real world, including parent and other agencies, as well as directly with the child. Yet they have often developed special skills in communicating with children and using therapeutic play. In early years work, teachers, nursery nurses, playgroup, parenting and family workers and so on provide group play for children and their families, with more or less awareness of the therapeutic benefits of play, although some workers provide play therapy specifically. Filial play therapy and similar approaches, as well as parenting programmes, help parents and carers to provide therapeutic play in the home. Residential child care workers may provide play as part of a thera-peutic environment. In education, therapeutic play is most likely to be offered by specialist teachers in classes and units, such as nurture groups, for children with emotional difficulties. Play workers and play rangers provide play out of school, often outdoors. Play therapists provide sessional work for indi-vidual children and also work in schools for children with learning or other disabilities. Hospital play specialists and child development centre workers use play in their work with sick, disabled and developmentally delayed children, as do some nurses and teachers who have acquired play skills. Some psychiatrists and psychologists use play methods in work with children and families.

The mode of work and its implications

Training for play therapy emphasizes the one-to-one play therapy session with a child over a period of time, although recent developments also involve exploring ways of helping parents and carers to provide therapeutic play themselves. Therapeutic play may take place in the course of the 'work of the day' in daily living or in 'play groups' in the broadest sense, as well as in individual 'direct work'. Sometimes groups of children, for example, children who have experienced bereavement, are brought together with a specific therapeutic purpose, in which play forms a greater or lesser part of the work.

Opportunity led work

Much therapeutic work is about providing primary experience through which the child who lacks an integrated sense of self can begin to develop and play. Sensory and interactive play needs to be part of a therapeutic environment for daily living, in which meals, play time, bath time and bedtime provide good experiences. Provision needs to be reliable and to give complete and uninterrupted experiences. For example, a planned mealtime with awareness, which includes cultural awareness, of the child's response to different food gives time for the child to enjoy and even play with food, providing a version of a good infant feeding experience. The sensory responsiveness of the whole environment matters, whether there are comfortable places to sit, homely rather than institutional smells and sounds, familiar and relaxing music, appealing toys and books, rocking and swinging things, and so on.

Being alongside children in their daily lives and activities gives many occasions for 'opportunity led' work, that is for handling and responding helpfully, rather than with an ill-judged hasty reaction, to the many unplanned moments that arise (Ward 2007). It may be in a room equipped for play or in some other setting such as a living room, classroom or hospital room, or outdoors in the natural world of sun, wind, water and trees. There may be only moments in which to make sense of what is taking place and to decide how to respond. The difference from one-to-one work is that the worker has to take into account what else is going on in the setting at the time and how other relationships are involved or affected. They may offer 'emotional first aid on the spot' (Redl and Wineman 1952; Redl 1966: 90) to a child's sudden anger or distress. Recognition and reflection of the child's feelings may help them manage the moment and move on. A worker can provide an attuned communication to what the child is expressing in words or in play, perhaps joining in with the child's play if invited, with their response expressed within the metaphor of the play, which may lead to an opening up rather than a closing down of communication. In this case it helps if there is protection from interruption which can be provided by other team members attuned to what is taking place.

Turn-taking games and action songs and games can support a developing relationship between child and worker, comparable to mother–baby play. This may sometimes mean careful 'reaching out' to draw a child lost in their own world back into communication, a version of animated baby play (Alvarez 1992). On another occasion the attuned worker may move quietly into view the next piece of jigsaw puzzle, Lego and so on, in 'socially unobtrusive object play'. This may help a child sustain playing and thinking at a time when they cannot tolerate more contact.

While the worker's reaction is spontaneous, it is not necessarily unplanned. It may form part of a pattern of work which has been agreed by the team on the basis of their assessment of the child. After an event or intervention the team needs to review what happened and work at together finding ways of going on helping. This thinking on the part of a team is important in enabling helpful interventions which can be managed by the team as a whole. Such team mental space needs to be valued and allowed for in the organization as a whole, so that the team containing the emotional distress of a child is itself contained. Group supervision as well as the necessary individual supervision is often helpful in making sense of the 'reflection process', the way in which the feelings belonging to children become enacted or mirrored in the team. Chapters 4 and 9 are largely about opportunity led work.

Individual and family work

The aims of individual work vary from a play-based assessment of a child's feelings about a particular situation, or communication about specific events or plans, which may also be therapeutic, to more formal non-directive play therapy which involves work with a child to help them through a time of emotional distress, disturbance or trauma. The length of therapeutic work varies according to the aims of work and the child's progress. It is often helpful to negotiate an initial block of sessions and to decide with others at the end of the period whether further work might be needed.

To determine whether individual play therapy is an appropriate intervention workers need to think about their own role and the role of their agency, and how it is likely to be perceived by the child and their family or carers. If they have other roles, perhaps statutory ones, workers need to consider if these may be affected by any revelations in the course of work, as well as affecting the family's perceptions of the possible outcome of work. They may need to consider whether there is support for the therapy from the family. A family which locates all its difficulties in the child may not want them 'cured', and may unconsciously sabotage therapy. Or they may be envious of the care a child is getting or may resent a child becoming more assertive. Other interventions, such as counselling, family work or family therapy, may be preferred or take place parallel to play therapy. Therapeutic play may be an important part of these other interventions (see Chapters 4 and 5). Often play therapy with a child is carried out alongside some other form of work with the family. Increasingly play therapists recognize their role in imparting therapeutic skills to parents and carers, for example, in filial therapy with foster and adoptive carers (Ryan 2004, 2007). In any case the play therapist needs to be developing a good working relationship with a child's family or carer before one-to-one play therapy is possible, and needs to maintain this partnership through ongoing review meetings at agreed points through the child's therapy.

Where a worker is one of a number of workers with the child and family there is a need to coordinate efforts. The network of professionals around a child and family can helpfully be included in an initial consultation process so that play therapy fits into the context of other work. Before therapy begins there is much work to be done with the network of support for the child, whatever that may be, in considering the need for therapy, the child's willingness and agreement, and in making arrangements which work, and which provide understanding and support for the therapy, including times when the child is rejecting both therapy and worker. It can be a struggle to ensure the reliability of sessions, for example, if a school event or other appointment is suddenly given priority. Therapy may be seen as a luxury when people are trying to manage a child's difficult behaviour and have other children to think about. It can be even harder if a child's feelings coming to the surface in play therapy and spill over at home or in school. Distressed or angry behaviour can be better tolerated by others if they are aware that 'getting better can make it worse' for a while (Kegerreis 1995). Unless carers, and more crucially the managers who have the power to make decisions, understand what is happening, the risk is that therapy will be ended prematurely. Parents, teachers, foster carers and residential workers may themselves be able to make a major contribution to helping the child if they are involved.

Since a child's feelings are linked to places, an important decision is where the play sessions are to take place. A worker has to weigh up the relative benefits of taking therapy to the child or taking the child to the therapy. Is the child more relaxed in a familiar setting or in a 'sanctuary'? A neutral setting gives a child more 'breathing space' away from the constraints of the real world. The child's home ground is familiar and might be considered, especially for a young child, if the child feels safe there. Often a school is a convenient place for child and worker, but the child's feelings about school and the particular room to be used need to be considered. A school or children's centre may be the least stigmatizing setting, rather than, for example, a child mental health or social services building. The room needs to be free from distractions and interruptions. Practical concerns must also be considered such as who is to bring the child, how feasible the journey, and how reliable the transport. The parent or 'chaperone' needs a comfortable place to wait, where the child can have access to them if necessary. There needs to be thought about the other occupants of the building, how they understand what is taking place, how much they need to know, how to react if the child leaves the playroom or runs off. If filial play therapy is planned, play sessions eventually move to where the child is living.

A weekly session is often the most feasible for both child and worker, but children with profound or lasting disturbances may need more frequent help if they are to feel contained enough to manage from one session to the next. Most workers offer sessions lasting from 40 minutes to one hour. Very young children and children with attachment difficulties may need a shorter session, unless parents are present. Sessions should be at the same times each week, to provide predictability in the child's life. The boundaries around therapy need to be very clear and consistent, including time and place and who brings the child. It is important for the worker to be reliable, and to be scrupulous about being on time and regularly keeping that time clear for the child. The child should, of course, see the same worker each time. The time of day and the transitions, emotional as well as physical, for the child require some thought and may need to be planned with others. A child may need to be released regularly from school. The detailed process of play therapy sessions, once underway, is discussed later in this chapter. Part of the essential planning for the work is making provision for supervision where the process of therapy can be thought about and understood.

Group work

Group work may be helpful for children who have had similar experiences, perhaps of bereavement or family break-up, when sharing feelings and activities in a group may help them feel that they are not alone, while mutual support and reflection in an emotionally containing group can often help them in managing their present feelings and in thinking about the future. Such groups may range from a small nurture or sibling group to a much larger group, and entail a range of play, games and activities, some more or less focused and directed (Silveira *et al.* 1988; Dwivedi 1993; Ryan and Walker 2007). Sometimes parents or carers are involved. Group psychotherapy provides non-directed play in which children with emotional disturbance are helped to think about themselves and their relationships in the group (Canham and Emanuel 2000). Here a combination of systemic and psychodynamic thinking often proves most useful.

Whatever the mode of work, the leadership of a group is crucial in providing emotional containment for the feelings expressed. In other than a very small group two co-leaders are necessary. One can be attending to 'task' aspects of the role while the other is attending to 'process', the emotional nature of what is taking place in the group. These roles can be shared over the life of the group. Symbolically the group leaders represent parental figures and children's reactions to them need to be considered with this in mind as well, of course, as the reality of the self that the leaders are bringing. Leaders need to meet after a session to reflect on what has taken place and to work together understanding its meaning. There will inevitably be (unconscious) attempts by the group to split the leaders, so that one carries good feelings and the other bad feelings about a particular child or interaction. Thinking about the (countertransference) feelings aroused in the leaders can be very helpful in understanding these projections and making them feel less like personal attacks but as expressions of children's feelings which need to be contained. Occasionally a group phantasy is created, where the only link to reality is provided by the leaders, who have the responsibility of ensuring that the phantasy takes a therapeutic rather than a damaging direction.

Supervision provides a further essential space for making sense of the work and helping it progress.

Play materials

Some workers are based in beautifully equipped playrooms. Others stagger from place to place carrying everything in boxes or bags. Others use everyday activities and spaces and playgrounds, including the outdoor world. Play material needs to be appropriate to the child's developmental level and needs (see Chapter 1) as well as their age. The kinds of play material and activities we offer provides the framework within which children communicate, helping them to show us how they feel and sometimes to re-enact their experience through their play. A warm comfortable welcoming room helps a child to feel more relaxed. Carpet and floor cushions mean that the worker can get down to the child's level. If the room has other functions a large play mat may delineate the play space.

When choosing play material we need to have the particular child in mind, ensuring that the child's culture is represented sufficiently for the child to feel the setting is familiar enough. I remember being reminded by an African worker that I had too many manufactured toys; her children would have felt more at home with natural materials, such as wood, stones and leaves. Brummer (1986) notes that 'play materials for black children must include the kinds of dolls, paints, masks and books which enable both child and worker to reflect on sameness and difference of colour'. Gil (2000) recommends that play material should permit expression of broad meanings (such as 'fire') rather than culturally bound ones ('Star Wars').

Clay, sand, water and paint, including finger and face paint, offer scope for sensory and embodiment play and can provide safe outlets for confused and angry feelings in messy and destructive play. These materials can be restored, which can help a child to learn that anger can be controlled and managed. (It may be a good idea to ask that the child comes in clothes that do not matter.) Sensory play might range from providing a bag of objects to feel or smell to singing and music, 'soft play' or play outdoors. Messy play can usually be offered in a playroom, or in activities such as cooking. Sometimes playdough, 'slime' or modelling material are more acceptable where there is anxiety about mess. A 'nest', cardboard box, play tent or other corner, with a blanket or rug and a range of books and stories allow a child to retreat to a safe space or to a missed experience of infancy. Some workers provide a real baby feeding bottle or a dummy while others prefer a symbolic toy version. Offering food and drink conveys a feeling of being cared for, yet may literally and symbolically represent taking in and keeping difficult things down, rather than letting them out by communicating feelings; there are choices to be made. A toilet should be near at hand.

Material for imaginative or symbolic and role play includes play people or dolls (ethnically appropriate), puppets, monsters and superheroes, face and animal masks, dressing-up clothes (hats and pieces of material), a medical kit, toy weapons or a punchbag, soft toys representing protective figures such as a lion or an owl, and perhaps items such as a magic pencil or wand, and musical instruments. Ordinary rag dolls, rather than miniature ones, and domestic furniture which matches them in size, such as a baby doll with a cot, help children whose capacity for symbolic play has been impaired, as Sinason (1988) found was often the case with sexually abused children. Larger dolls more nearly represent real people and the feelings that go with them. The dolls should have removable clothes, including day and night clothes. Miniature toys include doll families (including a baby and grand-parents), doll's houses (preferably two) and furniture, toy telephones, string, Lego or building blocks, a model 'village', miniature soldiers and vehicles (especially police cars, fire engines and ambulances), trains, and wild and domestic animals. Materials for writing, drawing and painting, and cutting and sticking are essential. Some older children may prefer, at least initially, a less obvious play setting, with more grown-up games and activities, although as they relax they may well turn to more childlike activities. It is important to use approaches with which both worker and child feel comfortable (Kerr *et al.* 1990). This is a long list and may be too much for some children who find over-abundance distracting. A carefully chosen but limited choice may help them to concentrate in play.

A playroom designed by Sarah Hemsby feels spacious and uncluttered, offering clear invitations to play. The door is painted with a picture of a mother and baby. A wall painting of a wood in winter is the first thing a child sees on entering; other pictures are a large Raymond Briggs 'Snowman' and a life-size painting in an alcove of a witch, lending the playroom an aura of magic, of being in a world apart. There is a sand tray; beside it are small baskets of miniatures, domestic and wild animals, dinosaurs and play people. There are painting and drawing materials, and playdough at a table. Elsewhere there are dolls, teddies and puppets, and domestic play equipment such as cups and plates, a small sink with water available, a doll's house, a large piece of orange material for dressing up, and a baby doll in a cradle near cushions in a corner for curling up in comfort on a carpeted floor.

Peripatetic workers are more constrained, providing materials in bags or boxes. One bag may contain painting and drawing materials, clay or play-dough. Another has puppets, masks, dolls and soft toys, monsters, baby play items, a doctor's kit and so on, for imaginative and role play. (A child can put the monsters back in a bag and pull up the draw string tightly!) A third bag might contain miniature toys, an ethnically appropriate miniature doll family and doll's house furniture, domestic and wild animals, cars and other vehicles, small blocks or fences. Workers who are using focused play methods need appropriate materials, such as pictures for the child to complete, or specially designed cards and games. Some workers, such as hospital play specialists, become inventive about providing play for disabled or bed-bound children. (Other chapters give more details.)

Developing skills in therapeutic play

The core skills of attunement and reflective listening

We need understanding of child development and play, especially of the impact of early experience and of attachment and loss. Infant and child observation (Miller *et al.* 1989) is an essential training in developing attunement, so that the nuances of an infant's responses in their relationship with their mother or other carer are available to be thought about and understood. This attunement, empathy and emotional containment have their parallel in the therapeutic process. An essential skill, one of the hardest to learn, is the ability to reflect the child's play. It contrasts with everyday behaviour where adults ask numerous questions or make comments which reveal personal opinions or judgements. Even praise, for example, 'That's a lovely painting' or 'I like your pretty dress', implies value judgement and needs to be avoided. It distracts the worker from noticing the child's real feelings and may push the child into wanting to please. Criticism is, of course, to be shunned. Yet it may involve a radical shift of approach for, say, the early years worker who is used to saying, 'That's not very nice' when a child is thumping a doll, and instead observes quietly 'You're hitting that doll baby very hard'. The discipline of reflecting rather than questioning takes practice. We can start by reflecting behaviour, for example, 'You're taking the monster to the sand – you're digging a hole – you're burying it deep down – you've got rid of it!'

The next stage is becoming aware of the feelings which the child is communicating and then reflecting these accurately, 'You don't like the monster – it's a bit scary – you're angry with it (as the child digs furiously) – maybe you're very pleased you've got rid of it?' It is not easy to empty one's mind of one's own thoughts and to make an internal space to focus on and think about the child, and to receive their communication. Tentative reflections of feelings leave the child able to correct us when wrong, for example, 'You look as if you're angry with that doll baby?' We stay with the metaphor of play, not making deeper interpretations such as 'That might be how you feel about your stepbrother', although we might sometimes ask 'Does it remind you of anything?' We sometimes fear being out of our depth. It does not matter that we do not understand all that a child's play may mean. The task in play therapy is not to interpret it to the child but to stay with children as they find it out for themselves. 'No man can reveal to you aught but that which already lies half asleep in the dawning of your knowledge' (Gibran 1972: 50).

The worker's use of self

Workers who value their own creativity and playfulness will be well placed to allow the child to use the freedom and creativity of spontaneous play, and to provide the conditions which make it possible. Noticing how a child makes us feel is an effective way of becoming aware of how a child may be feeling. It is important, however, to distinguish between the feelings which arise out of our own unresolved past experiences (the personal countertransference) and those which are felt through the child projecting them on to the worker (diagnostic countertransference). The more we have thought about our own feelings, the less likely is this confusion. This is why psychotherapists undergo personal psychoanalysis and play therapists have their own therapy as part of their training. Others workers using therapeutic play must find a means of getting in touch with their own inner world.

The worker who helps the child to explore deeper feelings by provision of a safe and accepting play situation, and by a willingness to join in spontaneous play, may unleash strong feelings, perhaps of anger, grief or fear. This can be alarming and we may feel overwhelmed. To become aware of children's painful feelings is a most painful experience for the worker and it is natural to create defences against feeling this pain. People in close contact with children over long periods, such as in residential work, can find the pain intolerable and without support they may tend to distance themselves and become unable to think about or contain the individual child's experience, or they may leave altogether. We must be aware of our normal desire to rescue children rather than to help them to confront their pain. We feel guilty that we are providing 'only' therapy, and want to reassure children that they are not 'bad'. Shirley Hoxter (1983) warns that fantasies of fostering the child (or anger with those who are looking after them) are a useful sign that we risk 'rescuing' rather than 'containing'. The notion of being a perfect parent matches the child's idealization, but is doomed to disillusion at the first minor frustration. It is vital to become aware of and take back this projection, so that we can help the child (whose projection it is initially) to take it back too and develop more realistic expectations.

We may be tempted to explain intellectually the reasons for the child's current predicament in terms of past events and other people's difficulties, or to blame other people. Social workers with heavy loads of statutory responsibilities may see the play therapy session as being 'the nice bits', while failing to take account of the fact that the worker in play therapy has to bear the child's unbearable feelings. The worker can feel inadequate and isolated, and risks colluding defensively with the powerless child's capacity for 'splitting' people into either good or bad, angry with a world which does not understand, and attacking it or giving up. These are unhelpful responses which avoid confronting the child's pain, and which do not offer containment. The task is to make sense of these feelings rather than act on them, to liaise carefully with others, without blame, in the best interests of the child.

We may become afraid of our own angry and punitive feelings towards the child as we receive the full force of the child's anger in play sessions and have to resist the urge to retaliate. Or we may be so busy defending ourselves and the environment from the child's anger that we have no opportunity to create the mental space to reflect on and to respond to the child's communication. The victim has become a persecutor. This can be alarming and we may feel overwhelmed. Some children treat us with contemptuous indifference, a communication of the rejection they themselves feel. We feel useless and helpless, even contaminated. In these situations we feel like giving up. If this were to happen it would confirm children's view that their feelings cannot be tolerated and are best dealt with by flight or projection on to other people.

Yet these feelings also offer the key to how we can respond helpfully. For example, children who create mess and confusion communicate this feeling to workers who in turn feel overwhelmed by confusion and their apparent failure to understand the child's communication. The child is forcing us to experience their chaotic feelings. Shirley Hoxter (1983) explains that somehow we have to bear experiencing both the child's feelings and our own until they have been 'modulated' enough to respond in terms of the child's communication. We need continually to remind ourselves that the attack is not personal but a re-enactment of the children's feelings towards parents whom they feel have let them down. It helps if we can recognize that the feelings we are experiencing are usually also those of the child towards a parent (transference), part of their 'inner working model' of the world. We must feel the feelings rather than defend against them, which means we may sometimes feel quite annihilated, but we must survive and still maintain our concern for the child. The task is to hold on to these feelings and to bear and think about them, until they become modified, in such a way that they can in due course be taken back by the child in a more manageable form. This 'containment' of the child is crucial and involves more than 'a good relationship'. Through such emotional containment the child can begin to hold on to both good and bad feelings rather than getting rid of them on to others, themselves becoming a container.

If the worker is to contain the child, they themselves must be contained. Their work needs management support; managers must understand and value the therapeutic work, and provide the structure and facilities within which it is possible for effective work to be carried out. This is in addition to workers' need for effective supervision from someone who understands the idea of the inner world and unconscious communication as well as the normal painful feelings which the work involves. Supervision helps to sort out the child's projections from other reactions and feelings of the worker, including those arising out of the worker's own past experience (Mattinson 1975; Hawkins and Shoet 2006). It is crucial if they are to continue helping children to cope with their pain. Sometimes colleagues supervise and support one another. Others look for supervision from an experienced and congenial worker either within or outside their agency.

Power and difference

Empowering the child

There is a potential tension between notions of childhood itself, with the 'competent social actor' view of the child demanding we listen to the voice of the child compared with the 'parental' view of a child as someone to be protected and looked after (Luckock and Lefevre 2006). Play therapy's emphasis on empowering the child through the therapeutic process means that this tension can be worked with. We now realize that children's expressed consent to and views of therapy need to be sought and considered (Carroll 2002; Jäger and Ryan 2007). This stance needs to go alongside attention to a child's whole communication rather than the particular words they use. For example, a child who says 'Go away' might mean just that, but equally might mean 'I am afraid you will go away and I want to be cared for, but dare not take the risk of admitting it, even to myself.' The worker's intuition and skill lies in understanding the meaning behind the communication.

Recognizing difference and oppression

The social context in which therapeutic play takes place requires much thought if it is to avoid reinforcing unhelpful differences between workers and children and their families in terms of power. Although there is more awareness than formerly of the importance of respecting difference, whether in gender and sexuality, race and ethnic origins and culture, class, poverty and disadvantage, disability and ill health, and attention to the way these are expressed in terms of power and oppression, this is not a straightforward matter in practice. A worker's own social background affects how they are and how they are perceived. White workers may unwittingly respond to a black child in terms of racist assumptions which are endemic in society and have become lodged in their unconscious. A 'colour blind' approach, on the basis that 'we are all the same underneath', may be at odds with the experience of a black or minority ethnic child, or one who is a refugee or asylum seeking, who has grown up under the constant threat of racist abuse or attack. The child may have internalized a model of a family or group living under siege or of their colour, or food and way of living, as hateful and contaminated. Similar unconscious or partly conscious attitudes may be held in respect of differences in gender, sexuality, disability, social class and so on, which make effective communication more difficult. Awareness of difference can feel threatening and cause anxiety, and may tempt workers to avoid areas of uncertainty. 'That is why people learning about this work need opportunities to reflect upon their own conscious and unconscious perceptions of "difference", which will be based in part on their own developmental experience, so that they can reflect on ways of acknowledging and overcoming whatever stereotyped assumptions they may hold' (Ward and McMahon 1998: 36).

Communicating with a black child

Although we may still hear of a black child trying to scrub themselves white (and shamefully there are still pubs called 'The Labour in Vain'), it is clear that despite the racism around them at both a personal and institutional level many black children have developed strong and positive images of black identity. However, this is often a complex identity, built to help the child survive (Maxime 1993). 'Many workers engage with these children as if they were white, thereby missing the stories of the children's struggle with obtaining a positive sense of their racial identity' (Thomas 1999: 77). If the help a black or mixed parentage child is offered at times of difficulty is framed in terms of an all-white or colour-blind environment that compounds their difficulty (Dwivedi and Varma 1996; Andreou 1999; Barn 1999). White workers need to undertake their own emotional labour (Gunaratnam *et al.* 1998). Not least, workers need to become 'culturally competent', understanding the ideas, beliefs and 'stories' which give meaning to behaviour for a particular group of people (Bailey-Smith 2001). For example, the symbolic meaning of animals may differ in different cultures; a snake may be either wise or dangerous, which may affect how we make sense of symbolic play (Gil 2000). Cultural competence requires curiosity, a not taking for granted of attitudes and assumptions. Play therapist Nina Rye (2004: 16) describes the effect of realizing that colour was a significant matter for a particular child:

> I had been puzzling over M's strange behavior in the playroom and I had given little thought to his appearance – he is brown in colour and has suffered racial taunts in his nice primary school – and even less to his absent father. In every session he carefully picked out first all the grey-green soldiers from the four colours of soldiers on the floor. On a sudden realization of my colour blindness, I commented 'You are looking for soldiers that are that colour'. He agreed. I added, 'Colour is important'. He replied emphatically, 'It is to me'.

As Lennox Thomas explains, in a racist society black and minority ethnic children are faced with the task of working out 'who will be kind and fair to them and who will not. This experience affects the degree to which they are able to disclose information about themselves honestly, or to make an identification with the white worker'. Instead they protect themselves with a 'proxy or pretend self, an internal split or "false self"' which ultimately may be unhelpful to the child. 'Unless the worker is able to understand the barriers that exist to communication and has the capacity to surmount them, the child will not be helped' (Thomas 1999: 66–67). We need to work on the assumption that we do not know everything, and to use our capacity for 'speculation, visualization and empathy'. 'The experience of working with cultural difference is part of the dynamic where not only the client might be different but where we, also, as workers are different in the therapeutic space' (Thomas 1999: 71). Thomas goes on to remind us that the worker needs 'to be courageous enough to stick with the painful material, even when the feelings evoked might be a sense of guilt for being white'. We need to ask ourselves 'how can I attune to the very many differences between us and how can I use those points of sameness between us in our contact' (Thomas 1999: 74–75).

The stages of therapy

Beginning play

The aim of a first session is for the worker and child to make contact, for the child to start exploring the play possibilities of the situation, and for the child to have enjoyed or appreciated it enough to want more. It can be an anxious time for both worker and child. Preferably they have met previously, on the child's home ground whatever that may be, and the worker has already discussed the possibility of therapy and the child agreed to come. While a younger child may be content to be told that this is a place where children come to play, older children are entitled to an explanation of why they are there. We may add that 'other people are concerned that you have worries that are difficult to talk about' and explain that sometimes children like to play or draw about their feelings and words do not have to be used. Often a child starts playing spontaneously as they are shown the toys and play material. The worker may say something like 'You can do whatever you want and I'll just be with you.' The worker needs to be sitting at the child's level, although respecting the child's personal space. Occasionally a child will be silent and immobile, and we can reflect in words how hard it can be to begin. On rare occasions we may judge that the child is too anxious about being in an unfamiliar situation, and it can help if we start playing, returning initiative to the child as they join in. Later in therapy the child's silence may have a different meaning, which we need to think about it and reflect in our own body language, and in our words or our silence.

The worker's role is to elicit play, to be aware of and to reflect the child's play, resisting any temptation to ask questions or to advise and direct. If the child invites the worker to join in play or to take a role, often either of the victim or the 'baddie', such as 'You be the child and I'll be the teacher', then we follow the child's directions. For example, I have been told to be asleep while the robber comes in the night and steals my birthday presents: I am then told to wake up in the morning and be upset, while the robber dances with glee. The symbolic significance of having had something good which is taken away is clear and I was able to feel and then articulate the feelings of loss. If the child gives us a role but does not tell us what to do, we can ask or perhaps play it in a stereotyped way, such as a nagging mother or a severe father. We need to be ready to drop the role at any moment, in tune with the child's play. With young children who are liable to confuse reality and fantasy it can be helpful to state, for example, 'I'm *pretending* to be your mum.' Engaging in role play is a delicate balancing act of joining in playing without losing the sense of our adult self and with it the ability to think about meanings.

We need to think about both the content and process of the child's play. It is always helpful to make notes as soon after the session as possible, as it is easy to forget or unconsciously alter what happened. Violet Oaklander (1978: 160–1) explains:

> I observe the process of the child as she plays. How does she play, how does she approach the materials, what does she choose, what does she avoid? What is her general style? Is there difficulty in shifting from one thing to another? Is she disorganized or well organized? What is her play pattern? How she plays tells a lot about how she is in her life. I watch the content of the play itself. Does she play out themes of loneliness? Aggression? Nurturance? Are there lots of accidents and crashes with planes and cars? I watch for the child's contact skills. Do I feel in contact with her as she plays? Is she so absorbed in her play that I see she makes good contact with her play and herself as she plays? Is she continually at the edge of contact, unable to commit herself to anything? What is the contact like within the play itself? Does she allow for contact between the objects of play? Do people or animals or cars contact each other, see each other, talk to each other?

The themes of a child's symbolic play in the first session often uncannily reflect their underlying problem, although this should not be assumed. The ongoing and changing themes of play over time are an important source of information about the child's inner world, and the child feels validated by our accepting and reflective response. This response is normally offered within the symbolism of play. We also need to attune to the child's feelings about us: for example, whether we feel we are being looked after, managed and controlled, feared or complied with, attacked or ignored. These too tell us about the child's inner working model of the world.

Even for workers who plan to use focused play methods it can be a good idea to be non-directive for at least the first session. The child has an opportunity to 'be' and to be accepted. If they have enjoyed play and contact with the worker they will want to return. The worker has an opportunity to observe and listen to how the child seems to be feeling and to give caring attention. Sometimes a child's own view of a problem will not be the same as an adult's. The worker can observe what the child's choices are, for example, drawing or playing with puppets, and what they are able to do, such as writing, which can inform choice of play techniques. They may say that they will play next time too but that the worker would also like some 'time for me', with some special pictures or games. A few older children cannot cope with initial free play and find a structured approach more comfortable. Tuning in to the child can guide the worker to the right methods for the child at that time. In all focused work it is important to give children the time they need, and to avoid pressurizing them to use a session in a particular way if they are not ready. Some children may take months before they feel safe to reveal feelings.

Control and limits

Some workers tell the child at the beginning that they will be there to make sure that play is safe and nothing gets damaged. It can be preferable to set limits as the need arises, making it clear to the child that they will let neither child nor worker be physically hurt, and preventing excessive destruction of materials. We need to decide how much destruction and mess we can personally tolerate and how much is acceptable in a given setting. Playing in a foster carer's living-room obviously poses different constraints from work in a specifically designated playroom. The session may be ended if the child leaves the room, although, once they know the child is safe, the worker may wait until the end of the allotted time for the child to return.

If play is messy and destructive the worker's task is to understand the feelings a child is conveying, perhaps feelings of being a mess, of anger, or of being frightened by their own or others' anger. If our reflection of this is 'heard' by the child this play may be helpful. If the child is so out of control that they cannot 'hear' the worker, and we become anxious that the situation is getting out of hand, then we need to intervene to stop the child, change the activity, or ultimately end the session. When the child is at a stage of testing limits we need to be ready to make it clear what the limits are and then stick to them, so that the child feels safe and contained. These limits may not be the same for every child. Part of the worker's skill lies in matching them to a child's needs, as well as what we feel able to cope with. The time limits of the session are an important part of the child's containment and should be kept to, even when the child is begging for longer. The child needs to be told when the session is nearing the end so that they can complete some aspect of play if they wish. A period of calm play at the end of a session, even helping to clear up, can help to ease the child's transition back to the real world and make feelings less likely to overflow elsewhere.

Dealing with the painful bits

The aim of work with a child is to help them to manage their emotional pain. It is important that this happens at a pace that the child can bear, which means 'tiptoeing up to the child's pain'. In this lies the strength of non-directive play therapy. As the tumult of a child's feelings pour forth in therapy it is very easy to become confused and disoriented as to what is happening. The worker may come to doubt whether there is any benefit to the child. Understanding of the stages through which therapy can move helps us to get our bearings. Moustakas (1964: 417–419) gives a guide. At first the child's feelings of anxiety and anger are diffuse and pervasive, affecting everything. They tend to be expressed in general ways such as apparently purposeless attacks on the materials or fear of everything. As the child experiences the worker's containment their feelings become more focused. Anger is directed at specific people, including the worker, or through symbolic play. Fears become fears of particular people and things. As the worker acknowledges these feelings the child's self-esteem starts to grow. At this stage the child often expresses positive feelings as well as fear or anger, mixed up together. For instance, at one moment the child may be feeding a baby doll and the next moment thumping it hard. These ambivalent feelings are expressed with great intensity at first, gradually becoming expressed in milder ways. Later, the child becomes able to sort and separate out positive and negative feelings about people and situations, in line with how things are in reality. Wilson and Ryan (2005) give a detailed and thorough guide to the developing process of play therapy.

Play disruption tends to happen when the child is overwhelmed by painful feelings. If children are upset their pain needs to be recognized. Even a brief recognition may touch quite deeply – for example, 'You're really hurting', or 'You're very sad about it.' It may *not* be helpful to distract them to something more pleasant. Sometimes we may need to sit quietly with the child, perhaps listening to music. How the child is at the end of a session is an indication of how helpful the child has found it.

Confidentiality

Confidentiality between child and therapist is not a clear-cut issue. The child needs to know how far the worker will tell other people about what happens in play sessions. We need to be honest about this, perhaps explaining that we will only tell parents or carers very generally how they are getting on, and that we will not talk to anyone without telling them first. The child may choose whether or not to talk about the sessions outside. It is a mistake to promise to keep secrets and a child may need to be told that some secrets are too big to keep. As far as possible, however, a child needs to feel that what they do and say in the play session is a private matter. We can help by asking the child's carers not to question the child about what took place. Certainly we need to know what is going on in the child's real life, such as a parent or carer being ill, a possible move, a planning meeting, parental contact, and so on. Some sharing of information about the process of therapy will be needed but how specific it is will vary, and needs careful thought. In residential therapeutic child care the expectation is that confidentiality is held by the whole organization caring for the child but is shared within it (see Chapter 9), and this may also be appropriate for an integrated network such a specialist foster care service, including the foster parents. For a child who has been bound to secrecy by an abuser, such sharing may come as a relief. The worker's 'duty of care' requires them to tell appropriate people if they have new information about abuse or they consider the child is not safe. They have to find a way of making this clear to the child. On the other hand, the detail of what happens in a session is better unshared, so that the child can explore ideas and feelings 'with no repercussions' in their external world (Hunter 2001: 38). For example, a child may vent their fury and destructiveness in the session but the worker's containment may free the child to try other ways of behaving at home or school. Usually it is better if drawings and paintings are not taken home but kept for the child by the worker. Hunter (2001: 50) reminds us: 'Confidentiality should not be a cloak for collusion nor an excuse for therapists not to shoulder ordinary adult responsibilities in relation to children. Nevertheless it is always difficult and debatable where exactly to draw the line.'

Endings

A child can feel abandoned when the worker is away, and earlier feelings of loss and non-containment are often aroused. The child therefore needs warning and preparation for the worker's holidays. One worker gives a child something small of her own to look after, or a 'thinking book' in which the child can draw pictures to show her. Another sends a postcard. On returning we may need to be prepared to deal with the child's anger at our 'abandonment'. This is an opportunity for the child to learn that anger can be safely expressed without it leading to retaliation or destroying the worker. This can be therapeutic, especially important if the play therapy experience is one which the child enjoys so much that negative feelings are seldom aroused.

The termination of therapeutic work needs even more preparation and thought. Ending ideally comes about because the aims of work, whether extensive or limited, have been achieved, and the child is better able to handle what comes next in life. This is not always the case, especially since it is often the adults in the child's life rather than the child who make the decisions. Parents or carers may want therapy to end, funding for therapy may stop, or a child may move home or placement, resulting in an ending which in the worker's and child's mind is premature. A sudden unexpected ending is even harder to deal with. Yet even premature endings need to be planned and negotiated as far as possible. We may need to negotiate to turn an untimely end into something more thoughtful, 'where there is some opportunity, even if painfully brief, to reflect on the experience of therapy and to contemplate how it feels to lose the relationship with the therapist' (Lanyado 1999b: 368).

In any case a worker may have quite mixed feelings about ending. In the same way as a parent is continually faced with the normal developmental task of helping their child grow from a secure dependence to becoming a separate and autonomous person, the worker who has become a significant figure to the child through their holding the child in mind now has to think about letting go. The child too has to let go of the therapist. Monica Lanyado explains the feelings involved for both: 'The complicated mix of anger, sadness, pain and regret, the inevitable feelings of there being so much that is incomplete – are all balanced by the awareness of what has been gained in therapy, together with appropriate excitement about what comes next.' The therapeutic relationship is itself 'a protracted transitional experience in the Winnicottian sense . . . in which, like the loved and often essential teddy or blanket of early childhood, the therapist is vital during the central period of therapy, in times of transition, pain and anxiety, but is also in time outgrown and left "in limbo" when no longer needed' (Lanyado 1999b: 360–361, 2004). A good ending is of great importance to a child whose previous experience of endings has been of painful traumatic separation or uncontained loss. This involves for both a mourning, a kind of internal 'resettling', in which what has been lost can be appreciated, without resort either to destructive 'spoiling' or idealization (Dyke 1984; Kegerreis 1995). As the end nears, a child may sometimes revert to earlier patterns of anxious or angry play, a sign of the anxiety raised by ending and the fear of change. The worker needs to remain confident that the child can face the anxiety of change and is ready for growth. Another child may start to come late or miss sessions, minimizing the loss through a withdrawal of emotional investment. The worker may also need to struggle to remain emotionally engaged. The child's symbolic play, often in visiting and leaving scenarios, allows a working through of ambivalent emotions which cannot easily be put into words.

We need to be able to experience and accept the painful loss of letting go so that we can receive and hold on to the child's feelings of loss. It helps to say 'I will miss you'. The child's sadness at ending needs to be recognized but also their growing capacity to contain experience and their readiness to move on. As play therapist Janet West assured Rosy at the end of their work together, 'You've got the playroom inside you; you've got the biscuits, you've got me, you've got your memories of what we've done together' (West 1984: 81). Writing a therapeutic letter to the child about the work achieved together gives a tangible memory (Marner 1995).

If therapy is a transitional experience, then there may be a case for something less stark than cutting all contact. As the parenting task is to let their children go while remaining 'the shore where casually they come again', so with therapy. We need to consider whether this is a collusive avoiding the pain of loss on our part, which is of no help to the child since it is a denial of the difficult feelings involved in ending. However, the possibility of some kind of continuing contact may provide 'a secure base to return to both in times of need and quite simply in terms of confirmation of the importance of what has taken place between them' (Lanyado 1999b: 366). West (1996) used ending to mediate reality into the play situation, the worker becoming a real person in Rosy's world. Together they prepared for ending, going out on a visit together, planning a 'party', photographs and a present for Rosy in the last session. Occasional contact or cards with friendly (rather than 'deep') comments kept alive a real relationship which in time the child would outgrow in the normal way. Others might prefer less change in role, allowing for the possibility of further work in a time of need. Each ending will be different and we need to remain thoughtful about how best to end work with a particular child.

Evaluation and research

We will not always know what happens next in the child's life story, or how far our work with them has made a difference. Anecdotally we have many stories of how much better a child is coping with their relationships, as well as some tales of struggle and difficulty. The hope is that a child has internalized enough good experience, of a good 'internal parent', to develop an inner world that is more trusting of both self and others, so that continuing growth and development take place:

> We do know from clinical experience that the non-directive process not only provides the opportunity to disentangle, interpret and dissolve symptoms, but provides many gains, particularly in the realms of increased sensitivity and capacity to think which are associated with growing maturity and creativity.
>
> (Lanyado 1999a: 365)

There is increasing research into the effectiveness of play therapy through outcome studies, including Bratton et al.'s (2005) meta-analysis of American play therapy outcome research. Another approach looks at children's retrospective views of their play therapy experience (Carroll 2002; Jäger and Ryan 2007) which can shed more light on how the process of play therapy is experienced. While more research is needed, numerous case studies bear witness to the power of play in healing the hurt child.

Chapter 4

Therapeutic play in early years

The emotional basis for young children's development

The value of early intervention

Traditionally children were 'seen and not heard'. They were expected to bottle up their feelings, receiving admonitions to 'be a brave boy' when physically hurt, to 'love your little brother' when being replaced by a new baby, to 'be a big girl' on starting school and saying goodbye to mother. Expression of pain and grief was seen as weakness; expression of rage and anger a sign that the child was bad or evil. This legacy is still with us, although much has changed. Grown-ups now openly recall the unhappinesses of their childhood years. The effects on young children of separation and loss, abuse and neglect are better understood. Yet acknowledging children's painful feelings is still rare outside the parent–child relationship, and some parents may not manage it. We find it hard to bear the idea that children are emotionally affected by events in their lives. The thought that a young child may be unhappy is so intolerable that we may demand that they appear always cheerful. People say (mistakenly) 'children soon forget'. Some children then develop a false self which conceals the pain within, while others are unable to repress their feelings which then spill over in troublesome behaviour. There are indications of widespread signs of disturbed behaviour in quite young children and it is clear that problems rarely disappear on their own. One major study in London found that '61% of problematic three-year-olds still showed significant difficulties on a clinical rating five years later' (Richman *et al.* 1982: 195).

There is abundant evidence that the early years are crucial to children's emotional development. Children's inner working models which determine how they view themselves and the world around them are largely based on the relationships formed in infancy (see Chapter 1). The strength for children who have someone who provides a reliable secure base – a secure attachment – is, paradoxically, that they feel free to play and explore the world. They do not have to spend time and energy monitoring the parent and trying to get their own emotional needs met. Studies of the pre-school years show that securely attached children are more confident with adults and with their peers, and that they tackle difficulties with more confidence and in the expectation that help will be available if they need it. It may be of course that such optimism is unrealistic. However, the securely attached child tends also to be likeable, which goes a long way to ensuring the support of others. Secure attachment confers not only social but also intellectual skills – the ability to think. The securely attached child is able to connect thinking and feeling, and is free to explore and learn. Parents whose own needs have not been met find it difficult to offer adequate nurturing to their children. Attachment theory and psychodynamic thinking not only provide a way of understanding what is happening between parent and child, but also indicate how help can be given to repair difficult or damaging early relationships. Early intervention can be extremely effective.

Acknowledging feelings in play

Any early years worker worth her salt can make a convincing argument for children learning through play. She can point to all sorts of cognitive gains, from learning concepts of volume and weight in sand and water play, experimentation and problem solving in play with junk materials, developing skills in sorting, matching and number (whether through doing jigsaw puzzles or making biscuits), to developing language skills through conversation, books and stories. She can show how play fosters social development as children learn to negotiate and manage themselves in a group of other children and adults. She will know that pretend play helps children learn about and try out significant roles such as father, mother or doctor. She may know (New 2000) about the many symbolic languages in which children can be creative and communicate. Asked how play contributes to emotional development, she is likely to pause to think and may suggest that play helps children develop self-confidence. Overall, her view of a child is likely to be based on whether their behaviour is acceptable and manageable, rather than in terms of the help needed to cope with specific emotional difficulties and anxieties. Difficult behaviour is seen as something to be modified rather than understood. Her ability to provide emotional support for a child relies on her capacity for sympathy, empathy and intuitive understanding, drawn from her past experience and personal life history, since this is rarely part of her training.

Children's disturbed behaviour is often quite disturbing to the workers who have to respond to it. It may raise feelings of anger and helplessness, for example, when dealing with a child who constantly grabs, pushes and hits. We may reasonably feel an urge to stop unwanted behaviour, to modify and manage it. For some children the provision of boundaries may be their main need. However, there can be an unwillingness really to listen to what the child is communicating. For example, if Rose is putting a doll to bed and smacks it hard, or Jamie kicks over the block garage Imran is building, an unthinking response might be 'That's not very nice, dear' (or even more unhelpfully, 'Say sorry' or 'How would you like it if someone did that to you'). What helps us most when we are feeling angry and anxious is to have those feelings acknowledged, and children have the same need. To Rose we might say, 'It looks as if you are really cross with that doll baby.' We could perhaps say to Jamie, 'I can see you're feeling very angry', although we could reasonably add 'I won't let you break up Imran's garage but you can have this cardboard box.'

Young children have a limited ability to talk about their feelings. Instead they use play. The special quality of play is that within its safe boundaries the child is free to be creative, to explore events and feelings, both conscious and unconscious. Rose who has a new baby brother may safely express her anger at being displaced from the centre of her mother's attention by smacking the doll baby. This may be enough to help her feel better and to go on loving her new brother. The adult's role then is to provide an interrupted and protected play space and time within which this play can take place. If we take the further step of making a space in our own minds to think about what she is communicating through her play, we have the possibility of finding the words to let her know that her feelings are acknowledged and accepted.

Creating and maintaining an inner mental space in the worker's mind is a fundamental condition of a therapeutic approach. It is no easy task. It is not only emotionally disturbed or damaged children who benefit. Normally developing children, growing up in ordinary families, also need supportive adults who are able to understand their states of mind and to provide an emotional 'holding environment' (Lanyado 1991). Bion (1962) called the process of being open to being stirred up emotionally by the child *reverie*. The task is to act as a *container*, tolerating without being overwhelmed by the child's feelings. We mentally digest how the child is feeling, sometimes consciously but often without consciously doing so. We become a thinker for their thoughts. By the way in which we respond we give these upset feelings back to the child in a more bearable form. The child then begins to hold on to and manage angry and anxious feelings, and no longer has to get rid of them by projecting them on to someone else. 'He takes in the feeling of "being contained", of being held in mind so that his anxieties can be tolerated and *thought about*' (Copley and Forryan 1987/1997: 241), and in turn develops a mind able to hold thoughts. So the experience of *emotional holding or containment* enables children to become a container of feelings, able to hold on to them and *think* about them. They become more emotionally integrated, developing what Fonagy *et al.* (1994) call 'reflective self function'.

Providing a holding environment

Space to think is the key. If we can hold on to this we will be better placed to insist on providing a high quality of child care and to resist narrow definitions of what constitutes learning. If the task is to help children develop and learn, we must also provide the essential pre-conditions for learning. As we have seen already, containment requires thinking, and thinking is the basis for learning. We must provide an emotional holding environment (Winnicott 1965) so that children are enabled to become thinkers. However, this cannot readily take place in the absence of a holding environment in the family, so that supporting and enabling families to do this must remain an essential part of our task. For parents who lack past good experiences and feelings to hold on to and draw on, emotional holding or containment may come from present experience. It could be from a partner, relative or friend – or from a professional agency. Like a set of Russian dolls, the parents are contained to contain the child. Similarly a holding environment for workers is vital if they are to maintain that inner mental space to think about and manage the feelings aroused by the work.

Assessment

Help is normally preceded by some kind of assessment of parent–child interaction, which might include use of Crittenden's Care Index for playful interaction (www.patcrittenden.com). More often it is informal observation, preferably by a worker trained in psychodynamic infant observation. We can observe the child's approach to play, how they cope with new situations and strange adults, and how they respond to brief separation and to the return of the parent, which gives some indication of their security of attachment. Story stem assessments (Farnfield 2001; Hodges *et al.* 2003) can often be incorporated into play. For example, while playing with farm animals the adult starts the story of the lost little pig who wanders away from their family. The child is asked to 'show me or tell me what happens next', the answer giving a glimpse of their inner working model.

In a play session we can observe parents' awareness of their child's needs, how much attention they give the child, whether they respond to the child's overtures, if they take over play, and if they enjoy playing. We can see how they cope if the child cries, such as whether they comfort in a positive way, how they manage their child's behaviour, and whether they enjoy close proximity to their child. Parents may also be involved during a developmental assessment of the child, which can be based on Sheridan *et al.*'s (2007) checklists (see also Chapter 1). This assessment can be used not only to assess any developmental delay but also to help parents to appreciate what is realistic for them to expect from their child.

Opportunity led work in early years settings

Play as symbolic communication

Play is crucial to symbolizing and internalizing experience. It is the child's way of making sense of experience, and therefore has to be child led. Where children have opportunities for play in a non-directed but safe group setting they may play out and master difficult or painful experiences, either by playing alone or by social play with other children. For example, soon after Peter's mother died he came into his playgroup, went to the sewing table and worked intently. 'I'm making a blue dress for my mummy to wear in heaven,' he said, while the worker helped Peter with his sewing.

John's mother was expecting a new baby. Maria Ulloa, a centre leader with psychoanalytic training, describes John's play and what she understood it to mean:

> I watched John (age four) playing with a wooden castle and banging it with a hammer. He told his friend that the castle was falling down and he needed to fix it. He started running round the castle pushing other children out of his way. He walked away pretending to hold a bottle in his mouth and went up to some other children saying that he was building a house to live in. He said to them it is better to stay out because it is dangerous being around a house that could fall apart. Perhaps the arrival of a new baby was felt as a real collapse of his world. By pretending to be a baby he established momentarily in his fantasy his status of loved child in his parent's mind. He kept other children away, who perhaps represented the new baby and possible siblings, or maybe in a form of identification with them, keeping himself away from the danger of his world changing or falling apart.

The worker's role here is to provide a safe space for play, and to notice and think about its meaning. At another time she may show recognition and acceptance of the feelings a child expresses in play, whether anxiety over a house move, anger over a new baby or grief at the loss of a family member. Sometimes she may join in and play too, but following the child. In opportunity led work (Ward 2007) the worker seizes the moment to reach a deeper level of communication. It may or may not have been planned previously but involves a rapid but thoughtful assessment of the situation and a judgment about what would be most helpful.

Reaching children who cannot play

Sometimes a worker may not know what is wrong but will start from a child's inability to play. Separation anxiety, which means the world feels too unfamiliar and dangerous to explore, is a common cause. What can help, especially with the youngest children – and is essential for babies and toddlers – is the provision of a secondary attachment figure who provides a secure base for the child. Playgroup course tutor, Bernie Ross, describes how she helped Helen on her regular visits to the group:

> Three-year-old Helen after six weeks attending playgroup still stood and watched. When I read stories in the book corner she sat silently beside me, her thumb in her mouth, with frequent whines and pointing to more books. Sometimes she watched other children playing. Children would join us, listen and talk, and go again. I said I was going to do a jigsaw and found a simple horse puzzle. Helen sat on my lap, her thumb came out, she took a piece and put it directly where it belonged. I continued to talk to her when I needed to do other things, Helen staying close by. The next time I was not there and she spent the morning watching. On my next visit she came straight to me and with a single word between thumb sucks gestured towards the book corner. She chose a book we had enjoyed and listened while watching the other children playing, before joining in a little more with puzzles. After several sessions like this Helen could sit and play next to others at the table toys or join a group with a helper doing some collage. When everyone had a drink and a biscuit, Helen would have a special snack from home, to help in settling her. One day children were chatting over their milk and, right out of the blue, she piped up to talk about the horses she likes. Her conversation was dotted with little giggles and stammers. I had to miss a couple of sessions but felt quite happy that Helen would cope. On my return she was pleased to see me and wanted to cling for a while. At milk-time she had no special snack but chose a biscuit from the tin and ate it all.

This effective piece of substitute mothering used play as the means of communication. As Helen's anxiety lessened she became free to start playing herself. Her acceptance of the playgroup's food indicated that she felt at home. At the same time, conversation with her mother had established that the family had recently moved to the area and that Helen was also attending a second nursery with a different and structured programme. It was not surprising that she was confused and anxious. Friendly and non-judgemental support helped her anxious mother to understand Helen's anxieties and to decide to withdraw her from the second group. After a period of absence through illness Helen arrived at playgroup with her mother:

> This time Helen immediately led her mum to the book corner, where out came the favourite books she always chose for me to read. Two hours and several quiet activities later Helen was contentedly playing with just her own mother. I assured her mother that she could go shopping if she wanted to but, although previously reluctant to stay, she declined, saying, 'I'm quite enjoying it myself now!' She later enrolled on a short course I was running about the value of play. She was a shy student but eventually began to air her thoughts. In the heat of discussion one day she blurted out, 'I'm terribly housepro . . .' and covered her mouth, bursting into giggles. 'I'm *not* terribly houseproud I meant to say!' 'Freudian slip!' laughed everyone, and I'm sure it was. Some time later Helen was happily settled at infant school and her mother became a regular helper at playgroup.

The similarities in the development of Helen and her mother are striking. Both were held within a containing relationship and both were given opportunities for play within its safe boundaries. As a result both became less anxious and more spontaneous, able to play and be more fully themselves. Helen no longer needed substitute mothering as her mother regained the capacity to 'contain' her. Although work with mother and child took place independently, the benefits to the child were all the greater because of the support the mother received.

In a less securely attached child the worker may be confronted by the child's difficult and chaotic states of mind, which require the worker to build a space in her mind to understand them. Maria Ulloa (2006) describes how she reached four-year-old Ellie, after several attempts to help her settle in other pre-schools had failed:

> Ellie came in clinging to her mother and gazing at the floor. She refused an invitation to join in the group gathering. As soon as her mother left she ran screaming to the far end of the room, rejecting my attempt to console her. I told her she was welcome to join the group when she was ready and left her for a little while on her own. When I returned I found her as before curled up and hiding her head between her legs. I asked her if she would like to talk about how she was feeling and she nodded.

I said that perhaps it is hard for her to let her mum go as she is afraid she can disappear. She did not answer immediately but then said, 'I don't know what to do.' I said that it is perhaps hard for her to decide what to do when mum is not there. If mum disappears she does not know what she wants anymore. I suggested that she hold my hand and we can both learn what to do when mum is not around. She accepted what I said and agreed to come to the kitchen with me to make some tea. I asked her what she would normally do at home and she said, 'I just watch television – all my mum does is watch television.' I asked if she played with her brother and with a serious look she answered, 'I hate my brother.'

For some weeks I tried to understand Ellie's state of mind. I noticed that Ellie did not greet her mother or show any enthusiasm when she returned at the end of a session. I realized that this very insecure attachment to her mother made it more difficult for her to find a secondary figure to trust and feel safe with. She was clinging at the beginning of a session and detached at the reunion with her mother; perhaps her way of avoiding the painful anxiety provoked by her mother's absence. The other workers decided to ignore her 'funny moods', probably their own defences against anxiety. This meant that Ellie was less likely to receive the warm response that she craved. The image of her mother in front of the television made me realize how difficult it was for Ellie to use anything other than a physical stimulus. I perceived her like a baby fixed in front of the television with 'nothing else to do'. Perhaps she had to spend long periods of time holding herself together, with the television providing a means of 'adhesive identification'. Her curled up body on arrival suggested a regression to this early state of mind where she was trying to contain herself. I had the feeling she was constantly angry with her mother but she seemed to have transferred some of this towards her older brother (who was close to her according to her mother). Little by little Ellie managed to trust me enough to join the group in simple activities. She trusted no one else until she left at the end of term to start school.

Banishing 'ghosts in the nursery'

Being open to a parent's communication, verbal and non-verbal, helps in understanding the meaning behind the child's behavior, which can then be conveyed back to the parent, as Maria Ulloa (2006) does here.

> Jake came in to pre-school, screaming and refusing to stay. His mother seemed anxious and hurried, and when asked said she had no idea what was the matter with him. Jake remained inconsolable so I went outside where his mother had stayed, to ask if anything unusual was happening. She said no but then remembered she was busy helping Jake's dad pack his bag ready to take him to the airport. I came in and said to Jake how painful it was, knowing dad was going away, to see everybody busy and daddy too rushed to say goodbye. He stopped crying and started to play, to his mother's relief. When she returned she talked about how hard it was for her as a child to say goodbye to her parents when they went away.

This work has some similarities with infant–parent psychotherapy (Stern 1985; Hopkins 1992) where work with the parent takes place in the presence of the child. A parent's feelings from a past relationship can sometimes unconsciously be transferred to the child. The child has come to represent a person in the parent's past or a part of the parent's hidden self. These 'ghosts in the nursery' (Fraiberg 1980) get in the way of seeing the child for the individual they are. The more malevolent the 'ghosts' are, the more damaging are they to the present parent–child relationship. As the parent is helped to make an emotional connection between her own childhood feeling memories and how her child is feeling now she becomes more able to see and respond to the child's distress rather than be puzzled and upset by the difficult behaviour.

Providing a therapeutic 'holding environment' – finding space for workers to think together

Barbara Dockar-Drysdale (1968, 1990) long ago suggested that emotional integration which was not reached in infancy, as appeared to be the case with Ellie, could be achieved later by the provision of 'primary experience'. This mirrors the essential features of emotional containment in infancy, above all the good experience of being thought about and responded to *as an individual* – of having the equivalent of the infant's good experience of feeding, sleeping, playing and being comforted. This is not easily provided in group child-care, where there is the temptation of falling into routines and a generalized domestic culture of care (Barnett 1995), which ignores the feelings of individual children, as the following example illustrates:

A student observing in daycare described her painful experience of watching two-year-old Jacob repeatedly being told 'good boy' for complying with routine demands for eating, toileting, napping and putting his shoes on, but who was never responded to on an individual basis. He remained speechless apart from himself uttering the words 'good boy' whenever he did anything. Presumably it was too painful for staff to put themselves in his shoes and think about his experience of being separated all day from people who loved him. Although Jacob seemed 'happy', we can surmise that the student was picking up his underlying distress.

What needs 'holding . . . is not only the individual child or parent and their own distress, but also the groups of children and their parents . . . as well as the group of staff, whose own strong feelings will be aroused through working with the children and their families . . . and who need some element of holding in their own right . . . if the anxieties inherent in the task are not to overwhelm or divert them' (Ward 2001: 33). This holding is mainly created by the forms of organization and by the process of management (Miller 1993). Above all, a staff team needs to have space to meet regularly, to think about what is happening and together to work at understanding it, as they did in the following example from Maria Ulloa.

Thinking as a team about Adam

Adam (age four) seemed not to play with other children, but only related to them by being bossy or bullying. He shouted and argued when asked to do anything although he could be affectionate to favourite members of staff. He disrupted any group activity. His mother was anxious about his worsening behaviour and sometimes burst into tears when talking about her concern for his future. Staff noticed that she appeased him by doing everything he wanted, and found themselves caught up in doing the same. His mother was visibly overwhelmed by Adam's powerful destructive feelings and they thought she felt helpless in containing them. Adam provoked the same powerful feelings in staff and the team gave time to reflecting on this. One was very distressed by his attacks; another, attempting to distance herself from his invasive attacks, said she 'felt nothing', except a desire to punish him. Thinking together helped the team decide to replace punishment with firmness and clear boundaries, which came as a relief to Adam. They discovered how terrified Adam was of his own emotions and phantasies. Once when he fell ill at school he kept saying in panic, 'I am going to die.' He was terrified of the 'wicked witches' in fairy tales. He was clearly dominated by a primitive kind of terror. He covered up his helplessness by his tough behaviour. Unable to cope with the burden of meaningless anxiety he projected all his feelings on to others, remaining mindless as a consequence and unable to benefit from the learning experience. The difficult task for the staff was to remain as thinking minds, making sense of his undigested knowledge. As they understood him better they noticed Adam became more interested in learning and showed some signs of sympathy towards littler children. Some of these thoughts were shared with his mother who communicated her sense of relief, especially as his behaviour improved.

Thinking as a team is not as easy as it may sound. It involves being open to powerful emotions. Anxieties we have experienced in similar situations earlier in life are often evoked, and particularly vulnerable spots may be touched. The particular value of thinking as a team is that it becomes possible to piece together different bits of information. In the case of Adam, one worker felt distress and another 'nothing'. While workers' own past experience will predispose them to react one way rather than another, what is also happening is that both workers were picking up aspects of Adam's feelings. Such different feelings suggest that Adam could not integrate his feelings and become a thinking 'self'. He had to get rid of his unbearable feelings into other people. Such splitting can get enacted within the team, with heated disagreements about how people see the child. If it can be recognized that the splitting mirrors the child's inner world, then the team can work at staying as thinking minds, as they did in this case, and provide the emotional containment which helps the child in turn become more integrated.

Team provision of a symbolic primary experience

An insecurely attached child will have an inner working model of themselves as unworthy of being loved, and will confirm this for themselves by behaving in a way that makes it hard to love them. Depending on the sensitivity of the parenting they received in infancy, this working model is more or less amenable to change. What helps is being allowed to go back to the point of breakdown and receiving a version of the primary experience of being cared for and thought about as tiny babies. Sometimes a team of workers may find a symbolic means of providing this primary experience. Rosemary Lilley (2001: 109–110) describes a family centre's work with three-year-old Karl who had been severely neglected and abused, and was now living in care with his aunt:

He would clear a table with a swipe of his arm, tread on other children playing and then vacantly chew a toy, throwing himself into a screaming ball on the floor if asked to help put right what he had done. We thought this seemed like the panic of an uncontained infant. Karl began to carry round a small soft doll, sucking and chewing its hands and feet. When he dissolved into panic on the floor his special worker spoke to him through the doll (a safe way of putting into words his unspoken fears) saying 'You seem very upset – here let me hold you – no one's going to hurt you here.' She cuddled the doll and laid it by his side. He wanted to take the doll home and we explained he had to bring it back next morning. The doll became a 'transitional object', taking some of the containing function of the centre home with him. The doll also provided a way in to more talking with him, which was needed before any transition such as going outdoors which sent him into further panic. When he hurt other children he would be held through his rage on our laps, as we told him we would keep him safe. Progress was seen when he began to do jigsaw puzzles, at first alone and then asking for help when he felt safe enough. He could not walk away from an unfinished puzzle. It was as if the puzzle represented having a 'whole experience' from start to finish, a compensation for his lack of nurture in infancy ... He moved on to building large Duplo brick towers ... Once the tower was higher than he was he took pleasure in carefully pushing it over, perhaps symbolizing his struggle for autonomy and control. His capacity to create havoc and pit adults against one another remained immense. Much staff time was put into thinking about Karl and his experiences, from formal staff meetings, group room meetings and end of day meetings, to supervision and more informal one-to-one exchanges.

Work with this unintegrated child demonstrates how a team that thinks together about feelings can resist 'splitting'. This containment, combined with their realization of the possibility of reaching him through symbolic communication, helped Karl to create his 'transitional object' and the beginnings of holding together his fragmented self. It was important that the symbolic significance of creating whole puzzles and building towers was understood, so that these activities could be protected from intrusion and seen for the progress they were. Together they provided Karl with a localized version of the primary experience he had missed in infancy. This was a start to the therapeutic help he would need for some years to come.

Of course, it is not practically or ethically possible (except in rare circumstances) to let a child regress completely. That is where the recognition and provision of a localized adaptation is helpful (Dockar-Drysdale 1968, 1990). Such a provision is both real and symbolic at the same time (a symbolic equation). Here is an example from parenting worker John Rivers.

Symbolic experience – looking after the cat

While working in a 'family day' programme I was asked to help a mother with her three-year-old son Lewis. She found him difficult and had come to believe he was unlovable. I think he had come to believe this as well, especially as his sister was getting more attention. The plan was for me to be in the room with his mother and sister but I would give him all his care, providing attention, boundaries, play, food and comfort. I would try and model for the mother that it was possible to love and nurture him – he was just a little boy and not the monster she had come to believe him to be. I also hoped it would take the pressure off her to manage him in our presence, so that she could feel held for herself and accept help for her ongoing depression. I had a good start for I found Lewis very likeable, despite his spectacular temper tantrums. I accepted and empathized with these, tried to understand his frustrations and was there for him afterwards. He seemed to attach to me quickly and stayed where I sat on the floor, rarely moving away to play with other children. He played with cars and other toys while I gave a running commentary, mixed with my reflections of the feelings he was showing. This would often leave me exhausted at the end of a five-hour day.

Lewis rarely spoke to me, but once or twice each day he would tell me he was a cat and direct me to stroke his head or give him a bowl of milk or food – I would break biscuits into a bowl. I believe this was his way of telling me he wanted somebody, probably his mum, to care for him, that he could be loved and was really very small and vulnerable. When he crawled around my feet, pushing cat-like against my leg, it felt like his way of reciprocating that care. I would be accepting no matter how much mess he made or how far he pushed the boundaries. I would not let him hurt himself or other children but always empathized with his struggles. His difficult behaviour started to change and his mother, who had been able to accept some help for her own difficulties, gradually started to accept him back. In a review meeting six months later his mother said it had been painful to see how quickly her son had allowed me to contain him, both physically and emotionally, when she had been struggling for so long. I think she was brave to acknowledge this and it showed how far she had come in her own understanding.

It is important to notice that the idea for the symbolic provision of good primary experience (here being looked after like a cat) came from the child and *not* from the worker. It is the worker's task to recognize it for the need it is, and to respond, making sure that they reliably provide what the child is asking for. This piece of work also demonstrates the need for the parent to feel appreciated and supported, so that envy of the worker's skill with their child can be replaced by relief and pleasure in being helped to build their own better relationship with their child.

Play to support the parent–child relationship

A 'holding environment' for parents

If parents are to 'hold' or contain their children, in the sense that Winnicott described, they themselves must be contained. Many mothers feel consumed by their young children and begin to lose their sense of self, and with it their self-confidence and self-esteem. The realization of parents' own needs for nurturing stems in part from feminist recognition of the needy child within the mother, described by Eichenbaum and Orbach (1983). Anne Jenkins (1989) recognized at NEWPIN that if the hurt child within the mother can be healed, mothers can go on to heal their own children. As Winnicott (1965: 49) acknowledged: 'Mothers who do not have it in them to provide good enough care cannot be made good by mere instruction.' We need to provide a holding environment for parents through which they feel held in mind, so that their anxiety is lessened and they can develop their own inner mental space to play with new thoughts and viewpoints. In this way we can help them understand their relationship with their children and make links between this relationship and their children's emotional needs. Then they can make use of more direct parenting help.

Parents with low incomes and who lack family support are often under particular pressure, as one child's play revealed. Doing pretend washing up in the home corner he threw the bowl of dishes across the room, saying, 'My mum did that this morning', which led to workers finding out she was worried about being caught for shoplifting. On being read the story of *Burglar Bill*, with its moral ending as the burglars return the stolen goods, another child piped up, 'We don't do that, we keeps it!' The centre was not only an important secure base for the children but also for their mothers. For example, the centre leader befriended a pregnant mother who found it hard to relate to her four year old, to the extent of taking her a clean nightdress every day she was in hospital, while also preparing her daughter for the baby by giving her a special doll to look after.

Reaching the child within the parent

A parent who has had an impoverished childhood may have few good memories to draw on. Sometimes their play needs require being met first, whether in a playing and playful group of adults, in a creative activity or even by being given their own version of Pinney's Children's Hours. Or a parent may be drawn into playing where the work is ostensibly with the child, as in the following example:

Rachel, aged four, was referred by her mother because she would not speak. As I visited them at home and started playing with Rachel it became clear that her silence was a response to her mother's demand that she talk, including to her strict grandparents, and that in a non-directive play situation she would blossom. I had a tiny mouse in my pocket who would come out to see what was going on, but was easily frightened and would run back to my pocket to hide if anyone came close or spoke to it. This matched what Rachel, on the other side of the room, was doing. I talked aloud about how the mouse was feeling but made no move to approach or question Rachel. She smiled with delight each time the mouse peeped out and when it ran away again. Soon she was quietly sitting by me, exploring the toys I was getting out. She was eager to draw with the felt-tip pens, although worried about making a mess. Later she was absorbed in play with a miniature village and people, arranging them on a tin tray covered with salt, for snow (it was winter). I sat on the floor with her and described what she was doing as she played. There was so much non-verbal communication between us that when she eventually spoke it seemed unsurprising and fitted into our pattern of communication quite naturally.

Rachel's mother was alternately sharp-tongued or complaining helplessly. Rachel could do nothing right. I realized that she felt that she had no control over Rachel or anything else in her life, and nothing seemed to give her any pleasure. As well as talking with her about herself and her own childhood I started to draw her into my play with Rachel, giving her a turn in card and board games such as Tummy Ache, and letting her win as often as Rachel. I would get Rachel's or my puppet to talk to her or tickle her, or need to take refuge on her lap. I read stories to which both listened. She began to smile more and sometimes the tone of her voice softened. When I was showing them how to play Clock Patience her face lit up and she said that she remembered playing that when she was little. As we drew on her good play memories of childhood, few as they were, the hurt child within her healed a little and became less demanding. She became more able to assume parental responsibility. She agreed to read to Rachel for five minutes a day and I think both enjoyed this time. By the end of eight weekly play sessions they were much happier together.

'Caught not taught'

In the following example a home visitor used play with dough to engage a two year old, giving an implicit rather than explicit message to the mother about the value of play:

I never thought the introduction of a mixture of flour, salt, water and food colouring, with a dash of oil and cream of tartar, could bring such contentment. I had been visiting Michael and his mother and found nothing to keep his attention for more than a minute or two. As he shouted and screamed for at least half the time I was there, I had to find something he could focus his anger on. I showed his mum the coloured dough and asked her permission to use it. She readily agreed. The morning flew by as Michael poked and prodded at the dough and eventually he smiled. The next week he took my bag and looked for the dough. He seemed to be a different child, quite gentle. He spent about an hour playing with the dough each week, which also gave me an opportunity to talk to him. This has been the pattern for seven months, although Michael doesn't look for the dough straightaway now. I introduce it when a tantrum seems imminent and it seems to be calming. About two months later I visited to find Michael unwell. I was delighted to find that, for the first time, his mother had made him some playdough herself.

The home visitor was careful to leave control with the mother and to seek her agreement, while demonstrating by example how play can be used to engage an anxious and angry child and make both parent and child happier together. Understanding was 'caught not taught'.

Filial play therapy

While play therapists may work one to one with pre-school age children, often while the parent is receiving their own separate form of help, there is a move towards including parents in a therapy session with their child. In filial play therapy ('filial' meaning 'relating to a son or daughter') a parent is helped to become the therapist to their child (Van Fleet 2005). This involves first learning to become better attuned to their child's emotional state and to provide and become involved in their play, either by experiencing it themselves, by watching someone else, or sometimes by being shown more directly. A further step is helping parents learn to name their child's difficult feelings and to reflect these back to the child in a way that helps the child feel understood. This provides the vital emotional holding which enables the child in turn to manage their feelings, rather than act them out. Filial play therapy teaches parents, individually or in groups, how to do this. Play therapist Nina Rye (2006: 14–15) describes her work with Zak and his mother as 'inadvertent filial therapy' since it took place almost entirely in the waiting room:

Zak was five, excluded from his first school, with a recent diagnosis of Asperger's syndrome and a history of witnessing domestic violence. His mother Karen was anxious to try 'anything'. Zak had great difficulty with transitions, especially leaving his mother. At school they used a quick parting – 'like ripping off a sticking plaster' Karen called it. Zak would be distressed but then appear to settle quickly. Surprisingly Zak came readily into the playroom, bringing his cuddly 'Kitten'. I had met him at his home the day before and he was curious about the playroom, which perhaps helped. But the next time he ran back to his mother and refused to leave her, so she came into the playroom with him. Before the next session I phoned Karen and we talked through what to do. I explained that although I could appreciate that the quick parting strategy usually worked for her I wanted to try something different, which would be part of the therapy. I asked her to follow any cues I gave but otherwise she need not say anything. To her credit she agreed. The next week Zak was playing at a table with bricks in the crowded waiting room. His mother smiled when I went in and I could see that Zak noticed. I greeted him quietly, sat down, commented a little on what he was doing, and said that I would return in two minutes and then it would be time to go to the playroom. Zak listened but did not look up. I returned, again sat down, commenting on what he was doing, adding that it was time to go to the playroom and I was waiting until he was ready. Zak looked even more determined to go on building, and he did so for a minute or two until disaster struck; his tower collapsed in pieces. His face crumpled and he jumped up, stamping and shouting. I reflected that he was very sad that his tower had broken. Zak threw some bricks onto the table. His mother looked alarmed but kept still, only her wide-open eyes and tightly crossed arms showing her agitation. I kept right on reflecting Zak's feelings of sadness and anger, until he was just placing bricks on the table, fitting a few pieces together, and eventually moved on to play with another toy. At this point I said that he could bring the toy to the playroom, but that it was time to go. Zak spoke to me for the first time that day, explaining what he was doing with the toy. A minute later he picked it up and walked in front of me to the playroom.

My routine from then on was the two-minute warning, then reflecting on his play while 'waiting until you are ready' and allowing him to choose what to take with him. The shouting, stamping and throwing faded away. Sometimes Zak looked upset, and sometimes it was not enough to bring 'Kitten' and a toy – the week after starting at a new school he needed to bring his mother too. But overall there was progress. He also became able to leave the playroom with only a few minutes delay and without becoming upset. I had to respect the strategy he developed for leaving, which was to place certain things where he wanted them for next time, as if to reassure himself that he was coming back. In fact the most important thing about his therapy seemed to be that he could manage transitions by using his own self-regulating strategies. I was pleased that he had made so much progress in five sessions. What I had not realized was the impact on his mother. In our progress meeting Karen told me frankly that she had doubted that my 'namby-pamby' approach would work! Once she had observed it and seen that Zak could leave calmly without going 'into one of his tempers' she decided to try it for herself. She described how she was naming his feelings, and enthusiastically gave me several reasons why it was so effective. I loved having a parent spontaneously find this out and come to tell me; usually I am the one doing the describing and giving reasons. But Karen had observed, experimented and worked it all out for herself.

From watching Nina, Zak's mother learned that noticing and naming feel-ings made a difference. She probably also learned unconsciously that it is possible not to 'collapse in pieces' like Zak's tower, despite her anxiety. Nina was doubtless also anxious but able to contain her own feelings along with Zak's and his mother's. Some parents need more help in becoming aware of the approach the therapist is modelling and benefit from some explicit discussion followed by help in practising themselves, as filial therapy can offer (see examples in Chapters 5 and 9).

In all of the examples described, recognition of the parent's anxieties and respect for their autonomy provided the emotional holding which enabled them to feel more sure of themselves and so to observe and learn how better to contain their children. All became more attuned and able to join in their children's play. Zak's mother learned the additional skill of naming and reflecting her son's feelings. Rachel's more emotionally deprived mother needed more help in having her own 'inner child' needs met before she could function as a parent rather than as a needy child.

Group work to improve parent–child relationships

Emotional holding for a parent may not always be enough to change their parenting significantly, as we have seen. An additional educational experience may be needed, preferably one that incorporates the idea of a holding environment into its way of working. It will be even better if it includes play. In play the player has mastery over the situation but feels contained within safe boundaries, which is the opposite of the experience of many parents. Through taking part in experiences which enable them to play, parents can begin to accept and to value the 'child' within them. This helps them to accept both their children's dependence and their need for some autonomy, ultimately making for a more secure attachment. Creative play at an adult level might include using the raw materials of children's play, or simply 'playing with ideas' in discussion. I remember a group of struggling young mothers trying out recipes for pink playdough for their children; the mothers found themselves making male genitals and shaking with laughter as they expressed their feelings about the men in their lives. Spontaneous play had broken through their reserve and provided a healing experience.

The examples which follow show some different approaches. All attend to the need to provide parents with emotional holding. Some programmes with the most emotionally deprived and needy parents offer more intense psycho-dynamically informed experiential group work to help parents make sense of past damaging experiences. All approaches provide an educational experience involving some version of learning from hearing new ideas, observing, being shown, discussing with others, and practising with support. Parents may dir-ectly be involved in playing with their children or they may be playing with ideas. The programmes aim to help parents become more attuned to their children, able to manage them and enjoy them, so that in turn the children's sense of self grows and their attachment becomes more secure.

Play and parenting workshops

Parenting worker John Rivers (2004) provides groups for parents whose children (aged four to eight) display difficult or destructive behaviour, including those with attention deficit hyperactivity disorder (ADHD). He uses Webster-Stratton's (1987) parent programme, which starts with an emphasis on play. His approach is facilitative, stressing that he 'will not be expecting them to do anything that they do not believe will work for them or that will not fit their home, beliefs or life style' and emphasizing parents' collective expertise. He writes:

> As I start to talk about the value of play it just feels almost frivolous after hearing how difficult life is for some of these parents to then have to tell them to go off and play with their child for fifteen minutes each day and that this will be the beginning of a new relationship that will help them shape their child's behaviour . . . As I look round the room I could see many thinking what is this fool talking about. It is at this point that I start to feel inadequate to the task. I try hard to remind myself that this programme works, that play is the right beginning, and that almost every time I have run this group I have felt this projection from the group . . . It is with all my fingers and toes crossed that I close the group and send them off on their homework: play with your child for a short time each day at a set time if possible, let your child take the lead but gently try to influence them into imaginative games or at least games that require conversation – definitely no computer games.
>
> While some parents start to enjoy their time with their child, many find it hard to believe it worth making the time and others say they do not enjoy it (and as children themselves many never really experienced playing with an adult). What really helps is giving parents the clear message that they matter and that they are valued. For the few short weeks that parents are attending my groups I try to give them a small experience of being nurtured and cared for. Making the room warm and welcoming, and providing food and drink is part of it. Also, as far as possible midway between each of the weekly group meetings each parent will receive a phone call from one of the group leaders. While this helps parents stay on track with homework or gives an opportunity to 'troubleshoot' difficulties, the most important aspect of these phone calls is that it gives a clear message that we are keeping them in mind, we are thinking about them and it matters to us how they are doing. In such a holding environment, parents feel emotionally safe enough to share some very personal and

emotive experience – their fears, anxieties and feelings of despair and hopelessness. The group leaders provide the containment, modelling how these feelings can be tolerated and thought about (for example, the parents' feelings of inadequacy, which the group leader may only become aware of when he himself experiences the same projected feeling and recognizes its origin!). Gradually parents become more able to provide containment for each other, and even for themselves. By the end many parents find their children more manageable and their relationships improve, although by no means are all problems solved.

The Child's Game

The play element of Webster-Stratton's programme has much in common with The Child's Game (Forehand and McMahon 1981) in which parent and child spend 15 to 30 minutes in a regular special time together (and similar to Pinney's Children's Hours, see Chapter 2). In a group, parents can practise in pairs (one as 'parent' and the other as 'child', giving each other feedback afterwards) before playing with their children at home. A few minutes may be enough at first. Rules for the Child's Game are as follows:

1   *Child's activity.* Allow your child to choose the activity. Do not introduce anything new into their play. If your child changes activities follow this but do not change the activity yourself.
2   *Follow.* Watch with interest what your child is doing – 'shadow' their movements or mood.
3   *Attend.* Describe aloud enthusiastically what your child is doing, giving a gentle running commentary on your child's activity.
4   *Join in and copy.* Participate in your child's play, by handing them materials or by taking a turn, or by doing what they do, or what they ask you to do. Be careful not to direct or structure play yourself. Remember that your child's play is to be the centre of your attention, so continue to describe their activity and not yours.
5   *No questions or commands.* Do not ask any questions or give any orders. (This is not so easy as it sounds.) These interrupt and structure your child's play.
6   *No teaching.* Do not use this time to teach your child or to test what they know.

Treasure basket and heuristic play groups

Elinor Goldschmied (1986) had the idea of providing Treasure Baskets containing everyday objects with varied sensory properties for babies, and went on (1992) to develop heuristic play ('heuristic' meaning 'discovery') where a group of young children was given a large number of objects and containers to explore and play with. A later development has been to include parents. In one group for families with children from 12 to 18 months, parents are invited to sit in a circle of beanbags (so that they are at their child's level) with their children alongside, providing them with a physical secure base. The children are free to go off and explore a variety of objects placed in the centre, for a 50-minute play time. Parents are asked to observe their child's play and be responsive without taking the initiative, and they are also asked not to talk with other parents, so that their children develop a sense that their parent is available. Some children sit and watch and others go off to play, returning to be comforted if upset. At the end of the play time adults and children help pack away the objects. After a snack the children sit and play with a worker. Meanwhile parents and workers have a drink, and go on to talk and think together about what the children have done and how they may have been feeling. The aim is to help parents focus on their child's interests and needs. After the session the staff have a time to reflect on the group and to note 'anything that may need to be said or changed for the following session'. Family worker Jenny Sanders (2006) observed children's developing attachment and exploration systems in play:

Seventeen months old Willow at first stayed with her mother. She then went off to explore, returning for 'emotional refuelling' from time to time, sometimes bringing objects to show her mother. Once she found some keys and stretched up pretending to unlock a door, and another time she gazed through a glass door, each time returning to sit close beside her mother. I wondered if her confidence in her mother's provision of a secure base enabled her to play with the idea of exploring a wider world. Esteban played closer to his mother. One day he found and stood on a tin nearby, maybe making him feel bigger and stronger. Once I caught his gaze and smiled at him, whereupon he snuggled into his mother. A short while later I started a game of 'Peep-Bo', and was met first with a serious look and then a smile, his mother watching too. After our game he picked up a piece of cellophane and looked at his mother through it, and they both laughed. Over the weeks a pattern emerged of the children returning to their mothers for longer periods, and with more apparent distress, but also seeming to do more exploring. This highlighted a paradox that the more secure the children felt the more they were able to communicate their feelings, which in turn created a sense that they were more vulnerable. Yet they were also exploring more freely, suggesting that they were in fact feeling more secure.

We can see from this account how real independence and autonomy depends on an initial state of dependence in which the child can trust that they will be responded to appropriately. The structure of the heuristic play group, together with the opportunity led interventions of workers, facilitates parental engagement and helps them develop more sensitivity and attunement, so enabling the growth of their children's sense of self and ultimately encouraging more exploration and play.

Mellow Parenting

Mellow Parenting (Puckering *et al.* 1996) is a form of group therapy designed to help hard to reach families with severe relationship problems with their infants and children under five. It is based on the work of NEWPIN (Jenkins 1989) which found that emotional help to mothers was not always enough to change their parenting (Mills and Puckering 1995). Parents spend mornings in an experiential group looking at their past and present relationships and how these may affect relationships with their children. Their children attend a separate play group. Parents and children meet for lunch, followed by structured joint activities, rhymes and games, with the aim of building a repertoire of mutually enjoyable activities. Then children return to their play group while their parents take part in a parenting workshop which might use videotapes of mealtime family interactions at home. Parents are helped to see what happened from the child's point of view. Then parents are given 'homework'. Mellow Parenting combines the emotional containment and educational aspect of good parenting programmes with the active inclusion of the children in the day's work.

Relationship play

A common issue in play sessions involving mothers and children is that mothers may experience their children as sibling rivals. They may express strong fear of the 'power' of their children. Again a structured approach can help:

An unstructured play group for families with children age four to six who had shown severe behaviour problems outside the home (both children and mothers, mainly single parents, had often had traumatic and unhappy lives) had the effect of deskilling mothers, who retreated to have coffee in the kitchen while the therapists played 'nicely' with the children. In deciding how to tackle this problem the team, with clinical psychologist Val Binney, were influenced by Sue Jennings's drama therapy and by

Veronica Sherborne's (1990) relationship play, in which the body is used as a play object. Their first experiments either led to explosions between mothers and children or, as in painting together, the activity was not intrusive enough to enable work on the relationship. The question was how to make the situation safe enough for both mothers and children to experiment with new behaviour. It was decided that mothers needed a place where they could work through their fears about play and touch. A discussion group was offered because it was recognized that these mothers disliked the intensive focus of individual work. A parallel play group of 45 minutes was provided for the children. This was followed by a 15 to 20 minutes structured play session with mothers and children together. The group was made up of five mother–child pairs. Experience showed that it was better if the worker with the children's play group did *not* take part in the joint group, avoiding the situation of mothers asking how their children had been and their jealousy on hearing that their children had been fine (Wright 1991; Binney 1991; Binney et al. 1994).

The aim was to improve attachment by helping mothers and children to catch up on the early experiences that they had missed, using games (Masheder 1989) involving physical contact and reciprocity. The time limits and opening and closing rituals of the relationship play session helped mothers feel contained. It would start with toddler games and work back to baby games, the content of sessions carefully graded to provide 'desensitization' through 'graduated steps to intimacy'. Without this it was found that the children became aggressive towards their mothers who would respond in kind with slaps:

The first four relationship play sessions consist of 'light' group work. Then there are three sessions of 'light' paired work. Four sessions of drama therapy exercises in pairs follow, with the final session being a party playing favourite games. First is a group warm-up exercise, such as 'Musical Knees', 'Pass the Parcel', followed by a game such as 'Ring-a-roses'. The latter sometimes becomes the ritual game that families choose to play every week. This is followed by games, played mainly on the floor, to encourage positive physical touch. Then come back-to-back games, fingertip play, such as 'Incy Wincy Spider', and traditional games such as 'Grandmother's Footsteps' or 'What's the Time Mr Wolf?'

(The first week the mothers are 'Grandmother', the second week the children take this role.) In later sessions paired touch games, based on the negotiation of power in an enjoyable way, include exercises such as mirroring, puppets or face painting. The child may be asked to draw round its mother on the floor, then mother draws round the child. Close body contact and eye-to-eye singing games, such as 'Rock-a-bye-baby' and 'Row, Row, Row the Boat', are only introduced after the fourth week. They are played first as a group and then in pairs and may become 'homework'. Then everyone sits on the floor and takes turns in telling parts of a 'good' story and a 'bad' one; they must end on a good note. After this comes singing of 'Rock-a-bye-baby', with the child sitting between mother's legs. Each session ends with a group 'yell' or an action story, such as *Thunderstorm*, designed to release the build-up of any tension and to prepare for leaving (Binney *et al.* 1994).

Group music and singing times, from infancy onwards, offer opportunities for body and eye contact between mother and child. Traditional rhymes and songs can jog memories of the parents' own childhood and lead to more singing and playfulness within the family at home. Those parents without this childhood memory of songs and rhymes are enabled to create the experience which will give their babies memories to hold on to, as well as enjoying the togetherness now (Shephard 1989). Dance therapy is based similarly on the belief that a relationship becomes apparent in the way that a parent and child move in relation to one another. It uses movement to create new patterns of relating. Bonnie Meekums (1988, 2002) used 'mirroring' to put mothers and children back in touch as they copy one another's movements. 'The dance enables stifled or inarticulate feelings to be expressed and to find an immediate response. It allows parents to let go of their inhibitions, their need to be like children and their fear of appearing childish, so that needs can be expressed and met in the same action' (Pithers 1990a). The child's sense of self is helped by developing their bodily awareness in relation to other people and the space around them. Work on the neurological benefit of sensory integration highlights the importance of movement and different kinds of touch and shows how parents can help, for example, through baby massage (Goddard Blythe 2004). Theraplay (Jernberg and Booth 1999) uses similar physical approaches to improve child–parent attachment relationships.

The relationship play sessions described led to improvement in mother–child attachment, although children's internal fears and extreme phantasies persisted. Essential to sustaining the relationship play was the separate mothers' group where they discussed subjects such as their 'terrible' children, their own childhood and the uselessness of men, and were helped to make connections between past and present – for one, how being 'locked up' as a child was reflected in her 'locking up' her own children. The team emphasized that the group leaders need support if they are to avoid burn-out from the stress of mothers' disclosures and projections (Binney 1991; Wright 1991; Binney *et al.* 1994).

Conclusion

The most significant developmental task for a child in the early years is the establishment of basic trust, which is the product of secure attachment. Only once a child has developed an inner working model of the world as responsive and helpful and themselves as worthy of love and care can they explore the world, developing autonomy and initiative. Much early years work is about supporting this process, both where initial attachment is secure enough and where it is not. Secondary attachment figures are crucial in providing a secure base for an infant in day care experiencing separation (whether or not the initial attachment is secure). Help to parents as well as the child is essential where the first attachment relationship is in difficulty. The earlier a damaged attachment can be repaired, the better for the child's future mental health.

If we remind ourselves that play is about feeling free to try things out without fear of criticism or failure because we feel safe enough and understood enough to do so, we can see how vital is the role of the worker or therapist in providing an emotionally containing relationship, a holding environment for the child but also for the parent. That provides the safe boundary – the 'playground' – which may be a physical space but is more importantly an emotional space within which thinking and feeling can take place and be connected. This chapter has explored a number of ways of working with parents and children, all of which aim to provide that mental play space within which growth can happen. Some ways of working are more obviously playful than others but the aim of all is to support child and parent's capacity to be more comfortably and happily themselves.

Often the work involves thinking about and acknowledging painful feelings such as grief and anger, difficult work for the child and for the parent. It is difficult too for the worker who also experiences strong feelings which at times can feel overwhelming. They need to work out where these feelings come from and whose feelings they are feeling. Workers need their own holding environment, a mental space where they can think safely about these feelings, free from other management requirements, and together make sense of what is happening. Team meetings are an essential tool for under-standing and making sense of relationships, without which the work cannot be effective. Remembering the idea of Russian dolls, if workers feel emotion-ally contained they are more able to contain the parent to in turn contain their child.

Chapter 5

Play in helping troubled families

A child's distress or difficult behaviour may be an indication that a family is in difficulty. If we see the family as a system with its own sets of values and beliefs, and its own 'scripts' for ways of communicating with one another and managing daily life, then the self of each member of the family will be influenced by the family pattern (Byng-Hall 1995). This pattern is largely brought by the parents from their families of origin and is learned by each child by living it. If the pattern becomes confusing or destructive, or if it is unable adequately to manage traumatic loss, then help to the whole family may be more useful than help to the child alone.

Family therapists have tended to treat children as miniature adults, perhaps because they are often more at ease with adults. By contrast play therapists tend to be comfortable with children but more anxious about working with adults. However, there is much to be gained by bringing together the techniques and skills of both. Play in family work and family therapy can achieve a number of aims. It can help in understanding the family's problem. It may be used to increase the ability of members of a family to communicate with one another, and to change their perceptions of one another and themselves. Creative and playful techniques such as family sculpting (Satir 1972) engage a whole family in seeing how they stand (literally!) in relation to one another. Play can change a family's view of what they can do as a family – for example, to find that time together can be enjoyable. It may be used to clarify and change alignments and boundaries in a family (Minuchin 1981). Where the child is scapegoated or used to carry the family's problem, therapy may be concerned with helping each family member to own their feelings and to stop projecting them on to the child. Where the child's emotional problems are judged to exist in their own right, play may help in involving the family in the child's therapy. In families with complex problems which have led to abuse or neglect, the family's difficulty needs to be assessed and understood, and help given to enable family members to provide adequate enough parenting, if possible, so that their child can stay in the family. At the same time the child's needs are paramount, as is the task of communication with the child's internal as well as their presenting self. The social worker, whose task this usually is, must make sense of and work with the whole family system (including the child) without losing sight of the child. Understanding and using play is one of their tools.

Play in understanding the family's problem

Penny Jaques (1987: 9–10), recognizing the value of play as a means of communication for children during family therapy sessions, provided drawing and painting materials, a doll's house with family, sets of domestic and wild animals, and modelling material. Play with wild animals might suggest a threat from outside to a child's sense of security, exemplified by the child who put domestic animals inside the fence with the wild ones outside. It may also express the child's own wild feelings:

> A six-year-old boy was anxious and clinging and hated to leave his mother's side to go to school. While his parents talked he made a series of Plasticine babies, and then took great delight in cutting off their heads, a clear communication about his envy for the one-year-old who could stay with mum all day, and quite a revelation in a boy who had shown no overt signs of jealousy and was described as 'devoted to the baby'. . . . Another five-year-old took six crocodiles and hippopotami and put them in the doll's house where the daddy doll was positioned watching television. He put the wild animals in a circle surrounding the daddy doll and then stood back gleefully . . . When his mother saw the set-up in the doll's house, she commented ruefully that six crocs and three hippos wouldn't stop her husband working too hard.

Jaques saw this as a crucial communication which transferred the definition of the problem away from the child to the father's unavailability, about which the boy was expressing his own and his mother's anger. The child's unconscious communication helps in clarifying the problem not only for the therapist but also for the members of the family. It provides a hypothesis for what is going on, although we need to look for a repeated pattern before coming to any firm conclusion.

Children's unconscious communication through drawing and painting in family sessions can help a family understand their child's deeper feelings about significant people and events. Jaques gives several examples. A girl who was aggressive and demanding after her father's death drew a happy girl skipping among flowers, then blacked out the sun and covered the picture with grey raindrops, perhaps her unshed tears. The communication may illuminate family dynamics. A four-year-old girl showed how her separation anxiety might be linked to her mother's unrecognized agoraphobia when she drew her house on wheels. A silent seven-year-old boy drew a ferocious shark, illuminating his family's need to be helped to permit the expression of strong feelings. The shark can be viewed not only in terms of the child's perception of threat from others but also as the projection of the child's own angry feelings. The process or way a child paints or draws can also convey information, inhibition suggesting anxiety or low self-esteem, messiness suggesting lack of self-control or inner feelings of being 'a mess'.

Using a more focused approach to a family session, Alison O'Brien and Penny Loudon (1985) would ask children to draw their family doing something, or at mealtimes or bedtimes, or to draw something that happened recently, a sad or happy time, school, or presents they would give each family member. Gil (1994) suggests a family picture developed from an initial squiggle, individual or family drawings of 'their family', or a portrait of a particular family member. Children can help draw a genogram, as well as set out figures or make models. This may help in uncovering needs for future work – for example, a child's need to be told more about his absent father. Even when specific tasks are given it remains important to encourage spontaneity and playfulness, with the worker remaining respectful of the family's ability to work on its own problems, with help. Parents need to be told that they and not the therapists are in charge of their children during a session, a process which supports their parenting role.

Asking children to draw their family may reveal their view of a problem. Occupational therapist Roz Smithson found focused drawing particularly useful if a child's free play repeatedly focused on less expressive activities such as a Lego construction, rather than communication or imaginative play. She writes:

Nine-year-old Simon was admitted to the children's unit because of enuresis, both night and day, sibling rivalry and temper outbursts. He was under-achieving at school and had poor peer relationships. Invited to paint his family he painted the title in a 'nice' colour, this was his word, perhaps representing his nice middle-class family. He painted his father first, with no arms and at a distance from the rest of the family (Figure 5.1). This could indicate that Simon viewed his father as emotionally distant. He told me they spent little time together. He painted his mother next, also with no arms. She was reported to have felt unable to love Simon because of all the pain he caused the family. Simon then painted his younger sister who was reported to be the dominant child of the family, and everything her parents could wish for, pretty, pleasant and intelligent. Not surprisingly there was rivalry between her and

Figure 5.1 My family, by Simon.

Simon. He drew his youngest sister next, a toddler, again with no arms but smiling. Simon said he felt able to relate to this sister the best. He drew himself last, again with no arms. This figure was standing on one leg and appearing to be squeezed in between his sisters. I asked Simon to tell me how the figure in the picture felt; he said he was squashed because there was no room for him. It suggested to me that he felt overshadowed and pushed out by his sisters. I asked Simon to speak as his parents, and when he found this difficult gave him a variety of phrases to choose from. He chose 'Let Simon come forward'. He added that he was not sure that his sisters would allow this to happen. With Simon's permission, themes which emerged within the individual therapy sessions were incorporated into future family sessions which were led by a colleague. In addition I worked jointly with Simon and his mother in several sessions to address other themes which emerged during the individual work.

While it is worth considering that 'no arms' might simply be Simon's way of drawing people, this account shows how the therapist was seeing this session within the context of what she knew of the family. It also illustrates how it was the meaning which the child gave to his picture, and his responses to the structured exercise, which were important.

A play task can be useful, both as a warm-up and in assessing a family's problem. Occupational therapist Pauline Blunden (1988) would ask a family to build a tower with 12 large wooden blocks. This is a simple task which even the youngest child can join in and gives an idea of the family dynamics. She observed who directs the building, who builds the tower, and who is passive or takes no part. She noted if they enjoy the task or if they get easily discouraged if the tower falls. With a similar aim, she would ask a family to sort a pack of playing cards into groups, giving a time limit. Other tasks might involve a playful discussion of family likes and dislikes or planning a family day out.

Play as family therapy

Visual techniques

Family therapy techniques such as role play and sculpting, or the drawing of a genogram, help adults as well as children to perceive and work on their relationships. O'Brien and Loudon (1985) use a variety of visual techniques in family therapy. A mobile shows how moving one part (person) affects all the others. Bursting balloons demonstrate the effects of cumulative stress.

Balancing scales to which weights are added for each complaint about a 'bad' child, as opposed to the 'good' one, help some parents to realize suddenly the devastating effects of their complaints. A family, made from modelling material, can be used to sculpt the family, to discuss family structure and to show how it changes with the family life cycle. Used with wooden rods to represent the structure or boundaries around a child (or their absence or inconsistency), a family unable to agree on setting firm limits for their 'uncontrollable' four year old were helped to see how lack of structure made their child insecure, and came to agree on a consistent routine. Other visual aids include a modelling material cake cut into segments, as well as gears, wheels, magnets, rubber bands, plant symbolism, knots, a Newton's cradle and nesting dolls. They provide concrete symbols (in the Piagetian sense) of family relationships which facilitate thought and foster playfulness, reducing feelings of threat and failure. Bonnie Eaker (1986: 243–244) values play because it creates 'enough emotional distance between family members for the truth to be spoken' and 'serves as a cushion in sustaining resistant families in treatment'. It can help parents who tend to intellectualize their difficulties as well as parents who have difficulties putting things into words. It can put parents in touch with the child within them and make them more able to reach their own children. Yet she warns against using family play therapy where abuse is suspected, if unlocking of family secrets might put a child at greater risk.

Family storytelling

Eliana Gil (1994) explores many aspects of the use of play in family therapy, including such techniques as puppets and storytelling. She describes how she introduces a family to storytelling with puppets by saying: 'I've brought some puppets today and I'm going to ask you to take a few minutes and choose the puppets that you would like to work with. Then I'm going to ask you to make up a story with a beginning, a middle and an end. There are only a couple of rules. You must make up a story, not tell one like *Cinderella* or *Pinocchio*, and you must act out the story with your puppets rather than narrate it' (Gil 1994: 47–48). After listening to the story she may enter the family metaphor, for example, by asking specific puppets to talk to one another or to comment on their own or another's behaviour or feelings. When the family is ready they may be helped to reflect on any connection between the puppets' story and their own life. Such an involving task frees family communication from distancing and blame, making possible some movement towards change. In Gardner's (1981) Mutual Storytelling technique the therapist goes on to tell a similar story but changes the ending to a more hopeful one.

Family play and games

Structured play and games were used with several large families with relationship problems where it was felt that normal family therapy would be too verbal and demanding (Martel 1981). Games included drawing their ideal home, or their dream island: using cards created by joint listing of 'feelings' in turn-taking games – 'I feel . . . when . . .', 'When I feel . . . I . . . and I would like people to . . .'; telling stories with hand puppets; sharing memories, things that had frightened, angered or saddened them, or future wishes; making face masks and enacting a play; making a cut-out family tree; sculpturing the family. When one family's commitment waned the workers drew a picture of how they saw each family member. These hit the nail on the head and the family re-engaged. The workers felt that the families gained more from experiential learning and the freeing effect of play within safe limits than from any interpretation or feedback they were given. Parents need to feel that they are partners in the process of change. Then they change in the ways in which they perceive and respond to their children, putting fewer projections and pressures on them and freeing them to develop normally.

A carefully designed play programme was used to help the parents and seven children of the very deprived Watson family to listen to one another, to appreciate each other's contributions and to begin to cooperate, raising their self-esteem, instead of seeing themselves as 'useless' (Martel 1981). The first session used 'ice-breakers', with everyone decorating a name card, playing statues and saying one thing that had happened that day. One room was turned into a 'huff' room, with a notice on the door, as people stormed off so often. Later, family members were given roles in dramatic play, a plane crash. The family had to decide where and when the crash happened, who was injured, and how they were rescued or escaped, and enact this with props. Other games were a cooperative treasure hunt, a home-made jigsaw puzzle where each member had a piece but could not let go until all were in place, and musical 'chairs' on pieces of paper, in which no one was 'out' but the paper got less. To show that girls were as good as boys, each gender made a board game in separate rooms. To give the family some positive feelings the three workers wrote complimentary descriptions on cards for the others to guess who it was, the owner taking the card home. They made a Watson family advertisement, each member saying something positive about the others, and then each member making a separate advertisement using these. Mimes, charades and acting in pairs, photographs and videotapes gave everyone positive attention. As the group came to an end the workers made up a song about the family, asking everyone how they wanted to be said goodbye to – whispered, shouted or sung!

Occupational therapist Susan Monson, with co-worker staff nurse Martin Elliott, took their inspiration from work with the Watson family in planning a final session with a family where conventional family therapy elsewhere had not worked well:

The family consisted of a mother lacking in confidence, an unsupportive father, a disabled child and a disturbed 'normal' child. The aim was for a final session that would encourage family identity and self-esteem and help its members to enjoy doing things together. We explained to the family that we had planned some activities mainly for the children but hoped they would all enjoy them. We introduced ourselves with a home-made jigsaw game. Then everyone took turns in being the leader in 'Simon Says'. Some of our instructions involved physical contact, such as 'hold hands' or 'hug each other'. 'Musical Islands' followed where everyone ended up on one island.

Next was a fantasy journey. Together we did a family collage on a large box to make a rocket, the family beginning to work as a team but finding it hard and needing help and encouragement. Then we told a story about the rocket journeying to another planet, after which the family were given roles in dramatic play, with a few props and dressing-up clothes to help. Mother, in a hat, was thrilled to be captain but a little unsure of her role. Father was steward and only stopped joking and teasing people to serve tea. The disabled child was the air hostess and sat on her father's lap shouting people's names. The other child was navigator, and was so carried away with the game that for a moment he thought it was real. We joined in, creating an asteroid storm by bombarding the rocket with rolled-up socks, suggesting that the family needed to cling together in the turbulence, which they found difficult to do. When the family landed safely, one of us took the role of a reporter and asked how the family had got on; the other took the role of a photographer and snapped pictures of the family. The captain said that all the members of her crew had done very well.

The session ended with a song about the family, with a verse about each. The mother kept the words and later sent a card saying how thrilled she was. We felt that the game had boosted her confidence considerably. Everyone, even father, had managed to enjoy doing something together although it was neither easy nor natural. Although ostensibly a 'silly game' the play session helped the parents take more appropriate control and to work together, so that everyone felt safer and happier. We felt that it achieved its aim in helping the family see itself more positively.

Such work draws from Minuchin's (1981) structural family therapy, concerned with spatial closeness and boundaries in families and redressing imbalances, and which is particularly appropriate for the application of play techniques. Sara Deco (1990) used family painting sessions to strengthen the boundaries between generations, to help a mother manage her child rather than be controlled by her. Where Minuchin would rearrange the chairs of family members in a therapy session, playdough or other activity could be used to bring all family members physically close to one another; if a child took itself away from the family then the therapist might ask the mother to bring the child back for play, giving her action a purpose.

Sometimes the need is not so much to put parents back in charge as to restore a damaged relationship between parent and child. Susan Monson gives another example of using play activities, together with other interventions, to help a grieving family following the death of a parent:

A family had suffered the trauma of nursing the father at home through a terminal illness. The middle child was deeply affected at the time but too young to understand or talk about it very well. She responded to the situation long term by acting out her feelings in difficult behaviour. This was mainly directed at the mother, while everyone else saw a tense and far too well-behaved child. Careful discussion with the family and the team led to individual play therapy for the child, meetings for the family, and work for the mother and child together which I took on. My aim was to help improve their relationship so that some of the positives could be shared with mother and more of the negatives shown elsewhere. The mother had some time on her own with the therapists to help her understand what was happening. I often use parents' memories of their own childhoods as a way of tuning in to their child's feelings and as something from their own lives to build on. An activity that has been enjoyed in childhood is usually a good one to choose. I also look for activities that involve physical closeness and those that provide an opportunity for fun; families with overwhelming problems have little experience of fun. In this case, activities included cooking, with mother and child making jam tarts and sharing the satisfaction of 'we made them together'; paper plate puppets which led to much laughter; drawing round each other's hands; and making shakers when each had to listen carefully to the other's sounds – helping them to listen to one another. Despite the complexity of the issues this simple approach, in conjunction with the other help, brought real progress. The family reported more balanced behaviour at home. They had been quick to follow suggestions on giving praise and using a firm cuddle to restrain any behaviour that got out of hand. They also began to understand how things like making a dreadful mess in the bedroom might link with the father's death.

The most encouraging change was the open affection between mother and child that replaced avoidance and hostility. In discussions the mother had some opportunity to express her own feelings and then reassurance was given that the reason for the difficult behaviour was not poor mothering but the closeness of the relationship and the things that had happened. The work then moved to the home and all the family enjoyed trying simple games and activities. They were able to suggest things themselves, like mime games, which enabled them to have fun together. The home-made playdough was popular with everyone! Special time with mum continued to be important but was balanced by family activities which helped with sharing. Individual play therapy continued during this period. Progress at home meant that the school had to start coping with some quite difficult behaviour. Partly because of regular liaison but also because the staff were so understanding, this behaviour was seen as improvement. This potentially awkward situation shows the importance of making time to talk with everyone involved.

While play helped a bereaved mother and children enjoy each other once more, the work also involved helping the mother develop some insight into both her own and her children's feelings, enabling her to respond to the meaning behind her daughter's difficult behaviour. In contrast to the same workers' more involved and to some extent directive stance with the space journey game, the structure and containment were provided both by the careful selection of activities that would engage the family, by supporting family members' autonomy, and by workers' attentive reflective stance, thinking about the feelings behind behaviour. There was also attention to linking this work to the individual therapeutic work for the mother, other family work and the play therapy for the child, and to helping the school also make sense of changes in the child's behaviour – a systemic approach that ensured that problems were not simply transferred elsewhere.

Involving parents and carers in a child's therapy

Parents and other family members may helpfully be involved in the therapy of children who have become the focus of concern, the 'identified patient'. Family therapist Barry Bowen draws on White and Epston's (1989) notion of 'externalizing the problem', which avoids notions of blame or failure. It unites the family against the problem and opens up new possibilities, tapping into a family's lighter, more optimistic side. Metaphor and analogy can be powerful tools, especially when the family's own metaphors are used (Bowen and Nimmo 1986; Bowen 1997). This is illustrated in his work with eight-year-old Kevin (Bowen 1996):

Externalizing the problem – 'hulk therapy'

Kevin had been living with his two brothers, his mother and her violent partner. He was excluded from school and had lived a streetwise existence, seeing himself as his brothers' protector and involved in violence His mother could not cope with Kevin's escalating aggression and dumped the children on their father and his new family. They could not cope either, so Kevin was looked after by his paternal aunt Joan and her gentle and organized family. She was committed to Kevin's welfare but sought help because of his tantrums, physical attacks on her and tormenting their small daughter. Kevin seemed to have internalized the violent models and limited impulse control he had encountered earlier. He told me violence was 'in his genes' and he would always be aggressive. I renamed the violence as anger; after all, he had plenty to be angry about. Kevin told me he liked watching *The Incredible Hulk* on television. The Hulk was a normal man until somebody made him angry. Then he suddenly grew into a green monster, lost control and smashed things, frightening people. Kevin volunteered the information that the man did not like being the Hulk. Wasn't Kevin a bit like the Hulk I wondered? Kevin thought he was more like the Part-Time Hulk as he wasn't angry *all* the time. I went on to ask what the monster does when he gets sad or upset, and wrote down 'shouting, spitting, swearing, messing about at school, breaking windows, shop-lifting'. We drew the Part-Time Hulk (Figure 5.2), big, with horns, an angry face, and carrying a stone to throw through windows. We drew 'the real Kevin', quite small and smiling, and eight years old – unlike the Hulk who, Kevin said, was only three. I said, 'The monster is only three but he frightens everyone, especially Kevin. You've got to beat the monster. Every time you beat him he shrinks and you grow a bit. How long do you think it will take to get the monster down a bit?' I told him that before he came back he was to draw another picture of the Part-Time Hulk and the real Kevin, checking with his family and his teacher on their size. He did this but the monster was still bigger than the stick figure, although it had shrunk a little. I sent Kevin

Figure 5.2 The part-time hulk, by Kevin.

a letter of congratulations but said that he still needed to work on reducing the monster. 'The trick is that if the monster gets smaller than you he will never beat you again. If you can get him down to pet-size you will get a certificate to say that you can teach people how to do hulk reduction.' Once Kevin became bigger than the Part-Time Hulk I sent him another letter and a monster-taming certificate, which was framed and placed on his bedroom wall. Once his anger was externalized it could be reduced to a manageable size.

The use of letters to the child after each session of 'hulk therapy' is crucial to Bowen's approach (Wood 1988; Marner 1995). It is a tangible demonstration to the child that they have been recognized and understood. Parents' role in joining in the game of beating the monster is important, and they usually enjoy it. They need to be present and contribute positive aspects of the monster/child. Each time they are asked how big the monster is. The method works in changing parents' (and teachers') perceptions of the child as well as the child's self-perception. At one level it is a behavioural approach but it also connects with less conscious phantasies, and replaces fear with hope. The metaphor is carefully chosen, based on what a child of this age might identify with. This technique helps children with conduct problems which conceal emotional difficulties, and children who risk being scapegoated. It requires, however, a basic commitment from the family to the child.

Involving a parent in storytelling in play therapy

Externalizing the problem through metaphor is intrinsic to storytelling, as it is to the symbolic expression of less than conscious feelings in play. Play therapist Deborah Hutton (2004: 5–15) used shared storytelling within non-directive play therapy to help a mother and child with relationship difficulties:

The Castle Maze

Nine-year-old Karen was referred for play therapy to counter her daily family experience of hostility, discouragement and criticism. Her parents were separated and she lived with her mother and younger sister, with contact with her father at weekends. Her mother had long struggled with parenting, unable to manage her daughter's angry outbursts and controlling behaviour, and her 'obsessive' tidiness. Karen had eight sessions of non-directive play therapy, usually choosing to use the sand tray and associated world materials (Lowenfeld 1979).

Both Karen and her mother Elaine then agreed to five joint play sessions. Karen was excited on seeing the sand tray but tempered her enthusiasm on seeing her mother's wariness. The therapist empathized with Elaine's uncertainty and went on to explain that they could choose what to do; her own role would be to watch and help if needed. Karen wanted her mother to decide but at first she refused, eventually suggesting making a castle, with a maze inside. Karen said that outside the castle walls was the beautiful land where everyone wanted to live, but to do this they first had to find their way through the maze. Elaine created the maze, with dead ends containing a monster camouflaged by plants. Karen helped add the monsters and gargoyles, enjoying the developing sense of danger and surprise in the story. Elaine thought about an escape route and added a King and Queen in a nice grassy place in the centre of the maze. In turn they moved characters through the maze trying to find and rescue the Queen, but each one was killed by a monster. Karen had the twins argue about the way and Elaine followed with an old woman who told them off for squabbling, both giggling as they recognized them as Karen and her sister. Elaine became a twin and helped Karen fight off monsters and rescue the Queen, but the King was angry and all had to escape, finally reaching the 'beautiful land' outside.

As they played, Karen and her mother made some spontaneous connections between the 'twins' and their real selves, without the need for any interpretative reflections from the therapist, who only commented on their difficulty in deciding who should lead the play. The symbolic content of the story reflected less conscious themes, reminiscent of Bettelheim's (1976) analysis of fairy tales where heroes overcome dangers and obstacles to achieve their goals. Karen's character needed help from her 'twin' Elaine in order to live in a 'beautiful land'. Elaine, however, had to struggle with powerlessness before she could help her children to escape. There is also some confusion about who the second twin is, Karen's sister or perhaps the mother herself who at that point does not feel strong enough to do more than argue with her daughter about the way, and later she might be the Queen needing rescue. The Castle Maze story provided an eloquent metaphor for the family's plight and suggested the nature of the work that was needed. Creating joint stories continued in subsequent sessions, with Elaine becoming more attuned to her daughter. However after a brief period of improvement, conflict returned to the household, a reminder of the difficulty in effecting lasting change in the inner working models (of both mother and daughter in this case) resulting from severely damaged attachments.

The therapist's non-directive, attentive and empathic stance, reflecting on the feelings aroused, provided the emotional containment which enabled mother and daughter to find a way of being more comfortably together, allowing the symbolism of the jointly created story to carry and connect their unconscious feelings, with glimpses of more conscious insight from the mother. This led to their improved relationship for a while. The empowering of both parent and child within this form of non-directive play therapy demonstrates one of the main features of filial therapy, which we consider next.

Filial play therapy

Filial therapy 'seems to address the difficulties of parent/carers whilst still being sensitive to the child's developmental needs' (Hutton 2004: 264). In filial therapy (Van Fleet and Guerney 2003) a parent learns specific child-centred play skills and undertakes therapeutic play sessions with their child. Parents are empowered to become the therapeutic 'agents of change' for their own children, without the damaging envy which their child's attachment to the therapist in non-directive play therapy can induce or the child's development becoming out of step with what a parent can respond to helpfully. A prerequisite is that a parent has the capacity and energy to be emotionally available to their child, if only for short periods of time. The benefit is that change within the child is matched by change in the family system, and so is more likely to be supported and sustained. A parent or carer is shown how to use non-directive play therapy skills of observing, listening, and reflecting aloud about how their child is feeling, and may be given an opportunity to experience the effect of these skills by taking the 'child' role. They go on to use these skills in a play session with their child, at first under the supervision of a play therapist, later as confidence grows, on their own. Ideally both parents provide play times for each of their children in turn. In the following case illustration, from play therapist Nina Rye (2005: 10–17) the mother was anxious to help her child and ready to learn the skills through which she could provide the emotional holding which enabled him to recover. Nina Rye's detailed account effectively explains the process of filial play therapy:

A case study in parental separation and school refusal

Nathan, now eleven, had always been quiet and 'good' at home. His younger brother had needed frequent surgery. His father had left home in an acrimonious separation and Nathan refused to have anything to do with him. At home he angrily demanded that his mother tell him what to do. He became disruptive at school and eventually refused to go. I met his mother Tina to discuss filial therapy, explaining how it can help re-create that moment-by-moment attunement and empathic response that mothers naturally engage in with their new babies. In a 20 minute Family Play Observation session in the clinic playroom Nathan initially resisted his mother's low-key invitations but within ten minutes moved to join her and his brother who were using playdough. His mother made a special effort to concentrate on Nathan while not ignoring his brother. Nathan gradually relaxed and concentrated on making a snail, eventually smiling and responding a little. She said later that she had wanted to ignore him, as giving him attention usually provoked a temper outburst, but she had thought about our earlier discussion of the value of positive attention and had risked something a little different. I affirmed this and explained how her skills would develop in filial therapy. She left feeling more confident about her ability to help Nathan.

Understanding the problem: an anxious 'controlling' attachment

I used the referral information, my interview with his mother and my analysis of the Family Play Observation to formulate initial hypotheses about Nathan. I wondered whether his role in the family had always been 'the quiet one' who was 'no trouble' (perhaps because of his parents' continual anxiety about his brother). His self-esteem from this role came at a price, that of his parents' positive attention. His sense of security collapsed when his parents' marriage broke down, and with it his coping mechanisms. He found it harder to regulate his feelings and became overwhelmed with anger at school (perhaps a safer place to express his feelings than home). This meant that he lost his role as the good quiet child, with a consequent loss of self-esteem. My hypothesis was that his attachment style was insecure ambivalent. I thought that he was not so much afraid of school as of losing his mother, having already lost his father. Only by staying at home and preventing her going to work could he have a sense that he could 'look after' mother, and so have his own attachment needs met. He became more controlling, desperately trying to engage his mother by demanding instructions about how to spend his time. My aim was for Nathan to regain trust and feel more secure in his relationships with his parents and become better able to communicate his feelings and needs, and so gain confidence and self-esteem. His mother wanted him to reduce his outbursts at home, start to talk to his father and return to school; she hoped that she could shout and argue less and enjoy time with Nathan. I hoped to increase her listening skills, to give her better insight into Nathan's worries and more confidence in encouraging his cooperation. Four skills training sessions concluded with a 30-minute mock play session in which I played a very reluctant and truculent Nathan, who kicked the beanbag, sat facing away from his mother and only gradually engaged in play. Having faced her 'worst case scenario' she was ready to begin play sessions with him. I observed her conducting four 30-minute sessions, giving her feedback afterwards.

Empathic responding

Nathan behaved very much as we had practised. He came in, strode to the end of the room and sat down, looking angry and half-turned away from his mother. She reflected that he did not want to be there. He sat without speaking for a while and then demanded that his mother tell him what to do. She repeated that he could do almost anything he wanted. Nathan looked puzzled and asked what he was supposed to do. She said he could choose. Nathan scowled. For 10 minutes he alternately asked and demanded to be told what to do, adding comments like 'This is stupid'. Tina sat patiently with her face and body towards him, reflecting his feelings of 'not liking this' and 'cross', and occasionally reminding him that it was up to him to choose how to spend the time. Her tenacity in empathic responding was finally rewarded when he moved to sit nearer her at the table. He picked up the playdough and they repeated some of the play from the earlier Family Play Observation, only this time Tina used empathic responses. Nathan stared at her and ducking his head to hide from me (I was at the other end of the room making notes) he whispered 'What are you talking like that for?' Despite her anxiety that he would become angry she resisted the temptation to answer as she would normally. Nathan stayed the full 30 minutes and left on time. In our discussion afterwards I affirmed Tina's use of filial skills in a demanding session, giving specific examples. Tina was pleased that Nathan had eventually chosen what to do and surprised that he had not 'blown his top' and stormed out. She worried that he had objected to the unfamiliar way she talked to him, and had left looking angry and might not return next week. I empathized with her feelings and let her know it was important to share her worries with me. I also said Nathan might need not to lose face by immediately making a big change, pointing out that he had chosen to stay the full time. He had shown a mixture of feelings, including enjoyment of her undivided and positive attention.

Staying with difficult feelings

Next time Nathan soon engaged with his mother, who was more confident and fluent in her responses. He relaxed and played more freely, with a board game and then some other toys. He pointed a dart gun at his mother (a symbolic expression of anger) who set a limit, saying this was not allowed when it was loaded. He did not become aggressive (as she later said she expected) and observed the limit thereafter. In his third session he chose the board game again. Tina was soon in the lead but was now skilled at staying with Nathan's challenging or difficult feelings. Rather than ignoring them or distracting him she reflected 'You worry about me being in front'. He accused her of cheating and then hit the dice bubble with some force. Tina said 'You don't like that, you like to win', and he replied 'Exactly', and they both laughed. He tried to prolong the session but his mother was firm about leaving. Once outside he refused to wait while Tina and I talked. She returned to say she could not stay and because of his reluctance to come to the clinic she thought it was time to begin home sessions. I felt we had not had time to prepare but I respected her decision. After a home session Tina came to the clinic to discuss it. When Nathan refused a play time I emphasized offering consistent weekly play 'appointments' but giving him some choice (and a measure of autonomy) about timing. This was successful but he chose to leave before his half-hour was up. I reminded Tina of the importance of Nathan experiencing her attunement to him, as she had when they had made eye contact over the board game and she had exactly reflected his feelings. I described feeling as if 'light and warmth had been switched on' and Tina agreed that it had been a turning point.

Changing relationships

A month later, Nathan agreed to one more observed session at the clinic. The same warmth and relaxation was evident. Tina was able to stay for feedback and then we met twice more. In our final meeting she reviewed the changes in Nathan and in her parenting. Nathan was back at school, participating fully and with no angry outbursts, and was playing with friends after school. He began talking to his father on the phone and enjoyed planning their visits. With fewer confrontations Tina said she felt more relaxed. She had been able to apply the skills she had learned on structure and limit setting by giving clear messages about how much time remained before bedtime. Then she had stood at the foot of the stairs and simply repeated that it was time to go up, and (to her amazement) both boys eventually complied without argument. Although their planned play sessions ended she was enjoying spending more time with Nathan as well as his brother. His mother's attunement and empathy gave Nathan the experience of having his attachment needs met, freeing him to enjoy other aspects of life. She struggled with the idea of giving attention to negative emotions such as anger which she would usually ignore (as behavioural therapists might also advise!). However, by attending to Nathan's discomfort and irritation she was able to give him the important message that she accepted that he had these feelings and she was no longer upset or overwhelmed. Although his mother's change of style was initially disconcerting, having all his feelings validated, negative as well as positive, had far-reaching consequences in developing Nathan's self-esteem. The potential of filial therapy to effect change in family relationships in a relatively short time is indicated by the progress made by both parent and child in this case.

Where a parent has the motivation and the emotional capacity to learn to become attuned and empathic in responding to their child then much can be achieved, as this case example amply demonstrates. The strength of filial play therapy is that it goes beyond the educational task of developing a parent's skills. It provides a holding environment for the parent, an emotional containment that gives them the experience of someone being attuned to and empathizing with their own feelings, without criticism or blame. A structure is provided within which the parent is supported to try out a different way of being with their child. This is the experience of play, of autonomy and creativity within a safe boundary, within which all aspects of the inner world of feelings, negative as well as positive, can be expressed and find recognition. As the parent experiences it they become more able to provide it for their child, to the benefit of both. The child's security of attachment is increased and with it their sense of self and self-esteem. Chapters 4 and 9 give further examples of filial therapy as well as other forms of parent–child relationship play in 'early years' work and in adoption and fostering.

Play in relationship-based social work with children and families

We cannot give what we have not received. If a parent's past childhood experience has been of misattunement, neglectful or abusive parenting and caring, especially if it is combined with present family experience of isolation and lack of support, then they may not have sufficient inner resources to make use of filial therapy or similar kinds of help. Often they need the long-term holding environment provided by an agency such as family centre if they are to bring up their own children well enough (McMahon and Ward 2001). However, it is sometimes possible in a shorter intervention to help the family itself to change and to sustain this over the longer term. The task of assessing a family's parenting capacity often falls to the social worker. Her skill lies above all in retaining the capacity to think in complex and messy situations, making sense of what she sees and experiences (which is why infant and child observation is such an important part of a social worker's training), and keeping her focus on the child. She needs to find the right distance to do this; too close in and she will be caught up in the multiple projections flying around between family members (usually indicated by an urge to identify with and rescue a particular family member – not necessarily the child); too far out and she will only be observing external behaviour without having the possibility of understanding its meaning (McMahon and Farnfield 2004). Although she works within a statutory assessment framework, it is the social worker's relationship with the child and family that makes the difference. As Clare Winnicott (1964: 45) long ago noted, the social worker differs from the therapist in that 'she starts off as a real person concerned with the external events and people in the child's life. In the course of her work with him she will attempt to bridge the gap between the external world and his feelings about it and in so doing she will enter his inner world too'. In the following case study social worker Paula Stacey (2002) gives an account of skilled work with a child 'at risk' and his family which enabled him to return to the care of his mother:

Family work with a child 'at risk'

Tommy's name had been placed on the child protection register because of injury from being hit by his mother Theresa when trying to control him. Tommy, aged eight, was temporarily placed with his maternal grandmother for three months or so until a core assessment could be completed and decisions then made about his future. His two-year-old sister remained at home with her mother and father, Tommy's step-father, who had recently died unexpectedly. Previous social workers, frightened by a very angry and violent little boy, had almost given up on Tommy, and a long-term removal from his family was imminent. I was the fifth social worker in eighteen months.

Experiencing the anxiety and maintaining a space to think

I first met Tommy at his grandmother's. He asked if I was his social worker, adding, 'I don't like social workers.' I thought about this for a moment, knowing that the family's relationship with social services had been difficult. I also realized that the family was on new ground suffering a loss, and I needed to be aware of their feelings. I asked Tommy if he could tell me why he didn't like social workers. He didn't reply but carefully studied me between looking at the television and talking to his grandmother. Grandmother was asking when Tommy could go home – his mother was not a bad mother and social services were wrong about her, and she herself could not care for Tommy indefinitely. I was aware that Tommy probably heard a lot of this sort of adult talk about conflict with social services and also wondered about how he might feel about her wish not to continue to care for him. I reassured grandmother that it was my view that children are best cared for in their families, but for the moment we need to work out what Tommy needs so that his mother can provide a good home for him. Meanwhile Tommy had fetched his toys and was making his army figures fly in the air and land on their feet ready to go and bash up another waiting figure. Other games followed, all with the same theme of power and indestructibility. I asked him which was his strongest soldier and he said, 'They are all tough.' I just sat and watched, understanding his defensive omnipotent need to be in control. He ignored grandmother when she asked him to stop playing and talk to me. I said that it was all right if he wanted to play. Tommy was now running round the room shooting at every object in sight with a large green plastic 'space gun'. He shot grandmother several times shouting, 'You've got no legs left, I've shot them off.' I was watching carefully, not saying anything, aware that I had not been shot – yet. I said I needed to go, reassuring grandmother when she again asked when Tommy was going home that we would be considering this but meanwhile she was doing a good job of providing Tommy with structure and consistency. I said goodbye to Tommy and made it clear I would like to see him again, perhaps when he is on an overnight visit to mum. Tommy dropped his gun and asked when he might see me again and I replied, 'Soon.' I left feeling warm towards him and pleased that he was my case. I think he had a sense that I had come to spend time with him, not to talk to adults. I then met his mother at her home to understand how she was feeling about Tommy after the death of her partner. She found it hard to engage with me, especially as her own mother was often present. I realized that grandmother had a powerful role in the family.

Understanding how Tommy made sense of events

I next met Tommy at school, the first of several sessions there. I told him I was curious about his family and asked him to draw a picture of his family with him in the centre. He put his name inside a drawing of a car, and I said, 'It looks as if you need to be protected.' He drew his mother in a bubble on top of the car, with his sister attached to mum between her and grandmother. He said they were 'protecting him outside the car'. His late stepfather was attached to mum but farther off and I asked about him, wondering how real his death felt to Tommy. He said, 'Mummy is sad about him dying and I think he is still near us.' When I asked where he thought he had gone, he said, 'To heaven,' pointing at the sky – at mum's he often slept in her bed because he was frightened his stepfather's ghost would come back and get him. He said he saw the ghost most nights. Then he said, 'Mummy had a baby and it died inside her – would it go to heaven even though it was not a proper baby?' I asked what he thought and he said, 'I think it would' and drew a baby in the top corner of the paper. When I asked his mother later she was surprised he knew about the miscarriage. I suggested that because Tommy hasn't always been able to depend on adults making sense of things for him he has spent a lot of time watching and making his own sense of what adults do and say. I thought he had done a pretty good job but now we needed to help him, and mentioned the ghost. She agreed. I felt that this gave us a shared task, establishing a real sense of the need to work together.

Doing something different – counteracting disintegrating forces

The opportunity for her to try something different soon came. Tommy was upset because his sister's wallpaper but not his dinosaur one had come. He was shouting at us, swearing and throwing things at his grandmother, ignoring her threats. I understood from what he said that he really wanted his mum to help him but her attempts to find out what was wrong were met with accusations that she didn't care for him at all. I decided that I should try to contain grandmother so that his mother could try and connect with Tommy. I advised gran that Theresa needed to take control of the situation and it is best if we just stand quietly in the background ready to support her. I encouraged Theresa not to give up but to try and calmly approach Tommy, as she (not me or gran) is the best person to help him find a way back in. I let Tommy know that he need not worry – I understand he is a good boy who is very upset. He eventually came and sat on his mother's lap and listened to her explanation, taking no notice of gran, who eventually couldn't resist commenting that it is not nice to throw things. I was pleased that Theresa had managed to take over the situation from her mother and to capitalize on her caring qualities. I made sure grandmother left the house with me, giving her a lift home, using the journey to let her know it was good to let Theresa deal with Tommy and that she had really helped her do this today. I explained to my co-workers with Theresa at the early years unit that she had managed to take control from her mother, and that this was an important theme to continue, including a session with grandmother to help her generate a different view of her daughter's parenting. During my last visit to Tommy at his school I began the story of the little pig who goes for a walk and gets lost (a story stem assessment), asking him what happened next. He made the mother pig find him, but after a quick hello he said, 'Oh no, the other piggy is lost and they went off to find it.' I thought about his story. It was good that he had been found but I was troubled by the short time spent on finding the first lost pig, followed by the loss of the second pig. I wondered if it suggested that Tommy cannot be certain that his mother will hold him in mind, giving an insight into a mother who has so much on her mind that she is not able to think consistently about her children in a reliable way. However, his play symbolized his understanding that he would not be annihilated – he would be found.

Given past organizational and individual pressures to move Tommy out of his family, an important aspect of my role in the beginning was creating and maintaining some stability for Tommy and his mother. I felt that my 'holding' of Tommy – making a space in my mind for him (Lanyado 1991) enabled him to experience an adult concentrating on him and his needs alone. Keeping the child in mind when others want to take decisions in the context of local authority care corresponds to Winnicott's (1965: 227) 'counteracting disintegrating forces in individuals and families'. I realized I was sensitive to his behaviour being misunderstood (and that this reflected aspects of myself both as child and adult) and I hoped he felt I understood him and that he could integrate this into his inner world. My role with Tommy was to be a bridge between his internal and external world, helping hold things together for him at a time when his fragile sense of self was under threat. I recognized his ambivalent attachment to his mother, involving his longing for but also fear of autonomy and individuation (a reflection of her own preoccupied attachment style). While 'acting out' he may have been fearful of a further separation from her. My alliance with Theresa enabled her to demonstrate some autonomy in her care giving towards Tommy. In thinking about her capacity to parent I had needed to think about the impact of losing her husband and unborn child, and her likely feelings of emptiness and worthlessness. By helping her see me away from her controlling if well-intentioned mother I could give her space to make sense of the various stresses in her life, allaying her fears that she is out of control. She then has more capacity to think about the needs of her child and more energy available for the task of caring, allowing her to try 'something different' from her mother's approach.

Resisting defences against anxiety

The system in which social work takes place means that unconscious processes add to the difficulty of relationship-based practice. Child protection referrals engender a level of fear and dread, which the social worker is in danger of projecting on the family, compounding their difficulties (Ferguson 2005). The main task is to contain the projections and to interject something good, being aware of the splitting processes at work which surface in the guise of 'well they just can't be helped, they are too angry', or 'their experiences of social work are so bad how on earth can I change that'. Clearly I am unable to change it but I can offer something different, which is to understand and contain some of my clients' difficulties that arise in daily life. If a worker is to be helped to be responsive to children's and parents' needs and so overcome defences against anxiety which inhibit thought (Menzies-Lyth 1988) she needs her own 'holding environment'. Containing my own anxiety in this case was initially a hard task. I had taken over at a point when fear and anxiety were experienced by family and workers alike. My own anxiety was from wanting to do something different which would be helpful for the family. My team manager was helpful in 'holding' me to go ahead and assess Tommy afresh. Discussing my anxiety in supervision and with colleagues enabled me to remain reflective.

My work with the family spanned nine months, culminating in Tommy returning home to the permanent care of his mother and his name being removed from the child protection register. Grandmother babysat his sister so that Tommy and his mother could have special times together. I also arranged for the family to have summer holidays together. The family knew long before my departure that I would be leaving. I tried to lay the foundations for this known ending, hoping that they would have a new experience of a good ending. I hoped that their readiness and capacity for moving on with their lives would prevail.

The worker could so easily have been drawn into the fear and chaos in the family. Instead she managed to find enough distance to resist being enmeshed, holding on to her ability to think about the unconscious meaning of Tommy's play as well as his carers' responses. While controlling behaviour and its failure is typical in families with an ambivalent preoccupied attachment style, she was able to understand the specific dynamics in this family and to find a way to help the family establish more appropriate and effective boundaries between the generations, so that all members felt better contained and understood. Her warmth, genuineness and emotional availability, and her hopefulness that families can and do have the resources to work with their difficulties meant that she established a good relationship with Tommy's family. For Tommy in particular she provided the inner mental space which enabled him to feel understood; she went on to help his mother do this herself, so that he no longer needed to 'act out' his anxiety. In order to do this emotionally demanding task of trying to understand others as she herself wishes to be understood, a social worker needs support and good enough 'holding' from her own organization.

Conclusion

Play is one of the tools for understanding and working with troubled families. It offers the worker and team an insight into the inner world of the family as a whole, as well as the particular inner worlds of its members. It can demonstrate the family system in action, making it possible to identify patterns and pressures, giving clues as to how help can best be given. Sometimes an intervention itself involves play, with the freeing of individuals from blame and the opportunity for spontaneity giving a family a different experience of how they can relate to one another. The safe boundary necessary for play is provided by the structure (which may be more or less focused or directive) and the setting within which play is offered, but above all by the 'holding in mind' the thoughtful inner mental space of the worker or team. This enables family members in turn to be thoughtful and perhaps 'try something different'. The greater the families' difficulties and anxieties, the harder is the workers' task of holding and containing. Families can be frightening to encounter and fears of contamination may lie not far beneath the surface. Workers' defences against anxiety, especially if they work within an unsupportive target-driven and bureaucratic culture, can lead to defensive practice which can blind them to the real needs of a child. Further, 'professional and family systems have a tendency to become enmeshed and reflect one another' (Ferguson 2005: 791). Where the professional system resists being drawn into the anxiety and stays supportive of the worker's need to be reflective then, as we have seen, much good work can take place.

Chapter 6

Therapeutic play for children with disabilities and illness

Children who have developmental delay and learning disabilities, or a physical disability, or illness, or a combination of these, have emotional needs related to their loss or lack of a fully functioning physical body, a container for the self, which they can take for granted. Their identity and sense of self, however strong, will be affected by their feelings about their body, and also by their vulnerability and dependence on others. They inevitably have less control over their lives than most children, and often fewer opportunities for the self-directing play which is central to the development of a sense of autonomy. As Erikson and Winnicott have shown (see Chapters 1 and 2), play gives children a vital opportunity to be themselves. This chapter considers the needs of disabled and ill children, especially their need for a sense of autonomy or agency, and how play can help. It shows how therapeutic play and play therapy can provide some measure of healing to children whose disability or illness involves emotional trauma, whether stemming from the primary trauma of their physical condition or from other aspects of their lives, such as damaged attachment, separation, loss or abuse, or from more than one of these.

Developmental play and the child's need for autonomy

While the old belief that developmentally delayed children do not play has been refuted (McConkey 1986), it is probably still the case that many learning and physically disabled children lose out on opportunities for play, especially the pretend or creative activities which are the prerequisites for symbolic thought and communication. If children naturally use play to help them make sense of their world, then a child with disabilities may be doubly handicapped if this need is not met. In recent years many children with disabilities have been integrated into normal play activities. Yet despite wider recognition of the value of play to children with disabilities there remains an underlying doubt that playing really aids learning, perhaps, as McConkey (1986: 86) suggests, due to 'the well-established tradition of the able-bodied doing things for handicapped people. The notion of letting handicapped children do things for themselves and in the way they want to do it is therefore fairly radical. Nevertheless, I believe we have much to learn by adopting this approach, particularly in the realm of play'.

Play is more than a technique to foster intellectual development. It is essential to the child's development of a sense of an autonomous self and so of self-esteem. A child with disabilities who is unable to achieve this through unaided spontaneous play needs help from an adult which fosters all the attributes of spontaneous play rather than taking them away even further. Although an adult provider and playmate may be needed: 'In our enthusiasm to help the child to learn we must not forget the voluntary and exploratory nature of play ... Our aim when we play with him is not only to help the child to want to learn new skills, but also to give him the feeling that he has some mastery and control over the things around him' (Newson and Hipgrave 1982: 67).

Non-directive regular special play times in which the worker or parent gives a reflective running commentary on what the child is doing (Pinney 1990) require a child to take the initiative, often an unusual experience for a disabled child who normally has to depend on others. The task is to attend to the minutest indication of what the child is interested in, following their gaze, carrying or moving them if necessary, using signing, symbols or mirroring their movements if words are not understood, and sometimes copying or joining in their play. Helen Cockerill (1992) found that her reflective commentary served to help restless and disorganized children to concentrate for longer and organize their activity, sometimes starting to provide their own commentary (Piaget's monologue, an aid to thinking). Sessions have a clear opening ritual: 'This is your special time – for the next 40 minutes you can do anything you want and I will look after you.' Limits are set as needed. There is a clear ending, counted down in minutes. The experience fosters autonomy and self-esteem – as one ten-year-old said, 'I like Special Times because here I am useful . . . everywhere else I am useless.'

The Newsons (1979) stressed the need to observe a child in a playful situation where their initiative is welcomed and the role of the adult is to help them to perform at their highest level of ability. The best early toy may be a not too life-like rag doll or teddy (rather than the usual posting box), enabling the child to re-create the events of their daily life such as washing, dressing and eating. We might use a basket of real baby equipment, a plastic bowl, flannel and soap, towel, potty, hairbrush, feeding bottle and doll, showing the child the things in the basket, observing what they use and how much of a sequence of events they can play out. This can help us decide at what point and at what level to join in to help the child develop more complex pretend play.

Attunement and 'scaffolding' in interactive play

The adult's task is to entice the child into playing. The best play material is of course another person. We may need to find ways of keeping interesting play material within reach of a child with limited mobility, or providing materials that are responsive to whatever the child can initiate, for example, toys which reward solving a practical mechanical task with a funny noise or a flashing light. Toys for pretend play are essential, preferably versions (of dolls, cups, saucepans and so on) that are more life size than miniature, as some children are only at the beginning of symbolic play. Unstructured and responsive materials such as water, dough, painting and fingerpainting, and sand (or safer variants such as dried tea leaves, or a bowl of large beans and dried pasta, seashells, or autumn leaves and conkers) encourage children to relax and play. It is important to provide materials culturally appropriate to the child and family – if food is precious then play with food may not be acceptable. We need to join in such play ourselves (for example, moving our fingers through the sand), so that children see adults modelling play.

We need to play at the child's developmental level, rather than pushing them too hastily to play at a more advanced level which they cannot sustain. At the same time we must remain observant and attentive to the child's slightest overture. Our response needs to be so gauged that it encourages further communication or play but is not so overwhelming that it removes the child's autonomy. By being in control of their play, children's mastery, however limited, of their environment increases. Such play is quite different from the adult-initiated and adult-controlled play of some structured developmental programmes, although the best of these allow room for the child's initiative and encourage the adult's responsiveness.

The adult provides the 'scaffolding' (Bruner's term) for the development of the child's own thought, initiative and action through thoughtful choice of materials and management of shared interaction. For example, we can start playing with a marble run to tempt the child into playing, followed by a gentle running commentary on the child's actions: 'You're putting another one in the hole, it's going down . . . down . . . ringing the bell . . . all the way down – lovely.' We do not ask questions since they put unhelpful pressure on the child. We avoid condescending praise such as 'good boy' but show our own enjoyment and appreciation of what the child is doing. As they begin to tolerate or even enjoy our presence, we join in, perhaps at first passing a marble, then posting one, to entice the child into a more complex turn-taking game (McMahon 1993).

Such play matches the way in which an attuned mother plays with her baby. She may reach out to engage a passive baby. Her use of repetition helps the infant to anticipate and respond, as in games like 'Tickle your Tummy' or 'Pop goes the Weasel'. The mother leaves spaces in the interaction for the baby to fill, to mutual delight, and responds to the child in her turn, often by imitating. She at first maintains the conversation, for that is what it is, but as the baby starts to take the initiative (for example, in a peep-bo game) the game becomes genuinely shared. She then provides the winding down and soothing necessary if the game gets too exciting. The same principles of attunement and 'scaffolding' are used in Melanie Nind and David Hewett's (1996) *Intensive Interaction* with profoundly learning disabled children. Such work demands a high level of observation and attunement, with the adult responsive to the slightest sign from the child.

Music therapist Wendy Prevezer (1990: 4) used the principles of early mother–infant interaction to initiate non-verbal 'conversations' between a child with autism and their worker or parent:

> We use three main strategies for this tuning in process, which in practice often overlap within one activity. These strategies permeate the way we use children's songs and rhymes, their active and lap play, and many structured and improvised games. In a child's first few sessions we experiment with a wide range of these activities, looking for a positive response, however small. The least structured way of tuning in to the child involves joining in with, imitating and later extending, his own spontaneous sounds and movements, and treating them as if they were intentional attempts at communication, even when they are clearly not. This child-centred approach provides the most straightforward way of drawing the child into a turn-taking situation. Most children respond by giving more eye contact, and eventually by using a wider range of sounds in a much more positive and intentional way ... The moment a child first realizes that he is leading or 'in control' is often visible on his face, and then his confidence grows ... The 'running commentary' involves using words in a simple extemporized song to fit in with whatever the child is doing at the time, whether it is jumping, rocking, or looking out of the window. The third strategy provides a more structured framework using a song with short verses, which are flexible enough to accommodate anything the child might do or suggest. For example, we might sing 'Pat, pat, pat your leg' or 'Crawl, crawl, crawl around', to the tune of 'Skip to My Lou'. One other important technique, used throughout many kinds of activity, is the leaving of 'dramatic pauses' before key words in familiar songs ... (which) seems to compel a child to 'slot in'.

Using an electronic keyboard helped Prevezer see and follow the child, while the parent or worker sat facing the child with the child's knees between hers. The basic strategies are widely applicable to children with communication and learning difficulties, and can be used on a one-to-one basis with the adult singing. Interactive games also help autistic children to respond to one other, for example, using a sand wheel with a small pot each, posting a bell to down a cardboard tube, pushing a ball or toy bus to each other, playing a few notes in turn on a glockenspiel, and rocking in a see-saw boat.

Play for children and parents together

Parents also need to play. Parents with young children with disabilities or developmental delay often find the task of parenting particularly stressful. It can be both physically and emotionally draining, with limited rewards when their children progress only slowly. Children with communication difficulties are often particularly unrewarding to 'mother' and this can lead to difficulties in attachment. Parents need to be emotionally held so that they can in turn 'hold' their children. In a family play group setting where workers and other parents 'in the same boat' appreciate their company, play and talk together, and help one another, a parent may find it a little easier to accept their child's disabilities. As parents find they have something of value to contribute to the group they may become more aware of the strengths they have as a family. Anxious parents can start to relax as they join in normal play activities, such as group collage, with other parents and children. The inclusion of siblings is important as so many miss out on parental time and attention – and on 'emotional holding' – because everyone's concern is focused on the child with difficulties. Music and singing in a group encourages physical contact and communication; sometimes a parent can physically feel their child relax. A time for rough and tumble play in a soft play area helps similarly. We need to work in partnership with parents, recognizing their knowledge of their children. Parents sometimes lose confidence in their own intuitive skills and find it helpful to realize (and be shown by the adult's modelling) that the process of attunement and interaction is familiar but may need to be made more conscious and explicit to match the pace of a slower developing child. Particular help may be needed if the child's difficulty is in interaction.

Interactive play for autistic children and their parents

Play and games which require interaction can help parents begin to get through to their children and have some success in fostering their development. They also help in strengthening attachment. Occupational therapist Susan Monson, working with speech therapist Margaret Petchey, starts from a similar approach to Prevezer:

In the hope that these early interaction patterns, normal for most mothers and children, could be taught to some extent to autistic children I worked on a one-to-one basis using musical conversations, give and take games, turn-taking and interaction activities. I was encouraged by the children's response but realized that it would be far more valuable for the mothers to be doing this so that they could enjoy a closer relationship with their children. I used normal and enjoyable activities whenever possible, in a structured step-by-step approach, but it was sometimes necessary to be very firm and intrusive for a few minutes. Autistic children need to be taught to play as they understand little speech and find it difficult to copy. The use of physical prompts and guidance proved a helpful technique and one that parents pick up easily. I worked increasingly with mothers and children at home, and all showed marked improvement.

A videotape shows work with four-year-old Jamie and his family:

Jamie is being helped to thread a wooden peg attached to a cord through the holes in a large flat wooden 'pear'. His mother holds him facing his father. She takes Jamie's hand, helping him push the peg through the hole. His father posts it back, wiggling it and calling to Jamie, who takes it and is encouraged to put it through another hole. His mother holds his hand but lets him do it independently whenever he tries. They play with a musical marble run, Jamie taking turns with his father as his mother holds and encourages him. He pushes large beads along a curly wire loop, his parents at each end urging him on. Rocked in a see-saw, he several times looks at his father, and does so again while being bounced astride his father's leg, as his father talks and his mother sings 'See-saw Margery Daw'. Jamie chases bubbles which his mother blows and looks at her when she stops. Father holds Jamie's hand, helping him to pretend feed a puppet from a spoon, while his mother uses the puppet to attract his attention. Jamie's parents were delighted with his responsive play and his play and communication continued to improve. Continuing support at home and in a small group with other parents gave the encouragement so important to the perseverance needed in reaching an autistic child.

Parents were involved in the last nine of 24 sessions of Orlaith Dignam's non-directive play therapy with an eight-year-old child with high functioning autism. To his parents' astonishment, Fred was just starting to play spontaneously, flying a toy plane:

Therapist: Oh the plane is flying.
Fred: [flying the plane into the sand]: Help me to get him out – help get me out.
Therapist: Oh, who's going to help him get out.
Fred: The cars help.
Therapist: The car is going to help the plane.

Supported by his therapist's reflections, Fred was building a sequence in his play. Another time Fred wanted to blow bubbles:

Therapist: You like blowing bubbles.
Fred: [sitting on a bean bag]: Gentle.
Therapist: You are being gentle. [As a bubble burst] It's burst.
Fred: Burst. [Then blowing bubbles at his father]
Therapist: [with animated voice] Fred, you are blowing bubbles at your father and he is blowing them back to you.
Fred: Giant.
Therapist: Letting us know Dad's a giant.

There are hints of the beginnings of the symbolic play which non-directive play therapy can encourage (Josefi and Ryan 2004). Through their involvement in play therapy, Fred's parents could both appreciate and be part of their son's real progress in communication and thought.

A note on sensory play

Sensory play environments are developmentally appropriate for some children and offer opportunities for playing and 'being' which do not occur naturally. Soft play areas of vinyl-covered foam shapes or air-filled mattresses provide a response to any movement. They are also a good place for interactive rough-and-tumble play between worker or parent and child (sometimes a way of reaching an autistic child) and encouraging interaction between children. Darkened rooms with coloured lights and soothing music offer womb-like comfort, valuable for anxious children in hospital (such as those awaiting surgery or babies on traction) or in an unfamiliar setting. With different music (or birdsong), and visual effects such as a rotating mirror ball, or a humming, vibrating tube of moving bubbles, the same room can be stimulating. Ultra-violet light and a resonance board intensify light and sound so that they can be picked up by sight- and hearing-impaired children. In her school for children with learning difficulties, Longhorn (1988) provided a sensory curriculum including touch, taste and smell. Newson and Hipgrave (1982) suggest ways to help children to get meaning from the use of each of their senses, from sand and water play to 'feely bags' and rolling in leaves (see also Chapters 1 and 2). Sensory play rooms, however useful, are a poor substitute for the real experiences of the outdoor world. Swimming offers freedom to play for many children with disabilities. An autistic young man's cry of 'Oh fuck' as a big wave broke over him while playing by the sea was a rare and significant encounter with the real world.

The emotional experience of disability

Learning disability, developmental delay, communication and language disorder, and physical disability or illness may be linked with emotional difficulties in varying ways. It may be that their physical or mental limitations have deprived children of the opportunity to experience the world and to develop their creativity and sense of self through play. We know too that disabled children are more at risk of abuse, and the resulting trauma, both within and outside the home. Early experiences of neglect or deprivation may, in some cases, have led to some potentially normal children being denied the physical or emotional nurture needed for normal development, resulting in learning difficulties. Experiences of separation and loss, of unresolved pain, anger and fear, may leave children traumatized, unable to think and to learn, sometimes even unable to feel, as they employ psychological defences to protect themselves against traumatic memories and further hurt. As Sinason (1992) reminds us, such stupefying experiences can indeed render a child 'stupid', a word which meant originally 'numbed with grief'.

Even in the most loving families, a child with an impairment painfully realizes that they are different, that they 'have not come out right' and are less than perfect. Perhaps they even have a subconscious sense that they should not have been born. This too is trauma. Valerie Sinason describes the 'handicapped smile' of some disabled children which conceals the pain of this knowledge and makes them more acceptable. This can involve 'cutting their real language and intellectual abilities' as they behave 'like smiling pets for fear of offending those they are dependent on' (Sinason 1992: 21). Some children do their utmost to defend themselves against the pain of having a damaged body, of being the helpless victim of what feels like an attack or punishment, which can only be understood as there being something bad inside them (Dale 1983). They develop an omnipotent 'second skin' and need someone to listen who can hold their feelings and not be too upset, as Susan Monson describes:

> Five-year-old Harry, born with cerebral palsy, arrived at school each day as Batman, or a pirate or a wizard. These characters were powerful or used magic spells, and definitely never did exercises or writing. He avoided physical therapy, saying 'Don't talk to me about my muscles.' In

play therapy he used a model family with themes of a granny who fell over and needed a stick, orphans starved to death; meals were spells poisoning people or making him fly. I reflected on his play, especially the disabilities and how the people must be feeling. The next week all the people had difficulties and even the dog needed a stick, meals were burnt but there were no spells. Recognition of Harry's feelings in therapy, matched elsewhere, was enough for him to leave his omnipotent magic characters outside school and risk trying the things he needed to learn. His imaginative play continued but was linked more closely to reality.

A more serious version of secondary handicap occurs where there is severe personality disturbance linked to the primary handicap: 'It is not that the handicap creates emotional disturbance as part of its process, but rather, that the burden of a handicap depletes what resources an individual has, leaving him or her prey to what is internally unresolved and disturbed' (Sinason 1992: 23). Fury, hatred and envy may lead to violence and aggression, grief and despair to depression and withdrawal.

The thought that a child may find their imperfection painful can be unbearable to parents and workers who are themselves struggling with painful feelings about the child's disability or illness, and who may experience the child as a source of trauma. How much easier is it then to deny the child's pain by making home or school a completely 'happy' place. Sometimes this positive emphasis is a real celebration of a child's individuality, of their abilities and strengths, which can only build a child's self-esteem. Yet if it goes beyond this to a requirement to be happy at all times, then angry, disobedient or jealous behaviour, or withdrawal and depression, may not be seen as the emotional communication which it is but as unwelcome behaviour to be modified rather than understood. Denial of pain is the worker's defence against anxiety and may pervade a whole organization (Menzies-Lyth 1988). It takes courage and imagination to provide the emotional support to workers which will enable them in turn to respond to children's communication of pain and distress.

Fear is often a worker's first reaction when contemplating work with a disabled child – fear of our emotional response to the impaired body which we cannot make better, fear of not being able to communicate, of not understanding possibly unclear speech. This too can render us 'stupid', leaving us with a silly smile on our faces, and avoiding the difficult task of struggling to make real contact with the person inside. We need to notice our reactions, conscious and less conscious, on meeting a child for the first time because they are a source of information which we need in order to establish real understanding and communication. Some of our reactions will have their origin in our own experience in family and the society we live in. Other reactions will be feelings which are transferred to us from the child. When we work with children with little speech this 'countertransference is a crucial tool to understanding', for example, the meaning of a child's head banging. 'One time when he banged his head I felt immensely sad for him and could speak of his longing to bang out the thoughts that hurt him. Another time, I felt angry and knew he was attacking me by hurting himself in front of me' (Sinason 1992: 323). A child's themes in play provide a further way for us to think about the meaning of their symbolic communication. I found all these ideas helpful in my play therapy with a number of children, but none more so than with Oliver.

Play therapy with Oliver

Oliver was ten years old and attended a special school for children with learning disability. He had cerebral palsy which meant he walked with a wide and awkward gait; his speech was unclear and he had not learned to read or to write more than his name. However, his bright gaze, a jokey sense of mischief and a certain charm in his manner when we met suggested there was more intelligence than was recognized. When I visited the family it was clear that his loving mother was near despair about his violent attacks on his younger brother Nick. She was clear that this jealousy or envy had begun with Nick's birth. Oliver was spending some nights at a hostel to give the family some respite, although his mother found this separation really painful and, as I learned from him later, Oliver did too. During my visit I found it hard to think amid the continual attacks on Nick; at the end I thanked Oliver for showing me what it was like in his family. Despite the violence it felt as if there were real affection between all members of the family. Their father was suffering from a degenerative illness and no longer able to walk far. I suggested that Oliver was helping the family to avoid thinking about their sadness at his father's declining health, and his mother instantly agreed. However, my role was to offer play therapy to Oliver at school. As so often happens, the first session encapsulated the core themes of the work to come.

Oliver took out some toys from my play bag and put a puppet on his hand, said 'Sooty' (a teddy puppet from children's television), and dabbed Sooty's eyes with his paws. I said Sooty was sad and Oliver nodded. I wondered why Sooty was sad. Oliver took a baby feeding bottle and a worn-looking miniature 'dad' doll, gleefully stuffing him into the bottle, while I said maybe Sooty was cross with dad and getting rid of him into the bottle. Then a female figure was stuffed into the bottle, and then a third figure, and swirled around. Then Sooty was held over the bottle, 'Wee-ing on them,' Oliver said. I said Sooty was angry with them, perhaps because they didn't know he was sad. In retrospect I was going too fast in interpreting play but it turned out that I was on the right track. The following week Oliver got a miniature male doll to pour imaginary orange juice, milk and coffee into a cup which Sooty drank and didn't like, and he threw the doll away. Then, as before, two male dolls and one female were stuffed gleefully into the bottle, with Sooty doing a long 'wee' on them. I said he was angry with them for not giving him the right food. Oliver then held Sooty with his head forced down and back, and I commented on how awful that must feel. With much effort Oliver then put the teat on the bottle and gave Sooty a good drink.

I think that Oliver's anger (and grief) with his damaged body and mind which could not find expression in words was acted out in his violent attacks. I hoped he could instead use the symbolism of play. One game Oliver played repeatedly. He would tell me to shut my eyes and go to sleep, and pretend that robbers came in the night and stole all the presents (my two play bags) so there was 'nothing left for Christmas'. He chortled with glee when I woke up and was horrified to find that everything had gone. He 'phoned' the police to tell them. Sometimes when I wondered who had taken the presents he would delightedly say, 'Me.' Later the game changed slightly; Oliver would say it was my birthday and bring me presents, enjoying my appreciation. He still came in the night and stole them, delighting in my chagrin on waking to find them gone, but he spent more time in giving than in taking away. Perhaps this game was about his guilt at robbing his mother of a perfect child but also his anger with her for giving birth to him and then 'replacing' him with another child? Afterwards he sometimes sat down and looked very tired, closing his eyes – but not as part of the game.

I didn't always hear what he said and felt very bad about this (and said to him I was sorry I couldn't understand what he was telling me), although I made a huge effort to listen which I found quite tiring. At the end of one session, after some concentrated play with doll babies in which they were alternately looked after, fed and put to bed and then hit or thrown away, but with milk for Sooty at the end, he went to sit at a nearby table and wearily put his head on the table and stretched forward with his right hand rubbing white against the table. He said he would phone his mother that evening (he was in respite care). He didn't move until I said he might be feeling quite tired as everything needed a lot of effort but it was time to go, when he quietly got up and came with me. (Another time it was Sooty who was floppy at the end of his time.) I felt the weight of his sadness and thought about the painful separation from his mother. I thought too about the immense energy he needed to manage daily life with a body that didn't support him adequately. Yet he still had hope; there was still food for him.

Another recurring game was Bad Limit (me) being taken to prison (behind a barricade of chairs) in handcuffs (a fragment of gold chain which I held together). I was sad in prison and Oliver was pleased and told me to 'cry a lot'. I pretended to cry and said how horrible it felt to be in prison all the time. Often he would delight in getting Sooty to put piles of poo and wee into my prison. I felt trapped and soiled. He drew Bad Limit with big eyes, which looked like a mother and child joined together by arms. Once he said 'Put me in prison' and we were both crying because we couldn't get out. This lasted some time and I felt I needed to bear his grief. He looked out of the window and I commented on his interest in the world outside but his sadness at not being part of it because his body let him down. Then he found out how to open and close the blinds, so I said that he could control the light coming into the prison, so there were some things he *could* control. Oliver then wanted me to write 'Oliver is bad, nobody likes him' and I said how horrible that must feel, as if he deserves being put in prison, but I didn't think he was bad. Towards the end of this session he asked me to read a story. Instead of the usual 'Angry Arthur' he chose 'Are You My Mother?' and listened carefully until the baby bird was safely back with his mother.

The prison sessions and very messy play, pretend and real (he covered my hands with mixtures of paint, water and dough) continued. I did as I was told except when it was personally invasive or too messy for me to think: boundaries needed keeping. I made clear to Oliver how horrible it felt but did not interpret back to him beyond recognizing his being pleased that I was feeling so messed up. One time he said, 'Stay in pieces.' I felt it important for him that I could tolerate the mess and survive, so that he might sustain the hope that he could do the same. However, I was quite anxious about whether this provided enough containment.

In the following weeks Oliver's own grief became more open. On his respite care days he would talk about phoning his mother, and I said he would miss her and she would miss him. He seemed very sad and when I said so he started weeping. I stayed with his sadness at being sent away, but talked through Sooty which Oliver could more easily bear. One day he played with the Red Riding Hood/Grandmother/Wolf doll and when I commented on the good and bad mother in the same person he began to cry again. Later he asked me to read him the book about cerebral palsy, as I had done sometimes previously. When he went I was left with the immense weight of his sorrow.

I continued to see Oliver for six more years. There is no easy coming to terms with disability; each stage in growing up makes new demands on the psyche. There is always the temptation to 'stay in pieces', with violent acting out, or a 'handicapped voice' as a defence, because that avoids the pain of thinking and being. We went on playing with an army of dolls and puppets whose symbolic meanings we shared. Oliver's symbolic play was often repetitive and violent; it became important not to join in and collude with its omnipotent defensive element. I needed to make clear that I did not approve of violence although I would try to name the feelings involved. We eventually needed to end our work together, which we did with mutual warmth. Oliver continued, not unsuccessfully, with his struggle to grow up whole.

In therapeutic play with children like Oliver, the worker walks a fine line between unhelpful reassuring and rescuing, which denies the reality of the child's pain, and reflections or interpretations which offer the child hope. Rescue is always an unhelpful collusion with avoiding thinking about painful feelings. However, it seems important not only to stay with the child's pain and grief but also to give hope that it is bearable and manageable. Alvarez (1992: 117) writes of the need to think in terms of 'overcoming' as well as 'defence', 'potency' alongside 'omnipotence', a 'sense of agency' alongside 'narcissism', 'structure and predictability' beside 'obsessional defences against fragmentation'. The therapist is both receiving the child's projections of damage and badness and also helping the child take in or introject from her something more hopeful.

Play for children with illness and in hospital

Hospital care for children has changed dramatically since John Bowlby and the Robertsons first demonstrated the harmful psychological effects on children of separation and loss (Robertson 1970; Dartington *et al.* 1976). The importance of parents' presence is now widely understood. It is also recognized that the stress of a hospital stay can be further reduced and a child's recovery speeded by the provision of play:

> Children visiting or staying in hospital have basic need for play and recreation that should be met routinely in all hospital departments providing a service to children. This applies equally to the siblings of patients and this is also a consideration for neonatal units. Play may also be used for therapeutic purposes, as part of the child's care plan and as a way of helping the child assimilate new information, adjust to and gain control over a potentially frightening environment and prepare to cope with procedures and interventions. There is evidence that play hastens recovery as well as reducing the need for interventions to be delivered under general anaesthesia.
>
> (DOH 2003, 3.7)

Hospital play specialist Nicola Phillips writes: 'An ill child, especially a child with a long-term illness, builds an inner world picture of themselves as an ill child and of adults as people who not only take care of them but can and do inflict pain. The role of the hospital play specialist is to support the child through illness and hospital admission by providing a relationship based on therapeutic play.' By accompanying the child on their 'illness journey' she can 'interpret this complicated environment in a way which corresponds to the internal world filter through which they see the external world'. From a position of understanding and empathy she gains an insight into the child's inner world, and she provides the acceptance and emotional containment which helps the child make sense of and cope with their experience. Nicola adds: 'In order to recognize the feelings that the child is communicating and then to hold them, I need time to reflect on the content of what the child has communicated but also on the nature of the therapeutic relationship. This includes reflecting on the feelings that I feel whilst with the child, since they provide an indication of how the child is feeling, a counter-transference which is often only recognized in hindsight'.

Children's need for autonomy and control

Play is a normal developmental need of all children when they are in hospital, as well as a means for coping with the specific emotional stress of their stay. Play may be used to welcome children, to help them to come to terms with the hospital environment, and to manage their fears about separation from parents and from familiar surroundings, as well as to prepare them for stressful procedures and to cope with their consequences, and to aid recovery. Even when parents are with the child in hospital, the child is separated from familiar aspects of life at home. Play can make a link between hospital and life outside. Play that is familiar comes as 'a welcome relief after all the strange sights, sounds and bodily discomfort' (Lansdown and Goldman 1988: 557). Children in hospital for long periods have a particular need for adequate opportunities for play so that their normal development is not interrupted.

We know that children who suffer least stress from a hospital stay are those who feel that they have retained some control over what was happening (Sylva and Stein 1990). Such control or autonomy helps the child maintain a sense of self, helping them manage painful experience. Diversionary play, although it has a role at times such as helping a child through a painful procedure, can be unhelpful:

> Play which takes the initiative from the child, and gives him a passive role – play which becomes a diversion and a denial of what is happening – does not help him to come to terms with current experience. This is one important reason why the adult does not impose his own ideas, but takes all his cues from the child.
>
> (Harvey 1984: 279)

Anxious children need play materials which are familiar, so it is important that they reflect children's different cultures. Unstructured materials such as sand and water enable regressive play without the child worrying about appearing 'babyish'. They can be soothing and relaxing for an anxious child, and can be adapted for children who are bed-bound, immobilized in plasters, or in isolation. Mobile children may have more choice in a playroom, different in tone from other clinical areas and offering the comfort of familiar toys and activities. There, play can be provided within a safe physical boundary, with an adult who is alert to a child's signals of unhappy feelings which need to be acknowledged and worked with, sometimes in opportunity led work and sometimes in planned individual play sessions. There has been debate about how inviolable the playroom should be as a sanctuary. Many consider that nursing that will not alarm or distress the child can take place in the playroom, where familiar surroundings can lessen the child's anxiety, but take the view that potentially distressing invasive medical interventions should not take place there (or in the child's bed space which should always be a safe place), but in a treatment room giving the child physical boundaries.

Working closely with other staff is important, especially where children need play taken to them in bed. The boundaries of play can often be provided by the worker's presence. A specific uninterrupted play time each day for children isolated in a bone marrow unit helped to give them some feeling of normality and a link with the outside world. Rosemary King (1988: 12) provided a variety of activities, including messy play, to stimulate learning but also to help children express emotion and cope with what is happening:

It is a positive way for them to 'unwind' from the stress caused by being on a unit such as this. I have found that a lot of children need much reassurance to use paint, dough and water as they normally would and still feel 'safe'. Messy play provides an excellent opportunity to use many of the threatening pieces of medical equipment in a non-threatening way, for example, syringe painting, water play, collage and printing. This also gives children a sense of control over these items, something which has been taken away in other respects, and gives them permission to express anger at the way the equipment has been used on them.

Ideas for adapting normal play activities such as messy play are found in *Play Focus* information sheets from the National Association of Hospital Play Staff (www.nahps.org.uk). Earlier sources on play provision in hospital are Noble (1967), Harvey and Hales-Tooke (1972), Lindquist (1977) and Weller and Oliver (1980).

The role of parents

It is important that the attachment needs of parents and children are supported, for example, through helping mothers hold their children and talk and sing to them as they would at home. Children may be confused by parents' loss of authority in hospital. Parents may find the hospital environment, where normal parental roles are removed or modified, both frightening and exhausting. Having an active role in playing with their child can give some relief, restoring their autonomy and self-esteem as well as their child's. Respectful recognition of the parents' role and awareness of differing attitudes to children, play and illness in families from different cultures is needed. 'Members of the oncology team can help parents by reassurance or by suggesting appropriate play techniques and approaches, but frequently we can stand back and learn from them' (Lansdown and Goldman 1988: 558).

Siblings

Play may help siblings who often experience loss of attention and 'containment' because of their parents' focus on the sick child. They may pick up parents' feelings of confusion and anxiety. They may also feel guilty, believing, through 'magical thinking', that they have caused their sibling to become ill. Group work, particularly for siblings of children with long-term illnesses or disabilities, can be helpful in reducing their fantasizing and their sense of isolation.

Focused play in preparing children for medical procedures

Focused play techniques, used imaginatively and flexibly, help prepare children for surgery or other unpleasant procedures. They aim to give children information about their treatment, offer choice where it is possible, reduce the anxiety of the unknown and allow the expression and containment of feelings. At pre-admission visits families will be shown around the ward and the anaesthetic and recovery rooms, and children encouraged to play with nurses' uniforms, gowns and masks, anaesthetic masks, bandages, stethoscopes, syringes, and so on. The hospital play specialist spends time with the child building a relationship and giving an opportunity for questions to be asked and responded to, whilst the nurse spends time with parents.

Individual preparation, normally on the day of the procedure, is preferable to group preparation 'which does not always allow for fears to be expressed and can result in anxieties being passed on' (NAHPS Guidelines, www.nahps.org.uk). Parents or carers need to be present and involved. The play specialist explains the procedure to the child using appropriate language. Tailor-made 'preparation books', short videos illustrating the procedure, or drawing body outlines may be helpful. A doll (which a child can relate to better than a teddy bear when they are trying to imagine what is going to happen to their body) is often used to go through the pre-operative routine. Procedures, such as injections or the insertions of lines, drains or catheters, are best demonstrated on an ordinary doll in the hospital corner of the playroom, allowing 'children to go through the event in anticipation and thus to have some sense of mastery over it'. Young children might be asked to help their 'sick' doll to overcome its fears. Anatomical dolls whose bodies can be opened may be frightening and are probably more useful in post-procedural play (Lansdown and Goldman 1988: 557). Children often have a fear of needles. Crompton (1980) reminds that practising injections on a doll is only really valuable if it permits the child to express fears rather than receive bland reassurances. As the child plays it becomes clearer what they have understood; misconceptions can be picked up, as well as some idea of what questions and fears remain. An empathic and imaginative approach helps a child face an injection before surgery, as hospital play specialist Joy Pearce (1990: 16) explains:

James was flitting from one end of the playroom to another in an almost frenzied state. I tried to get him to settle down by showing him some of our more interesting toys, and I tried to talk calmly to him but he could not keep still for a moment. After a while he walked over to the blackboard where there were some felt-tip pens and he began scribbling on a large piece of paper that was attached to the board. I asked him what he had drawn. He replied, 'My dog.' I then asked him if he would like to see a picture of my dog and he said, 'Yes.' I drew a picture of a large dog with huge paws and said that his name was Carlo. I then explained how Carlo had once needed to have an operation and he had come into hospital and the doctor had put Emla cream on his paws to make his paws numb. So when he had to have his injection he would not feel the needle, only a small scratch. James had become completely engrossed by this time and had relaxed considerably. We both drew the Emla cream on to the paws, and then we drew another dog and pretended that he was the doctor, drawing in his white coat and stethoscope. As I was drawing I was explaining to James that what had happened to Carlo, the dog, was going to happen to him. He was calm enough by this time to assimilate what I was saying to him. I tried to back up my preparation with the *Operation Book* but James refused to look at it, so I decided to leave well alone. After James had gone to theatre I asked his mother how he had reacted to all the medical procedures and she was quite relieved to say that he had coped quite well.

Play therapy with children undergoing serious surgery is particularly valuable. It needs a therapist who can offer extra understanding of the medical problems. Occupational therapist Sue Evans used focused approaches over ten sessions to help ten-year-old Michael come to terms with his damaged body and being different from his peers:

Michael was born with a deformed penis and had needed continuing surgery which left him depressed and angry. We used clay to create magic crystals to reveal places he would like to be (watching Saints with Dad) and places he wouldn't (injections, catheters, surgery, being alone). Then I joined him in throwing and splatting the clay, naming things he was angry about. When I encouraged him to paint his feelings as colours, he said, 'I'm no good at painting feelings but I can paint dinosaurs', and drew a tyrannosaurus rex saying, 'I'll eat you.' This gave me the cue for therapeutic story-making which Michael joined in enthusiastically. He began the story of Cera (a triceratops), who was sad because she was missing a bit of horn that tyrannosaurus rex had bitten off. A friendly stegosaurus helps Cera look for her horn (he drew a tail!) and they journey through Jurassic Park, where they get attacked by velociraptors until a helpful pterodactyl frightens them off. They find the horn but, I added, it is badly broken and cannot be fixed. Cera thinks about this loss. She can't fight but she can run and play, and if she is teased she can just ignore it. She'll still keep her best friends. Her family will be sad but tell her she just has to put up with it. In Michael's last picture Cera is proudly playing with friends who think she is so nice . . . but she still thinks of her horn. Michael was able to acknowledge some similar feelings to Cera but much was left unsaid; the story, and its theme of coming to terms with damage and difference, was enough. A further session focused on managing the pain of self catheterization. We used guided imagery, helping Michael use all his senses to imagine a special visit to watch Saints, which he went on to use successfully to distract himself during painful procedures.

Lansdown (1988) suggests further ways to help children create a mental barrier to pain from procedures: singing to and stroking, using counting games, puzzles, games, jokes and stories, video and listening on headsets.

Deeper fears of pain and damage, separation, loss and death

Reflective approaches can reach children's deeper fears of damage and loss, anger and guilt. Lynda Weiss (NAHPS) reminds us of Anna Freud's understanding that 'the response of children to surgery does not depend on the type or seriousness of the operation but on the type and depth of the fantasies aroused by it, mutilation, castration, abandonment and punishment'. Younger children fear separation, older children pain, mutilation and even death. While some needs can be anticipated by having certain kinds of play available, such as plastering dolls, the real need may turn out to be, for example, in a family where the parents' marriage is breaking up, the child's fear that mother will never return. Play therapist Jean Wilde describes how a child whose mother had died lay very still on the floor with his arms crossed. She did the same and role played his mother. She 'tried out' feelings with the child, saying, 'I didn't want to leave you. I had pains in my head but they've stopped hurting now', and explained that it was not his fault she had died. With another child she knew that his grandmother had recently died in hospital and was aware of the implications for his feelings about coming to hospital.

Guilt and self-blame cause huge distress, which may not initially be understood. Sinason (1990) describes how ten-year-old Jonathon's grandmother, who lived with him and his parents, suffered from headaches and told him his noisiness would be the death of her. She happened to go into hospital at the same time as he was having a tonsillectomy, which he saw as punishment for his speech organs. He became mute until helped by psychotherapy. A seven year old with his leg in plaster after being hit by a car was refusing to eat or talk. He drew several small cars and one large car. Asked why one was large, he said that was the one which had knocked him down, and went on to explain what had happened and how he blamed himself for running across the road without looking. After this he became more lively and started to eat (Harvey 1987: 5).

Containing terror and fury

Children's anxieties and fears may, however, be more readily accepted than their anger. A hospital's mismanagement of diagnostic tests meant that a child had to go home and return later. The furious child was told off by a nurse for banging her hand so much that she made it sore. The play therapist used the playroom for an hour's anger session where the child expressed her feelings in throwing, jumping and banging, feelings which were acknowledged by the therapist. They ended with music, a story and a cuddle. This was helpful to the child but staff were angry with the therapist for pandering, as they saw it, to the child. The therapist was able to recognize their projected anger and guilt at the hospital's shortcomings. This situation illustrates the particular difficulties of providing emotionally therapeutic play in a setting whose main purpose is other than this. We return to the need to allow expression of anger within the safe boundary of play with an emotionally containing adult. Materials (such as clay or playdough) which can survive a child's anger are helpful in allowing a child to realize that anger can be expressed without destroying things or people that matter to them. Dressing-up, doll play and hospital equipment allow children to play at being doctor or nurse and 'treat' dolls and teddies, re-enacting their experiences and working through their feelings of anger and fear. In another example (Sinason 1990), symbolic communication revealed a child's anger and her underlying fear of disintegration, which was understood.

Ten-year-old Mary needed a heart operation. In her drawing and plays she expressed the fear that she would lose her insides. Being shown educational diagrams of the heart did not help. She angrily tore the stuffing out of her teddy bear so that it lost its shape. Then she burst into tears. The hospital teacher helped Mary put the stuffing back in and sew up the teddy, showing how the stitches stopped the teddy's insides from falling out. After that Mary was able to face the operation more calmly.

Two further examples show how children's fear and anger with physical damage can find expression and containment in play. The work took place in a family play group in a hospital child development centre:

Three-year-old Emily developed epilepsy following a viral infection. The parents had a new baby while the child was in hospital. Described as having been 'a dear little girl', her violent and angry behaviour and temper tantrums alarmed her family and carers, and frightened Emily herself. Physical holding sent her into a frenzy, tearing out her hair, banging her head and poking her genitals. She delighted in messy play which appeared calming. She began to want a baby bottle and got into bed in the home corner. At lunch-time she wanted a baby cup. That happened for quite a little while until she began not to need to do it. At the same time her tantrums were becoming less frequent and less intense, and she seemed more in control.

We can understand this demonstration of Emily's inner world by noticing that people feel 'alarmed' or frightened, picking up her transferred feeling of feeling afraid. How frightening it must have been to have her body suddenly becoming a stranger to her, even apparently attacking her. At the same time her parents were less available through their preoccupation with the new baby. She must have feared, if at some less than conscious level, that her parents were attacking her and replacing her with a more satisfactory healthy baby. Her angry attacks on her own damaged body suggest her fury as well as terror with what has happened to her. Her ability to think has been replaced by overwhelming infantile feelings, which can only be managed by adults accepting her infantile state and allowing her to regress in messy play and being a baby again. This emotional holding helps to hold her fragmented self together so that in time she is able to do this for herself once more.

Mark, four years old, had been in hospital for much of his life and was 'frail' after recent major surgery, unable to cope with nursery school. He was slightly built but threw himself energetically into play, his mother watching anxiously. He rushed around giggling with developmentally delayed Kevin, but when Kevin clutched at his face Mark hit him hard, with real anger. Mark continued these sudden attacks, often for no discernible reason. We decided to invite both children to a shared play therapy session, with one worker for each child. At first they played independently but enjoying one another's presence. After some excited 'horse play' Mark hit Kevin in the face. I took him firmly on my lap saying, 'I won't let you hit Kevin. You need to sit down until you are ready to play again.' He quietened and I read a story. He and Kevin then found newspapers and 'read' peacefully, and later both painted. After a while play deteriorated again. I continued picking up Mark at the start of an attack, holding him firmly on my lap, saying calmly that I knew he was angry, it was all right to be angry, but I would not let him hurt Kevin.

One afternoon I had held Mark several times to calm him when he picked up a very large teddy bear. He started to undress him, asking for help. He said, 'You be the nurse', and he put the bear on the bed in the home corner and began 'examining' him. I fetched the hospital play kit which he used to give teddy injections and listen to his chest. I was saying things like 'It must hurt . . . I expect teddy feels like crying', watching Mark carefully, who was nodding. He fetched two long pencils and carefully stuck them into the bear's crotch. I continued reflective comments until he had finished playing. Later talking to his mother, she told me that the last of the series of reconstructive surgery Mark had needed on his penis had been extremely painful. After that cathartic day Mark coped much better with other children. I watched him play a complicated game involving cardboard tubes with Daniel, both totally absorbed. He started nursery school where he was much liked, to his mother's delight. She was relieved that they could go to the park without fearing he would push someone off the slide. In play therapy Mark always sought the hospital box and chose the same teddy, undressing it on the bed and 'treating' it. Once he lay down himself and asked me to be the doctor, which I did. Another time he told a passing child to be a nurse to teddy while he was doctor. He then told me to lie down and he examined and 'treated' me.

Mark's anger was at first diffuse but its recognition and containment enabled him to focus it appropriately. His repeated symbolic re-enactment of his operation and the recognition of his hurt and angry feelings, working initially within the symbolism of his hurt teddy, helped him express his pain and have it acknowledged. We learned only later that Mark had had a twin who had died in the womb. I wondered if his attacks on other children reflected his anger and grief at the part of himself that he had lost.

Facing death

Some children face their own death. Many terminally ill children live with denial and pretence, because the truth about their condition is too painful for the adults around them to admit to themselves or the child. In a well-meaning but often misguided attempt to protect the child, professionals and families enter into a 'mutual pretence' (Bluebond-Langer 1978) that everything will be fine and the child will recover. Yet it seems that children are usually aware of their impending death (Lansdown 1996), but go along with the pretence. While this could be seen as an effective and necessary coping mechanism, it prevents the child from having an opportunity to explore what death means and to prepare for it. Susan Monson writes:

Ruth has a rare genetic disorder which meant that she would slowly deteriorate before her premature death. She had been crying at school and was reluctant to go. I was seeing the family at home to help them talk about what was happening, and then began long-term play therapy with Ruth at school. Drawing *Faces*, she spoke about feeling frightened she might lose her parents, angry about school tasks becoming more difficult, sad at her body not feeling right, and happy if everything could return to normal. I said it would be wonderful if there was a magic wand to make things normal again, but there wasn't – she must feel so sad and frightened. Ruth drew a picture of herself inside a shape (it looked like a coffin) with a shadow round her. There was a ghost but she said she didn't know who it was – she was alone and falling and no one could help her. I reflected her feelings and made no other comment. The following week, at my suggestion, she painted a boat. She explained there was a storm. It was dark and the man was frightened, calling out he was drowning, but no one came to help him and, despite his lifebelt, he drowned. I expressed sympathy for the terrible situation he was in and the dreadful feelings he must have. Just having someone strong enough to listen and hold her feelings seemed to be helpful. After this she became happier and more animated, coping well enough at school. In supervision it was suggested that Ruth had needed to try and make sense of what was happening but could not burden her mother with this.

Recognition and containment of feelings, which include anger as well as fear and grief, require a worker who can bear to experience them. Hospital play specialist Nicola Phillips writes: 'One can only imagine that a child's inner world would be one of conflict and confusion.' A dying child's play with super-heroes changed from rescuing to attacking Nicola's play figures, which she understood as his awareness that adults could no longer save him and his anger at this. After several sessions in which this play was repeated, she talked to him about how angry the super-heroes seemed. Containing and then voicing these feelings enabled him to move to a place of acceptance. Crompton (1980) gives a poignant account of using drawing with a dying child and Dorothy Judd (1989) examines the demands of such work.

In a hospital setting it can be difficult to provide the worker with the emotional holding environment necessary if they are to receive and think about children's distress. Denial is an emotionally more comfortable response for staff constantly faced with potentially overwhelming anxiety and sadness (Menzies-Lyth 1988). Clinical supervision to explore the worker's feelings is essential, both to provide understanding of the child's feelings through their projection into the worker as well as more direct containment of the worker's feelings. A team approach can provide further space to think as well as giving mutual support.

Conclusion

When reality is painful and a child's future not bright we may sometimes be tempted to feel that it is kinder to leave a child in a state of not being able to think. This would also spare us the pain of facing these feelings ourselves. We must not be drawn into this trap. This would be to deny the very humanity of the child and their right to a full life, whatever it may hold and however brief it may be. We must hold on to our capacity to be a container for a child's most difficult feelings, able to bear them and think about them, and then when appropriate to return them to the child in a modified form, acknowledging pain and grief but also offering the child hope that they can bear them too and still find some richness in being themselves.

Similarly we need to think about the needs of families – parents and siblings, grandparents and in-laws – who have their own versions of loss of the hoped for child or anxiety about their child's future. Sometimes they need help from others to provide the emotional containment they need. Often we may be able to help parents support their child, with whatever modelling, guidance or support may be appropriate. Play together can be a way of both regaining autonomy and sense of agency, and of appreciating each other for who they are.

This is difficult work, and even more difficult for a worker on her own. Supervision, either individually or in a group, or both, helps us in bearing the feelings as well as in thinking about the process. We need to be aware of our own defences against pain and anxiety, which for many of us in therapeutic work are about being too close in (or enmeshed) rather than too far out. We need to find the right distance, one in which we are fully engaged in our relationship with the child (or parent) but retaining enough distance so that we can think. Working as a team and reflecting with colleagues can make all the difference to our ability to sustain the task. However, defensive processes, usually of the 'too far out' kind, also happen at an organizational level, which means that there is often real resistance to giving enough opportunity for reflective meetings in which people can explore together how the work makes them feel. It takes sustained effort to find ways to go on thinking and feeling together, without which we risk (in Valerie Sinason's phrase) stupefying experiences also rendering us stupid. Being helpful to others involves using ourselves.

Acknowledgement

With thanks to Nicola Phillips for help with the second part of the chapter on therapeutic play in hospitals.

Chapter 7

Therapeutic play for children experiencing separation, loss and bereavement in their families

The meaning of separation and loss for children

The most significant loss for a child is the absence of someone to whom they have become attached, a parent, sometimes a grandparent, another attachment figure or someone close such as a sibling or friend. Loss may come about through parental separation or divorce, or through bereavement – death. Children may experience other significant losses, for example, the death of a pet, loss of a transitional object, moving house and the loss of familiar surroundings, belongings and people. This latter is particularly severe if loss of country, and with it language and culture, is involved, as is the case for many asylum seeking and refugee children. Separation from an attachment figure may be brief or lasting, and can involve a change of home, temporary or long term, with different or unfamiliar people giving care. Understanding of attachment theory, specifically of the importance for their future mental health of an infant's attachments to their parents or caregivers, provides us with some insight into the emotional effects of separation and loss. Until the work of Bowlby, which together with the Robertsons' films revealed the damaging effects on young children of separation from their parents, there was little concern to minimize the need for that separation or to provide the secondary or substitute attachment figure that could help a young child manage the experience.

A baby first experiences separation anxiety as they become aware of their own existence separate from the parent. Separation anxiety is innate and normal, and has survival value, because the child is less likely to run into danger or get lost. Attachment seeking, holding on to or following parents, means that the child is more likely to get care. Separation anxiety starts at about six months and continues at a high level, only beginning to decline around the age of three as the child becomes more able to hold in mind the image and memory of the absent parent. Developing cognitive and language abilities, including a sense of time as well as memory, mean the child becomes more able to think and reflect, to ask questions and understand explanations. Later on as the child develops more autonomy, and becomes able to leave as well as be left, separation becomes less frightening. However, at any stage of life, including adulthood, separation may also be experienced as a loss of an attachment figure and involve fear and anger, as well as intense sorrow. These patterns are similar in different cultures, although ages may vary a little.

So a child's angry or grief-stricken *protest* in response to separation or loss of an attachment figure or someone important in their lives is a normal healthy response. It is painful to adults who witness it, even more so if they are also experiencing their own grief, and they may resort to denial of its intensity, suggesting that 'children soon forget'. Children do not 'soon forget', although they may be good at covering up their feelings if no one is there to attend to them with other than a false cheerfulness. What the child needs is comforting, the reassurance of familiar objects, routines and places as far as this is possible, tangible reminders of the missing person, such as a photograph or a pen, perhaps an item of clothing which retains their smell. The child's transitional object, the soft cloth or teddy, may help re-create an attachment figure in their absence. As Bowlby (1980) explains, the consequence of suppressing painful feelings, but also of a prolonged loss, is that the child moves from a state of protest to one of quiet *despair*, unable to hold in mind the 'good' attachment figure who cared for them as opposed to the 'bad' one who has left them (Robertson and Robertson 1989). The Robertsons' film of fostering two-year-old Thomas while his mother was in hospital shows how they prevented him reaching that state of despair. Thomas played happily right to the end of his stay, indicating that his carers were containing his anxiety, which did not prevent his distress becoming acute at times, leading to some avoidance (of looking at his mother's photograph) and some angry attacks on his foster mother. In the absence of emotional holding a child may move into a further state of *detachment*, appearing to be functioning more normally again but in fact with their emotions blunted and their ability to make relationships impaired.

Of course this is a similar process to the formation of highly anxious attachments and the consequences are similar. Although separation and loss threaten a child who already has a secure attachment, and certainly create intense pain, such children can also be more readily helped as they have an expectation that their feelings will be understood and responded to. Children with anxious attachments are likely to find separation and loss particularly damaging or difficult, as they have already devised strategies, such avoidant, controlling or caretaking behaviour, and ultimately detachment or dissociation, to defend them against the fear arising from their lack of a secure base and their painful feelings of being unworthy of care. If a child has previously experienced their parent as frightened or frightening (a 'disorganized' attachment), their relief at the separation or loss may be accompanied by the fear that they may be even less safe in an unfamiliar situation or setting. We can readily understand how the task of helping these children is so demanding.

The experience of bereaved children

When a child's parent or sibling dies the grief of the remaining adults is often so overwhelming that they find it difficult to recognize or cope with the child's grief. It may be thought that children do not really understand about death and that it would cause unnecessary pain to involve them in the parent's grieving, whether through going to the funeral or seeing the parent weep. If a child is not showing overt grief adults may not realize 'the depths of a child's misery, because children experience grief not as continuous but as sudden intermittent bursts of being caught up and overwhelmed by memories, which leave them feeling isolated and out of step with what is happening around them. Most youngsters can only tolerate short outbursts of grief and are easily distracted, which can make it seem that they are finished mourning long before this is actually the case' (Jewett 1994: 65). In fact the evidence abounds that children have the same reactions to loss as adults, although they may be less able to put their thoughts and feelings into words (Bowlby 1980). These reactions are initial shock and numbness, denial and disbelief, together with bewilderment, disorientation and loss of perspective. A time of intense grief follows, with yearning and pining, searching for the lost person, feelings of intense anger or guilt, mental disorganization, loneliness and despair. If all goes well some kind of reorganization and reintegration is reached (Kubler-Ross 1970; Raphael 1983). It is now recognized that grieving does not follow a simple sequence but that any aspect of grieving may recur at any time, over a prolonged period.

The work of mourning a loss involves a series of tasks. These are to accept the reality of the loss, to experience the pain of grief (avoiding both denial and idealization), to adjust to an environment in which the dead person is missing and, finally, to 'emotionally relocate the deceased and move on with life' (Worden 1991: 16). The notion of withdrawing emotional energy from the relationship with the dead person has been replaced by the idea of trans-formed but 'continuing bonds' (Klass *et al.* 1996: 19), a process of accom-modating to the meaning of the absent person in present life and reworking that meaning over time, particularly important for children whose cognitive and conceptual abilities develop as they grow up. Younger children with a limited understanding of time may also not have grasped the irreversibility of death, and expect the person to come alive again or to return from hospital. This is more likely if they have not been involved in the death, through seeing the body or coffin, or sharing in other people's grief. Young children under eight years are likely to use 'magical thinking' to make sense of incompre-hensible events. This may lead to intense guilt and extreme anxiety, as they come to believe that some perceived misdeed or angry thought of theirs, which is linked in time with the death, has caused it. If one parent has disappeared the child fears that this could happen again. The period of intense grief at losing a parent may be shorter for children than for adults but the whole grieving process may take many years and is renewed at the milestones in life, such as changing school, birthdays or the birth of their own baby, when the parent is again deeply missed (Hemmings 1990, 1995; Dyregrov 1991; Pennells and Smith 1999).

The death of a parent not only causes direct feelings of loss but often results in an upheaval in the child's world. At best the surviving parent has a changed role in the family. The child, boys especially, may be expected to take on a more responsible adult role, being told 'Look after your dad now', or 'You're the man of the family now', with its implicit denial of the child's continuing need to be cared for. For some the disruption may be more severe, involving new carers, perhaps eventually a step-parent, or a foster family. These secondary losses (Jewett 1994) are likely to intensify a child's sense of grief and loss, and to involve a loss of identity and self-esteem. This is exacerbated if a child is excluded from discussion and decision taking, and feels helpless to influence what happens.

The death of a brother or sister often results in the surviving child feeling guilt that they were not the one who died. Brothers and sisters are inevitably in competition with one another at some level. Death gives the survivor an unfair victory and a feeling of guilty triumph, as well as of loss, sometimes so severe as to lead to emotional disturbance (Sinason 1990). Again 'magical thinking' may lead children to blame themselves for their sibling's death. Before an anticipated death, siblings may have felt confused and isolated if parents were preoccupied, yet pretending all was well, fearing their own loss of control. Because of their own grief, parents may either not notice or cannot bear their child's equal need to grieve.

Bereaved children are likely to have feelings of confusion and bewilderment, of insecurity, of guilt, of anger, of isolation, and of loss of identity and self-esteem. These can be expressed in any number of ways, from nightmares, enuresis and crying, to withdrawal and depression, or angry and difficult behaviour.

Helping bereaved children

Working with the whole family

Mourning takes different forms as cultures vary, which means that as workers we have a task in learning about the meaning of mourning in that particular family and culture. Usually bereaved families experience a crisis of identity as well as a massive change in their structure and functioning, which places family members under great stress. New demands are made at a time when the family's coping resources are depleted. Any intervention needs to support the family rather than add to the pressure. Establishing a partnership between worker and parent, with the parent where possible doing part of the work in communicating with and supporting their child, helps enhance the parent's skills and self-esteem. 'It also assists the child to feel that this is not a problem that they are having outside of the family, but is one which is recognized as being part of the family's responsibility for all its members' (Hemmings 1992: 23). While there may be one-to-one work with the child it needs to be set in the context of the shared difficulty that the whole family is experiencing rather than as an isolated problem of the child. This is emphasized by the worker first meeting with the child at home.

Continuing contact and conversations with the family mean that the child and family can move on together. Since parents tend to underestimate their children's distress we need to help parents become more sensitive and responsive, as well as helping them manage their own grief. If difficult behaviour can be reframed as being about the child's grief, a parent may be able to respond more thoughtfully. For example, not wanting to go to school can be recognized as separation anxiety with fear of further loss, and then practical ways of managing this can be found. A parent can be helped to recognize that their child, however grown-up their apparent behaviour at times, may also feel like a vulnerable baby. Hemmings suggests that one way a parent can meet this need is by giving intimate 'baby-love' times, comforting the child through a more infantile experience of being bathed, cuddled and talked to, dressed and tucked up in bed. A parent who is supported to understand and comfort their child will, rather than feel helpless as experts take over, more confidently provide care in the future. For some grieving parents this may be too much to manage on their own at the time, so that play therapy sessions can help a bereaved child more immediately.

Non-directive play therapy

Children have usually learned that they are expected not to talk about their feelings, and they may also be quite protective of already distressed parents. In any case, a child's feelings may not all be experienced and thought about at a conscious level. Thus play methods have an important role in helping bereaved children to acknowledge and express their pain through the symbolism of their play, and to have it understood. Non-directive play therapy gives back a sense of control to a child at a time when so much of their life is out of their control. As always the therapist's role is to think about and bear the child's feelings, acknowledging and reflecting them as they are expressed in play. She will normally stay within the child's play symbolism, which means that the child can work at their own pace. A child's play themes may reveal where they are experiencing most difficulty, as illustrated by the following examples from Peta Hemmings, who provides a support service for bereaved families and people with terminal illnesses.

Self-blame and magical thinking

> Lee had developed nightmares and stopped playing out with his friends
> after his grandfather's death. He was alone in the room when his grand-
> father had a heart attack and called his mother, and then observed
> the family's panic and distress. In play sessions he armed himself with
> a sword, dagger, gun and invisible shield to guard a hoard of treasure
> from marauding pirates and monsters, which he vanquished. 'He even
> developed magical powers so he could fly away when the threat became
> too great, only to return and swoop victoriously on his attackers'
> (Hemmings 1995: 126). This omnipotent play helped compensate for his
> powerlessness in reality and his fear that he had been responsible. He
> needed much reassurance that he was not to blame.

Wish for reunion – searching

> Dean's father had died in a hospice. Dean (aged eight years) wondered if
> his father's room was empty but wasn't sure. In play sessions 'he made
> all the rooms in the doll's house into bedrooms and moved the dolls
> from bed to bed. Eventually all the dolls were crowded into one bed-
> room and he removed them one by one out of the house ... until the
> house was empty' (Hemmings 1995: 124). Following this he asked to
> visit the hospice where he searched his father's room meticulously,
> making certain his father was not there.

Anger

The sadness of a bereaved child is more readily accepted and understood
than anger. The expression of anger enables the process of grieving (Banks
and Mumford 1988):

> Sarah Mumford used a set of small knitted dolls to represent the family
> of a bereaved four-year-old boy who was living with foster parents. She
> wanted him to know that it was not his fault that his mother had died and
> that it was safe to express his anger at her leaving him, which she had
> not wanted to do. John named the dolls spontaneously and spent much
> time putting the mother and John dolls together and then separating

them. A doctor doll was told off and hit for his failure. John once expressed his anger by tying up the mother doll and dragging her round the floor. By the last session John had worked through his anger. He sadly kissed the mother doll goodbye and put her away in the bag.

Ending therapy as a managed experience of loss

Ending therapy will inevitably bring up feelings which resonate with the child's feelings of loss about the bereavement. Managing the ending of therapy is always important, but with a bereaved child it is crucial in providing an anticipated and well-managed experience of loss.

A play therapist's view of her work with bereaved children

Play therapist Clare Sheridan writes:

Thinking and experiencing death brings such powerful feelings that it feels safer to play your feelings rather than to talk about it, so non-directive play therapy is ideal with bereaved children. I speak from personal experience as my mother died whilst I was having play therapy myself as my own therapy requirement during my play therapy training, I was able to play my feelings and then talk about what I learnt from my play and from my dreams and thoughts in between the sessions. I played with sticky lizards and dreamed one hit me in the forehead, then I dreamt of planting seeds with Mum which grew with a golden glow to them. When I woke up I remembered her saying that I was the brave one that was always ready to take a risk. This was a great comfort to me. It also made me realize just how much work goes on in between sessions.

The child's journey in non-directive play therapy is whatever that child needs and only that child knows what they need on that particular day. They always show me, whether it is to sit quietly in the den and feel sad, or to make a pile of pooh, or to dress up as a character. I am their companion on their journey, to contain their feelings and to make sure that they are safe. I like to think about children's play using Sue Jennings' (1999) classifications of embodiment, projective and role play.

Embodiment play

Hiding objects in the sand, stones, sticks, toys, or more obviously skeletons, can relate to loss and death. I talk with the child about how we cannot see the object but we remember. Children often want to take turns hiding objects and I ask do they think it should be easy or hard to find them, which can indicate how the child feels about the loss. Sometimes we have to search for them at the same time and the child's hands meet mine under the sand. It can be a way of being close. One girl even said 'find me' the next time instead of 'find them'. Paintings and drawings reveal themes of loss. One girl whose father had died drew herself with a snowman on one side of the paper and on the other side a drawing of it melted into a puddle. We had a conversation about how it felt to melt away, and how it felt for her (on the paper) to have the snowman melt away, to only have it for such a short time, how he had melted and gone forever but she can still remember him and love him and always think of him. Feeling and experiencing sand, wet or dry, can release feelings. Wet sand becomes 'mud' or 'pooh' helping release 'yucky' feelings, fear, loss, internal pain. Several children have at various times piled 'pooh' on my hands and asked how much can I take, can I take more? They seem to be asking how much of their 'shitty feelings' can I bear to share with them. They often laugh a lot whilst doing the piling on of pooh – maybe they are relieved that I can cope with their feelings and want to share with them how they feel.

Projective play

Using small figures, animals, natural objects and small things either in the sand tray or on the floor, can help children project their feelings and tell their story through play. Writing their story down as they tell it can be very satisfying for them (Cattanach 1997). They like to discuss the story and sometimes may change the ending as the play therapy progresses. Using characters or animals in a story where they get buried is very common, often the character is the opposite sex to that of the parent or sibling that has died, maybe to make it feel even safer, or perhaps it is about the fear of the remaining parent/sibling/self dying. One boy whose sibling had died wrote a story of a cat that was frozen and none of the kittens could give it enough love to unfreeze it. When he chose to read it to his grieving mother she recognized herself as the frozen one and there was a definite improvement after that in their relationship. A boy whose father had died systematically took everything out of the doll's house and said it was an empty house. Then a small baby character wandered through the house looking for his daddy. This could reflect both his empty feelings and literally that his father was not in his house.

Some children are confused about the use of chemotherapy for cancer where a seemingly well parent has treatment and becomes more ill. Cups and saucers are used to make poison, sometimes for me or sometimes to feed baby with. Sometimes I have to die and then 'oh no, you didn't die' and then I have to have more poison. That for me mirrors the process of the parent who is ill for a long time and has to have horrible treatment and in the end dies anyway. In preparing for reviews we talk about any questions they need to ask about the illness and death of their parent.

Role play

Becoming another character, dressing up and being another person can free a child and release their subconscious thoughts. One boy dressed as the fairy godmother and we were chased by the witch and had to hide. After doing this repeatedly in several sessions he tied a sword to the end of the wand and vanquished the witch. We discussed how only in play can the wishes we really want to come true happen, but we can pretend and we can remember. Role playing hospitals, doctors and being buried are common themes with bereaved children. I have to accept nasty injections or have operations, sometimes I have to be angry with the doctor or to die and be buried.

Some focused approaches

There are many children's books and stories about death and loss (such as Susan Varley's *Badger's Parting Gifts*, and Michael Rosen's *Sad Book*) which can be helpful, either as resources available within non-directive play therapy or to use more directly. These and more factual information books, workbooks and resources are listed online (www.childbereavementnetwork.org.uk). *All About Me* is a board game to help children talk about their feelings about death and bereavement (Hemmings 1989). On landing on a square the player picks up a sentence completion card. These range from simple ones such as 'My favourite food is . . .' to deeper ones such as 'I feel really cross when . . .', 'The saddest day of my life was . . .' and 'When I need a hug I go to . . .'. Children find this game unthreatening and they relax and start to talk about feelings which may have been bottled up for some time. The game was initially invented to help one child in articulating the intense anger and frustration she felt at her mother's death.

> Michelle was getting into constant fights at school, especially with any-one who taunted her. The game gave her permission to feel and express her anger. She became able to talk about her mother. 'She visits her grave with her father and they cry together; they have learnt to share the emotions they both feel over their loss' (Hemmings 1989: 11). She also learned to deal with sudden overwhelming physical tension by aiming stones into the sea.

Other children have used punching a pillow (Jewett 1994). However, such physical release only supplements the child's basic need for their feelings to be tolerated and understood.

A bereaved child has lost trust in the future. Hemmings (1992: 24–25) might use a 'snowstorm' toy to acknowledge to a child how life has been turned upside-down, leaving them vulnerable to any new knock, such as a thoughtless comment at home, school or elsewhere, which sends everything swirling around again. Using drawing, and sometimes masks, she helps them identify which people they feel safe to talk to and how to protect themselves against hurtful comments. A 'transformer' toy helped a child understand that although his dying father's appearance had been changed by his illness it was still the same person and he had really died. Memory albums and memory boxes (Barnados) help in going on remembering as a child gets older:

> A ten-year-old boy had repressed his grief at the death of his much loved grandmother so that his ability to read and write was affected. The therapist's focused drama and play techniques included drawing a picture of the grandmother, burying her in the sand, and writing a memorial album using memories and photographs. The boy became free to mourn, freeing the family to mourn too and visit the grave for the first time (Nilman and Lewin 1989).

Unresolved mourning in a surviving parent which affects the ability of that parent to help the child to grieve can lead to angry behaviour from the child, a projection of the parent's anger, which may then be punished. Storytelling and story making can provide healing, as they have down the ages (Gersie 1991):

A four-year-old boy with behaviour problems had witnessed his father's accidental death. He was given help in six individual sessions, whilst his mother watched through a one-way screen. He used a frieze with illustrations of monsters from *Where the Wild Things Are* to express his anger at his father's death. In Sendak's (1963) story, Max is angry at being told off by his mother for his wild behaviour. In imagination he sails off to the land of the 'wild things' where he becomes their king, only returning when he becomes lonely, to 'his very own room where he found his supper waiting for him and it was still hot'. The mother's therapist then used the same story to show the mother that angry feelings could be safely expressed in fantasies provided they have a secure boundary (Muir *et al.* 1988).

Because focused approaches depend on initiation from the worker, they are potentially disempowering for the child who loses the ability to manage the pace at which they can express and manage their feelings. Their use requires a very sensitive and attuned worker who can introduce a technique (such as storytelling) at the appropriate moment so that it does not disrupt the thread of a child's play. Of course, the worker's choice and placing of particular toys or objects in the playroom may also mean that a child can make use of them within non-directive play. Alternatively, with a child able to use thinking, a technique can be discussed and explained to the child as helping with a particular aspect of their mourning, and then used with the child's consent.

Banishing 'magical thinking'

Four-year-old Susan had found her baby sister dead in her cot while her family panicked around her ... Her teacher was concerned about her soiling and self-harming and insisted the family get help. In individual sessions she rejected all play materials and sat silently colouring and cutting out. 'I decided to try a third object and introduced her to a fluffy rabbit puppet and a Russian babushka doll. I made up a story about the doll having lots of worries which made her feel very "jumbly" inside. Although the doll, Anna, looked just the same as all her friends on the outside, she felt very small and frightened on the inside. I opened up the doll to show Susan that inside was the tiniest doll.' The rabbit 'had extra long ears, which could hear children when they were upset and had special cuddles to comfort them'. As the story based on her experience developed, Susan watched with some animation. 'I suggested that she could help Anna by drawing some of the unhappy feelings she had, and cutting them out. We then placed them inside the smallest doll. At this point Susan took the initiative and placed the small doll inside the large one, and gave it to the rabbit to cuddle.' In a later session 'Susan was able to tell me that she felt that she had indeed killed the baby and that she should be punished for it.' Using dolls, they re-enacted the events of the morning of the baby's death and were able to 'clear away the troubling uncertainties about how and why people died', absolving her of responsibility. 'She was then more able to explore more fully the sadness and regret she felt when she thought about her sister. She derived great comfort from going to the grave and taking pictures she had drawn. She knew they would never be seen by the baby but she also knew that the gift made her feel much better' (Hemmings 1992: 23–24).

Traumatic loss and post traumatic stress

A sudden unexpected and catastrophic loss, especially one where the child was present and witnesses (or survives) something horrific, may involve overwhelming feelings of powerless and helplessness, creating profound traumatic stress, which interferes with the process of grief and mourning. Traumatic experiences include violence, rape, murder, suicide, death in a disaster, or violent conflict or war (Dyregrov 1991). They may also occur as part of experiencing a less violent death, for example, seeing a parent in acute pain or being the first to find the baby in a cot death. A few children are bereaved by one parent killing the other. Refugee children may have witnessed and experienced the most terrible events – humiliation, torture and violent death – and in addition have lost family, culture and identity by taking refuge in an alien and often hostile society.

Intrusive disturbing images and memories, often experienced as flashbacks, recur spontaneously or may be triggered by some environmental association, or they may recur when the child is trying to sleep or in dreams. At the same time there may be a numbing of emotional responsiveness, feelings of detachment from others or lack of interest in significant activities. A child may give a distanced account of what happened which lulls the listener into thinking the child was unaffected. Other indications are: being hyper-alert and 'jumpy', disturbed sleep, impaired memory or difficulty in concentrating, avoidance of activities that might trigger a traumatic memory and more intense disturbance if they do, and in older children guilt at surviving or fantasies of rescue or revenge. Post-traumatic stress disorder is diagnosed if a sufficient number of these symptoms of intrusion, arousal and avoidance is present for more than a month (Perrin *et al.* 2000).

There is evidence of the value of a debriefing interview, both individual and group, as emotional first aid, so that children can have adult confirmation of their experience (Perrin *et al.* 2000). Children must be in a setting where they feel safe, and their carers need parallel work in learning about children's grief reactions. As well as providing straightforward information which children need, debriefing uses methods which include drawing, redramatizing, even song and dance, to weaken intrusive memories as their expression becomes more symbolic (Dyregrov 1991). It has been shown to help alleviate some distress, although a few children have become more sensitized following group debriefing after a disaster. Children who have witnessed one parent killing the other are at severe risk of post-traumatic stress disorder. Dora Black (1990) considers a debriefing interview essential, once the child is with safe and familiar people, preferably immediately but if necessary even well after the event. She provides large rag dolls and drawing material so that children can show her what happened, which she puts into words. This, and the subsequent therapy these children need, is skilled work and requires a therapist who can bear the almost unbearable (Harris Hendricks *et al.* 1993).

The intrusion of dreadful images and memories makes it almost impossible for the child to work at the repeated remembering and reworking which is part of the normal mourning process. Their play, as well as dream material, is often repetitive replaying of the same scenarios, without any sense of development. Non-directive approaches have a number of advantages over the common directive approaches to treating children suffering from post-traumatic stress. The non-directive therapist's continuing observation and attunement gives her a better understanding of the child's inner world. Children are more likely to remain engaged in therapy because their defences are not attacked and they remain in control, working at their own pace. The therapist's presence as witness to the child's play enactments and the consistency and reliability of her attuned empathic response, together with the provision of the same (but carefully selected) play material in a familiar setting, helps the child by minimizing their anxiety and arousal, allowing cognitive processing of hitherto entirely sensory, bodily and affective memories (Ryan and Needham 2001). The therapist gives words to or names the feelings expressed in play, making them more conscious. Initially this may involve the child connecting one fragment of thought or memory with one feeling, and finding expression in symbolic ways which offer more emotional distance than in literal re-enactment. As an aspect of an experience is remembered and acknowledged, then the process of forgetting can also begin (Alvarez 1992). Further help may be needed as the child gets older and seeks more explanations, or if something triggers a recurrence. There is a continuing tension between the need to forget and the need to remember (Lanyado 1999), as the following case study from a play therapist illustrates:

Daniel and his mother were refugees, with insecure asylum status, from war in West Africa, leaving behind his brother and sisters and other family members. His father had been killed. In non-directive play sessions with his play therapist he used intense symbolic and role play, directing his therapist in what to do. 'There were themes of danger, fighting, death, terror and confusion in which things were not what they seemed. When I suggested that he was thinking about what had happened at home he agreed he was thinking about his dad being killed and was worried about his family still there. I reflected how he worried for them and maybe for himself too. Daniel continued to re-enact scenarios of fear and threat, with some rescue and healing, perhaps restoring some sense of control after events when he had felt helpless. But there was another aspect to his play. He was also interested in board games and had a natural desire to win. His symbolic play suggested to me that at times he was preoccupied with things of the past and fears for the future. At other times he tries to get on with everyday life, being interested and involving himself with activities in keeping with any other nine-year-old boy.

Group work with bereaved children

The group work process

Group work is often an effective way of helping bereaved children. The similarities in their experience may be greater than the differences. Bereaved children can feel very different from other children, even close friends, leaving them feeling isolated and vulnerable. They can find it helpful to realize that their experience is shared. In a safe group setting they may draw support from one another, find the information and knowledge they have been lacking, share their stories and realize that their responses to bereavement are normal and reasonable. Where their families are helped at the same time more open communication within families becomes possible.

Group work always needs much preparation if children are to feel safe and emotionally contained (Dwivedi 1993). As well as a providing a warm and welcoming physical setting, meeting children's primary needs for nurture and comforting, adults need to acknowledge that their own feelings will also be involved in the work. Often workers feel protective and are anxious that they will not 'make things worse' for the children or that they will be overcome by the children's expression of grief. Permission to feel both anger and sorrow is an important aspect of all group work, and it makes emotional demands on workers to be able to stay with the feelings. Planning needs to include specific and regular times in the programme when the workers meet to reflect on their own feelings aroused in the course of the work. Using the 'reflection process' (Mattinson 1975), workers can come to understand how their feelings and reactions tend to mirror a child's less conscious feelings, enabling them not only to become more in touch with a child's inner world but also to find the emotional strength to bear and contain these feelings. Individual supervision may be valuable but group meetings of the whole team provide a better match with the group way of working and enable more insight into group processes of bearing and containing pain, whether the child's or the worker's.

Group work programmes

Recent years have seen growth in the provision of group work for children who have experienced the death of a parent or sibling. Brothers and sisters in the same family can successfully join a larger group of bereaved children. The structure of group work tends to reflect Stroebe and Schut's (1999) dual process model of a bereaved person's need for continual movement between a 'loss orientation' to the past and a 'restoration orientation' to the future. (Numerous resources for group work, including books and stories, and videos of children talking about bereavement are listed online, for example, www.childbereavementnetwork.org.uk).

Pennells and Kitchener (1990) and Pennells and Smith (1999) provided groups to help children grieve for a parent who had died, helping them to express and deal with any fears and concerns, and to adjust positively to their changed life. Groups start with recognition of why they are there, and after introductions and ice-breakers, children begin to share views and feelings (perhaps using Hemmings's *All About Me* sentence completion cards). Listening to stories about death help children start to think together about their experience, while the metaphors (or animal characters) of the stories make this more bearable by providing some emotional distance. Further story making continues this process (Hogan and Pennells 1997), with the ultimate aim of children creating their own internal 'story' of their bereavement. Stories, drawing and painting, and bringing a memento to talk about, help a child in finding and holding on to positive memories of the person who has died, an important step if their previous final memory was painful. Later sessions look at more difficult memories, using a trigger video such as *That Morning I Went to School*, drawing pictures of what happened or faces to show how they are feeling, giving each child an opportunity to talk. Sometimes a child says she feels responsible, for example, 'If only I didn't go to school and helped mum more she wouldn't have died' (Pennells and Kitchener 1990: 14). Some tasks are individual, helping a child preserve a precious memory or contemplating their own future. These can lead into sharing thoughts and feelings together in joint activities.

Drama and role play allow group expression and symbolization of feelings,

helping turn those feelings from sensory memories to something more pro-
cessed and bearable. Children may role play how to cope with nightmares, so
realizing they have common fears. They might act out a funeral, especially if
they did not attend. They may role play how to manage angry feelings and
thoughtless comments from children at school. Sculpting gives insights into
how family members feel. The child places group members to 'sculpt' their
family before and after the parent died, then each in turn is asked how the
person they are representing feels. Another powerful exercise which may
arouse strong feelings is a guided fantasy in which they talk to the dead
parent, perhaps say what they would have wished, but then of course must
also say goodbye. This needs thoughtful 'holding' by the group leaders.

Children draw images and symbols of death, together creating a death
mural which symbolizes the whole group experience. This helps them explore
ideas and fears of heaven and hell, ghosts and angels, dreams and nightmares.
Factual information may be much needed, furthered by visits to a cemetery
or a stone mason. Information about mourning in different cultures and
religions is important (Ward 1995). The last sessions are oriented to the
future. A flower mural of feelings that can be left behind becomes a beautiful
flower, a metaphor for pain transformed into something positive. Children
may be asked to anticipate future loss situations (such as a sudden move to
an unfamiliar place), identify their feelings (for example, through an exercise
picking up 'feeling' cards, then symbolizing two feelings of, say, anger or
confusion in a drawing). They can be asked to identify (or draw in colour) on
a body outline where they feel those feelings, offering some insight into angry
kicking out or headaches. Practice in calming and relaxation exercises is
offered. They may draw how they will see themselves in a year's time, leading
to a positive discussion of 'how they will cope and go forward' (Stroebe's
'restoration orientation'). After a last session of fun, food and goodbyes
children leave taking their drawings or other work. Follow-up indicated that
the children were suffering less from crying, nightmares and enuresis, and had
more self-esteem. Children and adolescents both said how much the groups
helped.

Another programme offers more individual tasks. Children sculpt their
family with buttons on an outline family tree, choosing buttons to represent
themselves first and then members of their families, helping them think about
their own identity within their changing family. This needs a large number of
adults to listen to the children as they work. In another task each child is
given a piece of paper cut to their height, implicitly representing the child,
and encouraged to paint, using brushes, fingers and hands, being as messy as
they wish. 'Maria's picture resembled a child crying with large black foot-
prints all over it very carefully drawn. She had written the words dad and
dead on different parts of the picture' (Smith and Pennells 1995: 166–168).
Afterwards children needed help in sharing feelings with the whole group.
They were asked to write down one thing that had been helpful and one

unhelpful thing following their parent's death. These were posted into a box and each child picked one out and read it, leading to much about anger and the need to cry, as one said, 'I think it helps to cry so it takes all the anger out of us.' One of the strengths of this group work was the provision of a clear structure but with the minimum of directed activity. Once a task or activity had been outlined, children were free to develop their play and its symbolism. The workers' role was as active and reflective listeners.

A two-day residential programme for bereaved children (www. winstonswish.org.uk) makes more use of the symbolic power of shared rituals. A candlelight ceremony allows for the expression of sadness and gives permission to cry. 'One by one, everyone is invited to light their candle and given the option to say "I'm lighting my candle for . . . and the things I would like to remember about them are . . ."' (Smith and Pennells 1995: 183). After reflecting on sad feelings and being comforted, the candles are blown out, with each child encouraged to keep their candle to light on future occasions that they might choose. Parents have a parallel programme and are reunited at their children's 'graduation ceremony' marking what the children have achieved. A balloon ceremony ends the whole programme, each family member attaching two messages to a balloon, one to the person who has died and the other a wish for the future. All the balloons are released together, providing for some a symbolic letting go of grief and for others a way of keeping in communication with the dead person. The camps are not all sadness and grief; activities such as climbing and archery, a camp fire and a night walk are interspersed with feelings sessions so that children have fun as well as sharing intense feelings.

Group work was undertaken with five young children whose sibling had died in a cot death, following concern that through normal jealousy the children might have 'wished away' the new baby, resulting not only in guilt but in terrifying feelings of power; they might have fears that they too would die. Straightaway the children announced, 'We're here because our babies died', and wanted to talk about why they had died. They felt distressed, confused and, above all, angry. One child 'drew pictures of black monsters who would "kill everyone", including, it was made clear, the therapists'. Anger directed at the leaders in physical attacks was redirected to punching an 'angry cushion' which every child used at some point. Then the children drew pictures of their families, and several said that their families were 'looking for something that they've lost . . . but won't find it'. They drew their dead siblings and, again spontaneously, each child related where she or he had last seen the baby and how the baby had died. 'This was a very sad session, and . . . following these accounts of the babies' deaths, the group *all* en masse decided to go to the toilet, leaving the two therapists alone: thus we all had "a break" ' (Krasner and Beinart 1989: 14). With a little help the children made up a story about a princess whose cat had died. They said she would be sad for a long time although her parents had told her to try to forget her cat. One child was frightened that the princess would die too, but was reassured by a child less recently bereaved that the princess would grow up and become a queen. The children returned to the story, wondering if a good fairy could bring back the dead cat or 'magic' a new one into being the dead cat. With help, the children decided it would be better for the princess to love the new cat for itself. They seemed to reach the concept of the irreversibility of death as they decided that 'this kind of magic "couldn't really happen", but that the princess would never forget her old cat'. Follow-up found parents reporting their children were eating and sleeping better and were less anxious and upset.

Managing defences against anxiety in group work

Group activities and sharing of feelings mean that a child's pain can be expressed and find a resonance with other children's experience. When this is well contained it provides the child with a powerful validating experience of being thought about and understood. However, it is not always easy to provide containment for a group of angry grieving children. Parents and children reported good outcomes from the group work described. However, other groups can have more difficulty, with children silently avoiding engagement with the work of the group or at other times joining in angry acting out together. This is Bion's group defence of 'fight or flight' or, in Canham and Emanuel's (2000) phrase, a 'gang' rather than a 'group' state of mind. It is sometimes the case that children's disturbance is too great for them to engage in the group process. However, it may equally be that the 'holding environment' of the group does not provide children with a sense of a safe boundary within which they can explore their feelings. Group leaders can become too anxious and unable to remain thoughtful about what it is that the children are really communicating or too defensive to stay with the children's expression of anger or sorrow. The meaning of attacks on the leaders needs to be understood, not as a personal attack but perhaps as children's unconscious symbolic attack on their parents for dying or for failing to prevent another's death. If the group leaders can stay as thinking minds and survive attempts by the children to split or damage them, they may be able to provide the children with the experience of being held in mind, which can help them in turn to think and talk about their pain. Another reason for children's difficulty in engaging may be if insufficient preparation and support are given to the families, so that children are not fully supported in grieving. We need to remind ourselves that successful group work requires thinking about the circles of containment that are needed for the child, the family and the workers. Where the mourning process is well supported, the child's development of the 'coherent narrative' of their life experience, integrating thoughts and feelings, helps restore to some extent the child's faith that they can cope with their future. The threat that bereavement poses to a child's trusting and loving inner working model is held at bay.

Children in separation and divorce

Children whose parents separate or divorce suffer a form of bereavement. Such loss of a parent from the family gives rise to similar feelings and a similar process of grieving to loss through death, and sometimes it is more difficult to come to terms with than death. The loss may not be as final as in death, although some children do lose touch with one parent and experience the separation anxiety and grief which results from absence of an attachment figure. However, family break-up often entails conflict and intense acrimony between the parents, often for some time preceding the break-up as well as at the time, which complicates the emotional situation for the child. The separating parents, embroiled in their own conflicts, may be unaware of how their children are feeling and may underestimate their children's distress. Their own distress may mean that they find it difficult to give their children information and support. For the child, parental separation also involves loss of familiar patterns of roles and relationships in family life. It often leads to a change in circumstances, sometimes a move away from familiar places, away from friends and relatives, and a change in standard of living. Longer term, children may find themselves living in reordered families involving new relationships. More than one in three children experiences family break-up but most eventually resume a normal course of development, although perhaps with an increased sense of vulnerability and some loss of trust in continuity in their lives. A minority of children experience continuing problems, especially if they have been caught up in unresolved parental conflicts (for example, over contact), if there was domestic violence, if parental mental health or substance abuse was involved, or if there are serial separations and multiple transitions (Harold and Murch 2005).

Children's reactions to parental separation and divorce are likely to follow the general pattern of reactions to loss, with initial shock and disbelief, and continuing confusion, fear and anxiety about whether they will be looked after, much anger and great sadness. Young children, using 'magical thinking' to explain situations which make no immediate sense, blame themselves for their parents' separation; older children too may feel a sense of guilt. They may pick up notions of blaming, placating or rescuing their parents and punishing themselves. ' "The two walls of the house are collapsing and I am left trying to hold the roof up" is how one 12-year-old described his parents' divorce' (McFerran 1989).

Children in separation and divorce need an explanation of what is happening and why. They need to know that the break-up is not their fault. They need a reassurance, if possible, of continued love and care and reassurance too that both parents still love them. A complete and clean break with a parent, although considered proper in cultures where questions of family honour and shame are involved, has been shown to be damaging to the child. Also damaging is being recruited into parents' unresolved conflicts or emotional withdrawal (the 'silent treatment'). For example, a child may become protective of one parent which might mean refusing contact with the other, providing the child with a more stable emotional environment at the expense of the expression of their deeper wishes. Children need to be free to maintain a relationship with the absent parent (unless it is not safe to do so), and to have a means of keeping in touch. They need to have their feelings recognized, especially by their parents, and to have these feelings kept separate from their parents' conflicts. These are the findings of research studies, described in Walczak and Burns (1984), Lund (1984), Mitchell (1985) and Howard and Shepherd (1987) in Britain, and by Wallerstein and Kelly (1980) in the United States, elaborated by numerous subsequent studies (for example, Cockett and Tripp 1994; MacLean 2004; Harold and Murch 2005), including some which have sought children's views directly (Douglas *et al.* 2001).

Using play in ascertaining children's wishes and feelings

At the point of separation, conciliation can help families to make the least damaging arrangements for their children. It is essential to ascertain the child's wishes and feelings when considering their future care and their continuing contact with parents, especially where parents disagree. The 1989 Children Act requires that the child's welfare should be the paramount consideration 'when the court determines any question with respect to the upbringing and property of the child'. A court officer or conciliator is unlikely to have time for more than the bare minimum of sessions to establish communication (without putting 'undue pressure on the child') and to come to some understanding of how the child perceives the situation and how they feel, hence the need for establishing rapport quickly. This is not a straightforward task of asking children who they would like to live with. Children normally want their parents to resolve their conflicts and stay together. As we have seen they may feel confused and guilty about the separation and ambivalent about what they should do now. It is important to explain to children why they are being seen – for example, 'to have their say' or 'to help parents with their plans' (Garwood 1989: 30). Children say they prefer to be seen on their own, without parents and siblings, as they feel more free to express their views. Play, using mainly focused techniques within an emotionally containing relationship, can help children express how they feel and facilitates communication in the family, helping children relax and raise questions; for example, what a divorce is, whether they will still see their dad when they move house, if mum and dad will still be friends, and who will look after them after school. Play can help less conscious feelings find expression. This requires a setting offering comfort, quiet and privacy, with carefully chosen play materials appropriate to the child and family's culture. The worker follows the child's cues, whilst establishing mood, purpose and pace, providing direction without intrusion, and using empathic reflective listening. Direct questions are to be avoided and 'Can you show me?' is often preferable to 'Can you tell me?'. It is important to be responsive to distress or withdrawal, and not to push the child too far:

> One seven-year-old girl remembered a book, *Dinosaurs Divorce*, containing a calendar which she had subsequently copied at home and used to mark the days when she and her sister were due to visit their father. Two boys recalled how they had drawn a picture of their family home, before explaining to the conciliator about the changes that had taken place in their home. . . . One five-year-old boy, whose father sometimes travelled by plane to visit him, drew a picture of a plane . . . He carefully signed it and asked the conciliator to have it in the room when his parents next met to discuss contact. A boy of six used Lego to build the house where he visited his mother. He demonstrated some of his fears through his play and this helped his parents to understand his feelings and they subsequently modified the contact arrangements.
>
> (Garwood 1989: 32, 34)

Rosemary Gordon (1986) used wooden mosaics (shells, stones or buttons would serve the same purpose) to represent the family of ten-year-old Jenny, making patterns showing how the family used to live together and helping her talk about moves away, close relationships and new family members. Asked to show how she would like things to be, Jenny put her mother back in the family, contrary to reports that she no longer thought about her mother whom she had last seen five years before. Gordon and 12-year-old David drew a graffiti wall covered with all the words or slogans associated with family separation, such as 'tomorrow', 'school', 'being alone', 'fear' and 'death'. They played the *Faces* game, drawing 'what the face feels like when it thinks about . . . making a meal for the family, the past, facing a new family'. She asked David to show her how he would draw the family in shapes and colours, explaining that we all have our smooth sides and our jagged bits. He drew a perfect orange circle for mother; sister was almost a circle with points or 'grumpy bits'; dad was a few harsh strokes in the far corner of the paper. Gordon saw this as alignment with mother, showing David's need to sacrifice one parent for his dependency on the other. With seven-year-old Wayne, Gordon used *Faces* to ask 'What does the face look like when mum rings up?' Its confused and partly neutral expression suggested that he was distancing himself from the choice of one parent or the other by displaying little emotion. Mixed and ambivalent feelings can be revealed by portraying separate expressions on opposite sides of the face, or in two drawings of parts of the body, one of 'the bits of you that want to go' and another for 'the bits that want to stay'. Other play methods, based on ideas from Jewett (1994) and Oaklander (1978), include role play, body sculpturing, music, and talking about angry or sad feelings as shapes or sounds. Brigid Kroll (1994) used genograms to help children think about family dynamics, or an eco-map – cutting out shapes representing chosen people to lay out on the floor, then asking questions such as who would the child take with them, who would worry most, who needed rescuing, and so on. Or they would play the *Holiday* game, finding the accommodation was not big enough and needing to think how to divide family members between two smaller places.

While children find great relief when their views are heard and their feelings recognized, they may value the opportunity to express more complex feelings. Kroll (1994) describes children's different adaptations to parental separation. A 'parental' child hides her vulnerability by caring for others. Playing Winnicott's squiggle game, a 'parental' girl repeatedly drew a worm and demanded that the worker turn it into a snail. Kroll understood her to be telling her about the vulnerable bit of herself and asking her to do something about it. A 'despairing' child, full of grief and sorrow, may resort to manic defences such as a preoccupation with order. A 'retreating' child, full of separation anxiety, seeks the solace of infancy. An 'angry' child may express anger overtly or in passive aggression. Anger is invariably a part of grief, which children need to be able to feel and then express physically (by punching a pillow or cushion, tearing up newspaper, kicking a can, hitting a bed with a racquet or bat), writing all the bad words they can think of, drawing, painting or modelling their anger. They can put their anger into words and say them to the source, such as speaking to the figure in a drawing, or to an imagined person sitting in an empty chair. However, children need also to be able to reflect on their anger, on what causes it, how they feel and how they express it, which is where symbolic play is helpful, as Kroll (1994) describes.

Play techniques in family sessions

Where parents are committed to take joint responsibility for the issues their children raise and for making decisions about their children's future, a family interview or meeting can improve communication between parents and children and help parents work out a solution. Children need to be willing to come. Even pre-verbal children can absorb a great deal through the tone and manner of what is said, and parents may learn from observing their reactions. Garwood describes how a young child's play in the room where his parents were meeting became more frantic when their voices were raised. His parents were able to notice and recognize this. Lisa Parkinson (1987) suggests using play materials, such as houses, play people, finger and glove puppets, and paper and drawing materials, to rehearse with a family how they will manage a contact visit. Jigsaws, with figures that fit into a wooden frame, can help children and parents to look at who fits where in the child's life and to realize that each has something different to offer, helpful to separated fathers who often have no clear role in the divided family. Parents and children who have not seen each other for a while might draw where they live now and ask questions about each other's drawings (see Chapter 5 for other ideas).

Play therapy with children experiencing parental separation

Some children, seriously disturbed by family conflict and break-up, may benefit from a longer period of play therapy. Such children often feel torn in two, not only externally through conflicting loyalties to warring parents but also in terms of their internal world. If one parent comes to represent what is 'good' and the other what is 'bad', there is risk of one parent being idealized and the other denigrated, with a corresponding split in the child's internal world. This splitting is liable to leave the child in Klein's paranoid-schizoid position, with bad feelings unbearable and so projected out, rather than moving towards a more mature integration of good and bad aspects of the self. Oedipal conflicts exacerbate the difficulty, for example, when a boy's identification with the good aspects of his father are attacked by his mother's anger with the bad father who has 'abandoned' them, so that the child too sees his father as bad and so internalizes a view of himself as bad. Therapy can provide the emotional containment which helps a child tolerate both bad and good feelings, representing them symbolically, making them thinkable and so enabling the development of a more integrated sense of self.

In the following case study, children's counsellor Lesley Aberdein used a non-directive play therapy approach to helping a child who was experiencing difficulties as a result of parental conflict and eventual separation:

Jason, ten years old, was distressed by violent rows between his parents. He would try to stop them by creating a distraction, usually something particularly naughty. His younger sister would go upstairs, open the windows and scream. Counselling was offered to parents and children. I saw Jason weekly in the playroom. Jason's parents split up, eventually divorcing and setting up house with new partners. Two sessions in the playroom after the parental split are summarized here.

Jason arrived with mum who said he was desperate to talk to me, adding privately that he had behaved very badly that morning. Later Jason explained that mum had told him he was just like his father and complained that he did nothing but think of dad. Jason spent the session painting and cutting out a horrific, ugly, monster-like mask, which he finished and put on. I asked if he ever felt like the monster and he agreed. He felt sure mum saw him as a monster because he was always being naughty, and because he wanted to be with his dad. For the last few minutes Jason thwacked the punchbag with venom. I asked him if there was anyone he would really like to thump, and he replied, 'Everyone in my family.'

A week later Jason came in with dad, holding his hand tightly, smiling and clearly delighted. Dad left, promising Jason he would see him soon. Today Jason wanted to paint. His painting looked like a cracked window which I reflected. He agreed, then began to colour in one of the cracked pieces a different colour. I asked why part of one window was different and he replied that that was dad's. Like the window, his family had split but it was dad who had left. It was his fault and so dad's part was a different colour. I suggested that just as broken windows could be replaced by new ones, a broken family can also be replaced. The new family, like the new window, would not be the same as the old one but it could eventually be as good as before. Jason looked at me long and hard, then said, 'We had a window which got broken once. We got a new one, and' (here he paused, then continued in a definite, set tone) 'it was exactly the same as the old one!' Jason was not ready or willing to accept the parental split and remained very angry with dad. After this, Jason began to paint again. I looked at it and confessed I found it difficult to make out what he had drawn. 'Look, there's the flowers round about. Does that give you a clue? It's a coffin'. I asked who was in the coffin. 'My family. My family is dead.' We talked about how he felt about the break-up. He expressed anger towards mum who had a boyfriend and would not consider a reconciliation, despite dad's wish to return. He moved to the sandpit and began to bury every single toy. I suggested that there were times when he felt like burying himself away from all the unhappiness around him. He agreed and said, 'Sometimes I just feel like hiding so that I can't see or hear what they are saying. Then when I come out I'll find the family is like it was before.'

Jason at first used the opportunities in the playroom to express his anger at the loss of his family. His monster masks also suggest feelings of guilt and badness, an identification with the father he longs for but also fears being like. His ambivalent feelings are accepted and acknowledged, using the language of their symbolic expression. Although Jason spoke of his anger with both parents, his painting revealed a profound sense of grief and loss as he recognized the death of his family. His grief received recognition and acceptance. Through the emotional holding environment of the therapeutic relationship Jason was able to make use of symbolic play to help him to express and integrate his feelings, becoming able to put them into words where they could be thought about.

Group work for children of separating parents

Children say they would like to meet others in similar situations. Group work helps them realize that they are not alone in their experience of family break-up. It gives an opportunity to talk about things that may be difficult, forbidden or taboo elsewhere, to share feelings, and to learn that the break-up is not their fault. They can learn too that they are not passive victims but can make choices and act on them. The large numbers of children involved in separation and divorce make group work a feasible way of supporting them. Group work with sibling pairs can help them realize that they are a unit and have one another for support at home (Regan and Young 1990).

A group work programme

A suggested programme for a children's group from a divorce court service (*What About Me?*) starts with introductions and ice-breakers, followed by trust or relationship games (from Dearling and Armstrong's *Youth Games Book*). Using a play street map, miniature houses, cars, and play people, children are then asked in turn to show who they live with, where the other parent lives, and what they do when they see them. Or children might draw the two homes showing the people in them. Older children can draw a genogram or family tree, or use mosaics, showing who lives with whom. They can draw faces to show how they feel, for example, 'When I think of school', 'When I feel lonely inside', 'When my parents fight', 'When I go to bed at night'. Younger children may use outline faces to indicate happy, sad, angry or puzzled feelings, while older children can use sentence completion games with phrases such as 'I get angry when . . .', 'My biggest fear is . . .', 'The trouble with dad is . . .'. Feelings can be expressed in listening or moving to music, using musical instruments, using clay or playdough, or drawing them in shapes and colours. Children can make each other into shapes – for example, 'the sad shape I feel when dad doesn't turn up as promised'. Older children may use the group members to sculpt their family. They go on to think about 'What can we do with angry/sad/happy feelings?' and how to tell a parent how they feel, for example, saying 'Mummy, this is my sad shape'. Ways of dealing with anger can be explored. The 'empty chair' can be used to express anger with someone or to practise something that needs to be said. Children can pretend to be the parent or person responding, which can also give a useful insight into their feelings. There may be group storytelling or role play, such as the *Divorce of the Three Bears*. Children might listen to a story, such as Althea's *I Have Two Homes* or Brown and Brown's *Dinosaurs Divorce* for younger ones, Wilson's *Suitcase Kid*, or Blume's *It's Not the End of the World* for older children. Many of the activities suggested for bereavement group work may be helpful. Other programmes may be less structured or based entirely on non-directed play.

Reflecting on group process – the leaders' task

Whether group work has a more or less structured programme, the group leaders still have the task of maintaining a holding environment for the whole group, making it possible for children's difficult thoughts and feelings to be shared, heard and accepted. They need to remain thoughtful about the group process and the meaning of children's individual and group communication. It is often helpful for the group to have two leaders, who alternate between leading activities and attending to the meaning of what is happening. They will also represent a parental couple and so carry projections or transferences based on the children's experiences. This is likely to include some version of splitting, with each leader carrying different projections, maybe one attacked as the bad angry parent and the other protected as the good caring parent. Group leaders need to be in good communication with one another so that they can avoid re-enacting the parental break-up. They also need to pay attention to the children maintaining a 'group' rather than a 'gang' state of mind (Canham and Emanuel 2000), noticing when the group is resorting to fight or flight, pairing or splitting within the group, or becoming overly dependent on the leaders (Bion's basic assumption activity). These defences against anxiety occur when the group does not feel safe and contained. Again the reason needs to be understood so that leaders can better articulate and so contain the anxiety. Feelings put into words or expressed symbolically are less likely to be acted out.

Conclusion

As this chapter has shown, there are different ways of using play in being alongside children who have experienced separation and loss and being receptive to their communication. It may simply be the provision of a 'third thing' (Clare Winnicott's phrase) – perhaps a toy or an activity, something that we and the child (or group of children) can focus on, easing communication.

Symbolic play enables the expression of less conscious feelings in the presence of a receptive worker, a process which in itself is healing. Some very distressed children will benefit from a longer period of play therapy so that they can work through complicated and ambivalent emotions.

Each child's experience of separation and loss is individual and unique, and the meaning of that loss needs to be understood. A broader understanding of theory and research can inform our thinking about a specific loss but it is no substitute for engagement with the child's particular feelings. Our openness to what a child is communicating means that we must also be open to being stirred up by the child's painful feelings. It matters to be able to hold on to and think about those feelings, rather than resort to a defensive reassurance of the child or a distancing from their pain. We need to be aware of our own feelings and working at understanding their origin, whether as a communication from children's present experience or from our own history, or in combination. It is here that knowledge and use of the self are crucial to the work. No amount of structured programming will substitute for the emotional holding environment provided by workers capable of thinking about the meaning of what a child or group is communicating. If we are to provide this containment we need to be in good emotional touch with one another, helping each other to think about process and noticing where we may be using defences against anxiety. Supervision – both individual and group – and consultation have an important role here.

An experience of separation and loss, however painful, is not necessarily damaging to a child's secure attachment and to their inner working model of the world as one which they can trust to love and care for them, although it can certainly threaten this, for a time at least. Where families, schools and communities can be supported to provide emotional containment, their children may manage a painful loss. However, children who have experienced separations and losses in infancy or who suffer repeated, sometimes traumatic, losses have much more difficulty in developing an integrated sense of self. Their inner working model is of a world that cannot be relied on and their view of self is that they are not worthy of love or care. The help they need is much more complex, which is the subject of the following chapters.

Chapter 8

Therapeutic play with children who have experienced continual trauma and loss

A number of children have lived in families and the wider world in which they have had insufficient protection or care, and so have had to find their own ways of managing to survive in dangerous environments. Deprivation, neglect or abuse means they have experienced continual trauma and loss. Some have lacked 'good enough' parenting for most of their lives. They have lived in families where domestic violence, parental substance abuse and mental health problems, such as psychosis, self-harm or periods of depression, are common place, often with cycles of damage and deprivation going back over the generations. Parents are unable to hold in mind their child as a person in their own right but see them in terms of their own phantasies and needs, as a 'ghost in the nursery' (Fraiberg 1980). Parents who are emotionally unavailable leave children feeling abandoned, rejected and frightened. Domestic violence, even if not directed at the child, leaves them unable to receive relief of their fear from a frightened parent. Some parents and carers are directly frightening, terrorizing through bullying and physical violence and abuse, including sexual abuse. Sometimes the danger comes from outside the immediate family, as in some sexual abuse as well as bullying or gang violence. Dangers include social services and multiple moves in the care system. The immediate family may be socially powerless to protect their child, whether through poverty or otherwise living on the margins of society, sometimes as part of a social group experiencing extreme racism, oppression, social conflict, persecution or war.

How seriously a child is affected depends on whether there is an available attachment figure to offer care and protection and to be able to bear to think about the child's experience, that is, to hold the child in mind. Where this exists the child tends to be more resilient (Fonagy *et al.* 1994). Children who experienced damaging attachments are more vulnerable. How a child is affected also depends on how predictable the danger is from the child's point of view. The predictably dangererous carer can be managed to some extent by the child learning to become completely compliant or by caretaking (looking after the carer), whatever will keep them safest – that is, by developing a 'false self' which involves denying aspects of their real selves but leaving them with some capacity to think. The unpredictably dangerous parent or carer is managed by the child tuning in to their emotional state and being for the most part angrily coercive, that is, highly controlling, with a disarming sudden switch of strategy to being charmingly seductive. Crittenden's developmental attachment model helps illuminate these patterns (Figure 1.1, p. 13). Another crucial factor is how early in life the child was affected. A child who was initially cared for well enough to develop some sense of self may find ways to manage fear, although, of course, continuing trauma will take a psychological toll. The child whom no one has ever held in mind and whose self has therefore remained fragmented is in a state of continuing terror, helplessness and inability to think, devoid of strategies.

Some children are still living with their families, although often the family structure has changed as adults or children have left or been added. Others move between their family and foster care or a residential home or school. The most emotionally damaged children require therapeutic care in every aspect of their daily life. When this is not available, they ricochet through a series of failed placements or even adoption, in the process becoming ever more disturbed. Play approaches are important in contributing to an assessment of a child's needs since they offer access to the child's inner world, to the child's inner working model of themselves and the world. The results of assessment need to inform treatment. However, treatment invariably needs to go beyond offering play therapy or psychotherapy. The child cannot change unless their experience of the world changes. Play therapy will rarely achieve this alone. It needs to be part of a much larger programme of continuing work with the child's network of care, including family, the school and the child's carers, whether residential or foster or adoptive care.

As workers we may experience considerable anxiety as we search for appropriate skills in communicating with children who may have been abused. Our own reactions to abuse are invariably strong, and feelings of anger, disgust and revulsion may cloud initial judgements of the best way to help. The child who perceives a worker's shocked reaction will beat a rapid retreat, confirming their impression that the subject is not acceptable and cannot be discussed. We need to be in touch with our own history and aware of our vulnerable areas so that we are less likely to be taken by surprise and more able to offer an open and accepting response to children's communication. We need to empathize with a child's pain, anger or confusion and resist any urge either to rescue or to retreat into so-called 'professional' distancing (Hoxter 1983). We must stay in touch with our feelings aroused in the work, able to reflect on them rather than act on them. These feelings are often a communication from the child, a projection or 'transference' of their feelings in relation to the significant people in their lives, providing us with essential information about their inner world and the kind of help they need (Copley and Forryan 1987/1997; Hardwick and Woodhead 1999). The best clue to how children are really feeling lies in how they make us feel, whether it is useless, no good, wiped out or annihilated, helpless or 'bad'. Play may contain this indirect communication even when it offers little that can be interpreted as a direct communication.

To stay in touch with the child's sometimes quite horrific experience may take all the emotional strength we can muster. We will feel sickened, contaminated, confused and helpless, but unless we can endure these feelings without defending against them the child will not believe that their experience can be endured or that they are worth anything. The task is to survive, with our capacity for concern for the child remaining undiminished. This offers the child hope. Support in the form of supervision and consultation needs to be available as a matter of course to help us understand the feelings aroused and to use them in the service of the child.

We first consider how play approaches and non-directive play may contribute to assessment and then examine the part of therapeutic play and play therapy in treatment itself.

Play in assessment of the child's inner world

Non-directive play in assessment

As workers we may understandably feel anxious about our ability to make an adequate assessment of a child we are meeting for the first time. There is a temptation to reassure ourselves by preparing all sorts of tasks and activities which risk distracting us from the task of paying attention to how the child is. To understand a child's inner world and their working model of attachment simply sitting in a playroom with them will tell us a great deal about how they expect the world to treat them. A securely attached child is free to explore and play while an anxious child needs to be constantly monitoring their attachment figure, fearing abandonment or threat. If we say to the child 'Explore the room, play with what you like – I'm just going to sit here', then procedurally the child has to fall back on past relationships as a guide. We soon pick up something of the child's expectations. The worker 'may have a sense that the child wants to please her or take care of her in small ways, indicating compliance or caretaking', suggesting a defended attachment, 'or quickly find herself in a struggle for dominance more typical of coercive children. Frightened, possibly "disorganized" children, may find the confines of the playroom too threatening and the whole session is spent negotiating with the child about boundaries or, in everyday language, trying to keep the child in the room' (Farnfield 2001: 66).

Social workers have a duty to establish the wishes and feelings of children involved in care proceedings, and to ensure that they understand as far as they can what is happening and why. Some more integrated children may be able to think about these questions and put them into words, perhaps with the help of a 'third thing' to ease communication (such as an eco map or flow chart, see Chapter 2). Most children, however, have some ambivalent feelings, many below the level of consciousness. Play, especially symbolic play, frees them to express their feelings and fantasies. Non-directive play sessions can work well as assessments, sometimes in parallel with a more direct interview which can be carried out by a different worker. Occasionally some direct questions may be included in the play session, although this takes great skill in avoiding disruption of the child's self-directed play. The main risk is that the worker's mind becomes preoccupied by their intended question or activity, impairing the ability to provide an inner mental space to think about the child's communication. Non-directive play can provide the emotional containment which makes the assessment process more bearable, giving the child autonomy within safe boundaries, important in reducing their sense of powerlessness. A non-directive approach means 'the child is largely free from the effects of suggestion and coercion' (Ryan and Wilson 2000: 277), which make it more acceptable as evidence in court proceedings, although symbolic play requires careful presentation which avoids over-interpretation (Ryan and Wilson 1996).

Story stem and other assessments

Narrative stem exercises often work best if they are introduced as unintrusively as possible at an opportune moment when child and adult are playing together. Using miniature animals or dolls the worker starts to tell a story, for example, setting up a family of pigs and saying, 'This little pig goes off for a walk . . . oh dear, (s)he's lost, (s)he doesn't know how to get home. . . . Can you show or tell me what happens next?' The child's response often provides a useful glimpse of their inner working model of attachment, which can help the worker in forming a hypothesis. Does someone in the family come to rescue the little pig? Does the little pig manage to find its own way home and, if so, what is their reception on return (pleasure, anger, not noticed)? Does someone else rescue the pig? Or does someone or something threaten or kill the pig, or, as one child said, 'He just died.' Catastrophic fantasies such as these tend to appear in the stories of the most traumatized children. While the *content* of the stories indicates the extent of a child's expectation of protection and care, the *way* children tell their stories is also diagnostic. A coherent story, even if a sad tale, suggests a child able to integrate thinking and feeling, which suggests a secure enough attachment to someone or somewhere past or present. By contrast an unfinished meandering story without direction suggests a child with a preoccupied or ambivalent attachment – they are lost in feelings without coherent thought. An avoidantly attached 'dismissing' child may change the story or cut it short, avoiding any engagement with feelings. Using several of these stories (Bretherton *et al.* 1990; Hodges *et al.* 2003), together with further play observations, we can look for repeating patterns which can help us either to confirm or to revise our hypotheses. The Separation Anxiety Test uses photographs in a similar way (Wright *et al.* 1995). For older children and adolescents a number of autobiographical and attachment interviews have been developed, including a useful Attachment Style Interview (Bifulco *et al.* in press). For the youngest children observation of the child in the equivalent of a Strange Situation (for example, reunion with a carer who returns to collect a child) provides useful clues to the child's models of attachment. In any case it is always important to get the child's history, which in itself can show to what extent the child has experienced dangerous environments (Farnfield 2001).

Communication through play of possible sexual abuse

Ferenczi (1984) wrote of the harmful effects on children of the 'confusion of tongues' in sexual abuse, in which the language of tenderness becomes confused with the language of sexual passion. The sexual abuse of children became widely recognized in the 1980s, creating a furore as society was forced to contemplate its existence but at the same time wishing to deny it. Social workers and others were pilloried at the time for their investigations, but research in subsequent years made clear that sexual abuse of children of all ages is widespread, occurring at all levels of society and across cultures and time. What has changed is recognition of the human rights of the child. Young children may not be aware that the abuse is wrong although they may know they do not like it. Older children are often torn by conflicting feelings. They may feel it is their fault, especially if some pleasure has been involved in the abuse. They may feel it is all they deserve. They may have been bound to secrecy and told of terrible consequences for the family if the abuse is found out. They have been manipulated and lied to. Sometimes the abuser is the only person in their lives who gives them any kind of nurturing, however distorted, which compounds the child's confusion. They have experienced adults with enormous power over them, their trust has been destroyed and they are not likely to trust readily any adult. Looked at in terms of Erikson's tasks of emotional development, instead of basic trust the child learns mistrust, instead of autonomy the child learns shame and self-doubt, instead of initiative guilt, and instead of industry inferiority. The child reaching adolescence experiences role confusion instead of developing a sense of identity.

Workers in daily contact with normal children are in a good position to be alert to signs of distress in a child. Young children who have been abused are often confused, angry and unhappy, with low self-esteem. Bentovim *et al.* (1988) notes that sexually abused young children tend to show sexualized behaviour, and regressive behaviour such as wetting, soiling, eating problems and sleep disturbance. They may have fears of specific rooms, such as the bathroom, or of particular people, such as men of a given size or hair colour. Older children have much stronger feelings of stigmatization and shame, of having a terrible secret to hide, of feeling dirty, powerless and betrayed. They have found that the most important adults in their lives are not to be trusted. Worse, they come to believe that it is their fault that they have not been looked after so their self-esteem is low. Some children find it difficult to concentrate at school but others find escape by putting their efforts into high achievement. Their feelings may be variously expressed, in 'acting-out' unmanageable behaviour, in withdrawn and depressed behaviour, in tummy pains or illness, or in highly conformist 'good' behaviour, perhaps staying close to the teacher. Girls are likely to end up as typical 'victims'; boys are more likely to identify with the aggressor. However, factors other than sexual abuse can cause these sorts of behaviour and a worker or teacher is simply alerted to the possibility. Familiarity with normal development and play leads workers to notice a child whose response to adults or whose play is unusually sexualized and goes beyond normal mummies and daddies, or doctors and nurses, play. Four-year-olds are interested in sexual differences and may explore them in play, but a detailed enactment of sexual intercourse or of sexual variations is unlikely and should raise questions as to the source of their knowledge. With children of primary school age, as well as being alert to more general signs of distress, workers may become concerned if they observe sexually explicit play in the playground or if a child behaves in a sexualized way towards other children or seductively to adults.

Whilst children's play may give warning signals it can also be a way of listening to the child and finding out what is wrong. The early years worker can use reflective listening as the child plays spontaneously, for example, about monsters who come in the night. With school age children who are more likely to draw attention to their plight indirectly, it may be helpful to create a play situation in which the adult can be involved alongside the child, perhaps drawing and painting, or using clay, puppets or stories, showing a readiness to accept whatever the child's communication may be. For example, a ten-year-old girl had been attending a primary school unit for disturbed children with no apparent suspicion of abuse when her teacher happened to suggest she drew her dream house. She drew a house with windows, with patterns of dots and colours. In the garden to the left of the house she painted 'mum's towel' and her 'sister's swing'. On the right she painted a big black rectangular towel which she labelled 'dad'. On an intuition her teacher started to talk about having her own bedroom where you don't have to let anyone in; people have to knock and ask. She asked, 'Does anyone come into your room when you don't want them to?' The child replied, 'I've got a terrible tummy ache' and put her head in her hands. Her teacher sat quietly reading to her, avoiding further intrusion but alerted to the possibility of abuse. If a child creates the story we need to keep to the symbolism. For example, one child told a story about a princess who had to kiss the prince and did not want to. The adult said, 'It sounds like the princess needs some help to stop the prince,' telling the child, 'I would be unhappy and frightened if that happened to me . . . Has anything like what happened to the princess happened to you?' (Peake 1989). We need to relieve the child of responsibility by saying, 'Some secrets are too big to keep.' Repeating what the child says or reflecting back what they are doing shows that we are listening carefully, are not in a hurry, and are not shocked or frightened by what they have to say.

Willies and marys

Early years workers may be the first people outside the family that a child gets to know, and therefore also the first people to have a chance to recognize when a child may have been abused. Observation of a child's spontaneous play can alert workers to the possibility that something may be wrong. A boy's frightened reaction to the television set in the home corner led to finding out that his father had made him watch video 'nasties'. His mother had not understood why he was frightened to go to bed at night but could now protect him. Workers in one centre provided special one-to-one play times using a box of toys in a quiet corner of the playroom. Other workers would recognize what was going on and subtly minimize interruption or distraction. Going at the child's pace and responding to their overtures in spontaneous play helps children to communicate about what is troubling them:

> Lisa's mother was worried by her four-year-old daughter's nightmares and agreed to one-to-one play sessions. Lisa said spiders had frightened her and 'I don't like willies by my face.' In a cooking session making jam tarts the worker announced, 'You can lick it in a minute' (meaning the spoon) and Lisa said 'I don't want to play the licking game.' Playing with playdough, she made a pastry man with a big mouth, a belt with a huge buckle and a long stick 'to make you do it'. She insisted that the man had a big willy, 'cause they're always big ain't they?' The worker echoed her words, showing that she was listening and not shocked, and copied the pastry man in a drawing with Lisa blacking in the eyes and the big mouth. She drew black squiggles at the bottom corner which she said was 'the mess, 'cause you see there's always a mess after'. The worker later took the pastry man to show to the child protection conference.

It may take a long time for children to show what is happening to them:

> Social workers were already anxious about three-year-old Nina and the centre was finding her behaviour manipulative and unpleasant. Nina's mother was fond of her, but she was an alcoholic and had a volatile

relationship with another man Rob as well as Nina's father, and was often bruised, comatose or absent. Playing with the toy box Nina said the big soft owl who likes children was 'crying . . . afraid of the dark . . . Jack Frost killed him . . . there are witches in my bedroom'. Later she said, 'There are snakes in my bedroom, they sleep behind the chair.' A doll was 'crying cos no one loves me'. She drew eyes, with 'big drips', saying 'Rob makes her sad', and 'Rob's long face with all his mouths'. Playing with the doll's house, Nina told the Rob doll 'Get out of my bedroom', putting him in bed with mum. She took another man doll and tried to take off his trousers, saying 'He goes in my bed and wakes up in the morning and puts his trousers on.' Amid mounting concern, all staff were made aware of the need to listen carefully and one reported the following conversation. Nina talked of her dark house with monsters saying, 'The goblin touched my mum and Mum's mary.' ('Did he?') 'Yes.' ('What did he do?') 'He touched my mary.' ('Mm?') 'Yes, he scratched me.' ('Who was this goblin?') 'He had a mask on but it was my dad.' Later Nina told the centre leader, 'I've just told Tina my secrets.' ('Have you?') 'Yes, I've told her I've got a goblin in my house.' Then she abruptly changed the subject and chatted about a little dog. Nina's drawings continued to show mum crying or not well, and everyone being sad. Through these months a series of child protection meetings involving the network of agencies working with the family monitored the situation closely, aware of the indications of sexual abuse but lacking real evidence on which to act. This is a common situation which causes great anxiety for all concerned.

Using knowledge of child development, children's memory and pretend play

We need an understanding of the stages of a child's development, including intellectual and language development and play (see Chapter 1), if we are to assess accurately what a child is communicating whether in words or actions. The quality of children's memory is an issue of particular importance. Evidence suggests that what children remember is not essentially different from what adults remember, especially for central events in their lives. In recognizing pictures and faces, young children under five do as well as older children. There is evidence that children can remember things from their earliest years, even abuse which they were not aware was such at the time. This occurs mainly in procedural memory but some children retain images, and memories of sounds and smells, and for very young children imaged memory may be dominant. Young children may have difficulty in remembering details of events, such as places and times, if these are asked as abstractions and out of context. They do much better if given the opportunity to relate a familiar sequence of events, such as going to bed, using 'script' or episodic memory (Fundudis 1989; Crittenden 2000). Any adult questions must be open ended, with no hint of a suggested reply. Young children are more likely than older children to agree with an adult's suggestion, probably because of their experience of the power of adults, but even so they seldom go along with major suggestions that they know to be incorrect. Children under five usually respond honestly to the question as they perceive it. However, if they are able to anticipate the expected answer they may give this instead. Older children are more able to resist suggestions but are capable of lying, and may do so for many reasons, including fear and guilt. Hesitant and confused accounts are more likely to be true than a coherent, 'pat', unemotional one. There are numerous pressures on children not to be truthful. An allegation of sexual abuse leads to immense pressure on the child, within and without the family, so that denial and retraction commonly follow. Whilst each individual situation must be carefully evaluated, children are far more likely to lie in retracting and denying abuse than in making an initial allegation.

A common concern is that children may be unable to distinguish fact from fantasy. Young children cannot fantasize about events completely outside their experience although they may make wrong interpretations of real situations. Nina's goblins, in the preceding example, are a case in point. Whilst the goblins, known about through books or television stories, are fantasy representations of alarming people, touching her 'mary' (a dialect word for vagina) is most unlikely to occur in stories and more likely to be based on experience. Her statement cannot, therefore, be dismissed as fantasy and needs further investigation. Lack of sexual play does not mean the child has *not* been abused, neither does explicit sexual play mean the child *has* been abused, but used with other indicators they can help to build up a picture of the child's experience.

Therapy through play for abused and traumatized children

The task of therapy

Therapy can normally only take place when the child is safe and no longer living in a dangerous environment. Until then children need all their defences. As long as the child is safe, part of the task of the therapy might be to help the child manage a transition, or series of transitions, when the child's relationship with the worker may be the one stable factor in their life. Not all children need therapy if their carers can provide a listening containing experience. 'It can be a message of rejection to a hurting child: "I cannot bear to listen so I'll send you to a professional"' (Hunter 2001: 23). However, some more integrated children may find great relief in a short period of one-to-one therapy while more seriously damaged or 'stuck' children will need a longer and more intensive therapeutic experience.

The aftermath of recognition of an abusing or otherwise dangerous environment may sometimes be as traumatic for the child as the original trauma, often involving separations and loss of a member of the family. Therapy may need to address both. It needs to go entirely at the child's pace and can continue for a long time before the child plays out any specific episodes of abuse. (One problem which sometimes arises then is further disclosure of abuse. The worker may have to act, especially if another perpetrator is involved.) Therapy is dealing above all with the child's general feelings of hurt and damage; the word trauma means wounded or pierced. We know that early and continuing trauma affects the brain, sensitizing it so that it becomes prone to hyper-arousal under any stress. Therapy therefore needs to provide a calm and soothing environment. Wilson (2006) describes trauma as a nonsensical experience, that is, one devoid of meaning. The child has experienced *unbearable betrayal* (by those who should be caring for the child), *immobilizing powerlessness, outrageous intrusion* (forced intimacy of the child bodily or mental space removing what little control children have over their bodies and over their lives), *intolerable anxiety* (of death or annihilation, and perhaps of losing control in excitement which is not understood), and *impossible comprehension* (although the child has usually tried to give the experience meaning by their feeling of somehow having deserved it, adding to their hurt). The child's life has been based on lies, not only self-protective lies following threats of harm but the more serious denial by the abuser of the child's pain and distress which leaves the child doubting the reality of their experience (Hunter 2001: 90–91). The task of therapy is to give back meaning. In attachment terms this is about helping the child internalize a coherent narrative of their life, that is, to connect feeling and thinking in reflecting on their experience.

Materials for play

As well as a range of play material (see Chapter 3), some workers also have available some particular toys, based on Madge Bray's (1991) toy box, used widely at the time to help children disclose sexual abuse. These include 'nice' and 'horrible' toys, snakes and worms, a knife, scissors, spiders, a crocodile, a plastic winged bat with a big mouth, a big tongue monster, a hammer, a mask, a play medical kit, a piece of sheepskin, two pandas 'hugging' each other, dolls with a happy face on one side and a sad face on the other, a big-mouthed doll, a Red Riding Hood granny doll that turned upside down becomes a wolf. The anatomically complete dolls once popular in work with possibly abused children are considered too provocative. Many toys enable symbolic expression of anger, for example, a Rambo puppet with boxing gloves. Other items might be an old camera (some children have been used for pornography), a whoopee cushion (giving permission for 'rude' things), books containing anatomical drawings, such as Rayner's *The Body Book*, special drawing and colouring books, and jigsaw puzzles of people whose clothes can be removed. Stories with which children can identify provide a symbolic mode for working through feelings. Older children may like fairy stories, such as *The Ugly Duckling, Snow White* or *Hansel and Gretel*, or stories of good triumphing over evil. Younger children need stories nearer to home such as *Can't You Sleep, Little Bear?*, which provide openings to explore important matters. Some stories have been specially written about sexual abuse, such as *I'm Glad I Told Mum*, Rouf's *Mousie* and *Secrets*.

Therapy for more integrated children with moderate trauma

Remembering in order to forget

Where the child's family or carer provides continuing care and concern, or can be helped to do so, and when the danger to the child has been limited in occurrence and duration, a brief period of play therapy may be enough to give many abused children enough confidence to continue with their daily lives. Through symbolic play, within an emotionally containing relationship with a thinking worker, a child can give meaning to their experience. 'The more mildly traumatized patient, whose disorder is affecting his personality on the neurotic level, may need to remember the trauma in order to forget' (Alvarez 1992: 151). The task of therapy is to restore the child's trust in appropriate people, to give appropriate power back to the child, to respect both their bodies and their minds and so restore their self-respect, to help the child manage fear, to accept anger, grief, disgust and other overwhelming feelings, restoring the capacity for normal relationships of mutual sharing and care.

We need to let the child know that we recognize that bad things have happened to them, avoiding collusion in keeping it secret, so that they can raise the subject when they wish. Children need to understand that they are not to blame, that they are right to tell, that they are not responsible for what happens to their family, and that they have a right to protection. Therapy needs to restore children's feeling that they are normal. Parents or foster parents may be involved in some parts of therapy to help them to understand the child's feelings. Sometimes taking the therapy to wherever the child is living makes this process easier (Weinstein 1987), although it is arguable that the child's home should not be the place where painful feelings are stirred up (Doyle 1987, 1990). Further help needs to be available at future stress points. The child's first need in therapy, however, may be less about the trauma of abuse and more about their current experience of separation and loss, as the following example shows.

Not being good enough and not being wanted – fear, anger and grief in role play

The more integrated child with some good early experience is often ready to make use of symbolic play, including role play. A play therapist discusses her work with two children, one in foster care and one in kinship care, who both used role play to explore their feelings about losing their families:

Cindy, aged five, and her younger sister recently came into foster care. Cindy role played with me saying, 'You're my little sister and we have lost our mum,' ending with her taking me by the hand and saying, 'Come on, we're not good enough, we've got to find a new family.' Shooting with a pretend gun, Cindy said, 'I'm going to shoot mummy x [foster mother], I'm cross with her, she's bad, she won't throw the boys out' [foster mother's own children]. Cindy then turned on me, demanding to know why I didn't throw out the hats that didn't fit her. I acknowledged how angry she was at having to share mummy x and also share me with the other children. Underlying this was her fear that she was not good enough for anybody and would ultimately be rejected.

Another time Cindy directed me to come to the 'shop' (with a particular doll, which appeared to stand for her), and say that the doll had lost its mum and Cindy was going to look after her. Cindy as foster mum became more and more impatient towards the doll and then yelling 'I can't cope, I can't give her what she needs,' she called me back. Another version of this involved Cindy alternating between being a child, who tried and failed to be good, and a foster mum who got crosser and crosser for no apparent reason. This culminated in Cindy as foster mum shouting down the play telephone, 'I can't look after her any more, I can't go on, she's got to go. They've got to find a new family, I don't want her, I've chosen the wrong one, the other children don't want her.' Cindy looked sad and said, 'No one wants us, we're not good enough.' I empathized with her feelings. She had at this point just moved foster placement and the sentiments expressed were, from her point of view, essentially accurate. To try and give false reassurance or to tell her it was not true would have denied her feelings and implied that they were unacceptable, compounding her belief that she was 'not good enough' for anyone to want to keep. She then made an idealized family, Cindy being a loving foster mum to the dolls. She made the telephone ring. 'Hello. Yes, they're having a meeting to decide if she can stay.' (This undoubtedly referred to a review meeting she supposedly knew nothing about.) Cindy was not sure what the answer would be. She sighed and said tiredly, 'It's going on years.'

Mary, aged eight, lives happily with her grandparents. Early on she made a story in the sand tray. She created a home for a family of seals, father, mother and baby. The baby got separated from its parents and was put into a different enclosure, where the parents can see her. They try to get in but the baby doesn't want them to. 'She likes it living away from her mum and dad.' The mother later gets in but Mary said the dad wasn't allowed as 'the government wouldn't let him'. (Her dad had been in jail.) Another time she chose small figures and made the child hit the mother. I wondered aloud what was happening. Mary said, 'You've got to guess.' (She was quite angry with me for not understanding all her unspoken needs.) I commented that the girl seemed very angry with her mum, to which Mary replied emphatically, 'Yes.' I speculated that maybe the girl thought that her mum didn't want her. Mary replied, 'Well you've got that right at least!' Recently Mary, now a year older, has spoken more directly of her family and the person she refers to as her 'ex-mother'.

These are two hurt and angry children. Cindy shows both her anger and her underlying fear at not being wanted by her mother, although on the surface her play is about rejection by foster parents and therapist. Mary is angry with her mother for not wanting her and not being able to meet her needs for mothering. Like Cindy she projects some of this anger on to the therapist. The therapist's role is sometimes a direct empathic reflection of the child's feelings, sometimes an acknowledgement of the child's feelings through playing roles assigned by the child.

Realizing, symbolizing and conceptualizing anger

A non-statutory agency team describes helping Paul face his anger, so that he could learn to manage it:

Eight-year-old Paul had been physically abused and had witnessed his brother being sexually assaulted by their father. Both children had been threatened with knives and locked in dark bare rooms. In one year in care Paul has had four foster homes; his brother has been placed separately. We work with both children individually. Paul was able to talk freely about events but spoke in a very matter-of-fact tone, as though they had happened to someone else. At first he rejected play therapy, not being able to cope with free play where he felt out of control. He preferred the structure of expressing his thoughts through drawing, writing or questionnaires. It was a year before he was ready to share his true feelings. One day the words started to come flooding out and Paul became oblivious to any other work. Using a large floor cushion to represent dad he climbed on a cupboard to jump on him, stabbed and shot him, bound him up like a parcel and hung him from a curtain rail. He tied the toy guns, knives, snakes and spiders around the cushion with a camera placed to take pictures if dad tried to escape. He wrote on the cushion 'Dad Jones leave him here', and on paper to his brother wrote 'This is for you I hate Dad, bastard, wanker'. He left his 'display' until the next week so that his brother could see it and know how he felt. When Paul returned we took photographs. Since then, Paul has learned that in his sessions it is acceptable to express angry and destructive feelings in ways that are not allowed (and which he does not allow himself) at school or at home. He often tests his foster mother's and our own rules but the attractive side of his personality is emerging. We have frequent discussions with his foster mother about our work with Paul and she understands that what he does with us is quite separate from what she provides.

That it took a year of structured work before Paul felt able to reveal his anger emphasizes the importance of going at the child's pace, however slow this may seem. Collaboration between therapists and foster parents was important so that each could understand the other's role and set appropriate and different limits. Hunter (2001: 35) reminds us that 'a child needs to know that the adults work together behind the scenes' but it doesn't mean the details of therapy are shared. 'Therapy often captures the distressed part of a child and frees their life for other more positive experiences.' Dockar-Drysdale's (1990: 120) stages towards integration illuminate the process of Paul's anger work. First he had to *experience* and *realize*, or become aware of, his anger, which he then *symbolized* in his 'display'. Finally, by writing and taking photographs he was able to *conceptualize* it, that is, put it into a form in which he could think about it and talk about it.

From anger to grief

Role playing with role reversal can be helpful. The abused child might become the powerful controlling monster and worker plays the role given by the child, usually the victim, as Anne Bannister (1989: 80) describes:

> 'I'm frightened,' I say (as the child), 'I'm going to tell Mummy.' 'No you're not,' says the child. 'Mummy will be cross, you're feeling mad'. . . Because the child has told me I'm 'feeling mad', I respond to the monster's attack with gusto and a battle (which did not happen in the real abusive situation) ensues. My child puppet may eventually lose the battle for this is the element of realism. But next time we play the game the child may want to play herself and actually express some of her anger that she could not do at the time of abuse.

Bannister (1989: 90) tells how one little boy repeatedly placed a 'boy' doll in a cradle and then attacked it with a 'daddy' doll. Because the child was tearful the worker picked up the doll to protect it and the boy stopped playing. 'It was suggested to the worker that next time she should allow the attack to continue but express sympathy with the baby. "Poor little boy, he must be feeling very frightened and lonely" she said as the "daddy" doll attacked the baby again. The boy began to cry, as he had not done before. He seemed to experience relief from his pain and was able to start to share his feelings.' This reminds us to stay with the child's grief and fear, often more painful to think about than anger. As feelings become more thinkable the child can make some kind of sense of their experience and start to move on.

Therapy with children experiencing multiple trauma and loss

Forgetting in order to remember

It is a much harder task to heal the child who has experienced multiple traumatic abuse and loss, sometimes from infancy, 'where the trauma begins to colour the whole of the personality' (Alvarez 1992: 152). Lack of self-esteem is pervasive and extremely damaging. Whilst some children remain passive and frozen 'victims', others exert what power they can and become bullies or seducers of other children. For example, one abused girl's figures of the 'monster' and the 'ballet dancer' illustrate how she internalized her parents so that they became part of herself – father is a menacing sexual gorilla, while mother, the dancer standing on one leg with arms raised, is both seductive and helpless (Hunter 1986). Identification with the aggressor, familiar from hostage situations, is a defence against the terror of complete helplessness and dependence, turning the child into an 'ugly restless predator with a poisonous bite' (Hunter 2001: 116). This may be concealed beneath a compliant false self or simply lie alongside the needy child who longs to be cared for. Or the child may attack their own thinking ability, through drugs or self-harm, becoming their own abuser. Even more damaging is lack even of a sense of self in some fragmented children who have suppressed all feeling by dissociation and eventually become emotionally and cognitively blunted, devoid of any real feelings or sensations.

All these children need a longer and more intensive therapeutic experience, which may include play therapy (Cattanach 1992; West 1992; Ryan and Wilson 1996; Wickham and West 2002; Rymaszewska and Philpot 2006) or child psychotherapy (Hunter 2001; Cant 2002; Lanyado 2004), as part of therapeutic care in daily living. The child 'may need to forget the trauma in order to be able to remember' (Alvarez 1992: 151). The worker has to become the container for the child's projected unbearable feelings, holding on to and tolerating them without retaliation or placating, and over a long period, without passing them back to the child even as a reflection. This provides a version of the soothing and nurturing good mothering experience that the child has missed. 'While this non-abusing world is built up the therapist may have to respect the child's need to keep out both abuse and the past.' From this 'safe and protected and hopeful perspective' (Alvarez 1992: 161–162), the child can start eventually to digest feelings and begin to think and remember. Alvarez reminds us:

> A.thought becomes thinkable often by a very slow gradual process, a process which cannot be rushed. . . . The 'remembering' may involve a million tiny integrations taking place, each one under conditions where other aspects of the abuse, other integrations, can afford to be forgotten. The abuse may have to be explored one aspect at a time; for example, through doll play the child may explore what it feels like 'to be told to lie down and to have to do something when you have no say in the matter?
>
> (Alvarez 1992: 153)

We need to keep a firm boundary between a thought or fantasy and an action or deed. We also need to stay with the symbolism of play without any attempt to interpret its meaning (which to the child can feel like an attack), except in a way which offers hope. Similarly, if we say 'You seem to find it hard to believe I won't reject you because you attack me', the child hears only the rejection. Instead we need to say something like 'You are finding it hard to hope that I will go on being here for you.'

The following examples of longer term therapeutic work illustrate some children's emotional responses to abuse. They emphasize the difficulty of the task of therapy and the slow pace which it may require. For sexually abused children whose every conceivable boundary has been breached in the past safe boundaries are vital. We may need to place limits on behaviour in the session, including if the child tries to touch us inappropriately, even in play. The child may be inviting (or think we are inviting) an abusive relationship, which may be the only kind they know. We need to recognize and resist colluding in what is an enactment rather than a working through. 'Some children seem quite unclear where they end and you begin' (Hunter 2001: 96) and use projective merger which can feel almost unbearably intrusive. A child who has developed an identification with the aggressor may be literally sickening to be with, as child psychotherapist Margaret Hunter (1991: 297) describes:

> Julia unrelentingly attacked, denigrated and humiliated the 'babies', attacked the mother-doll's breasts with the sharp points of a pencil, and forced a sharp scissor between the mother-doll's legs. The babies were made to put their heads into the toilet to eat their food while she laughed and sneered at them . . . I had a sudden terrible realization I was about to be sick. I had to forcibly distract myself by looking out of the window for a few moments. The feeling passed, and I was again able to talk with her about a mother who bears babies but does not feed them, who forces them to resort to a toilet for food, to their own waste products because life-giving milk is withheld.

While play therapists may not offer this level of interpretation they share the need to be able both to feel the child's pain and endure, 'and not to vomit it out' (Hunter 1991: 298). Here are two examples of workers containing a child's feelings of confusion and mess.

Anger and confusion beneath a compliant false self

Alice had been abused from infancy until the age of eight when she went to live with foster parents. She protected herself with a false self. If her foster parents told her to go and play in the garden because she was noisy she would go out and run in circles with a fixed smile on her face, being 'good'. In the residential therapeutic community she told her worker about her abuse while buying Coca-Cola in the supermarket; at home it was a reward for sex. Alice would tell people in a distanced matter-of-fact way, avoiding pain. She was so confused about her identity that in a game touching body parts she was not able to put her hands on her head or her nose. She does not know where she is or even *if* she is. Alice loved the playroom and the idea that there she has those 40 minutes a week to *be*. Her therapeutic care worker described her first playroom session with Alice:

> Usually a very delicate child, Alice slopped paint on to the paper. When she had finished and was about to give her painting to me she checked

herself, saying, 'I don't have to. It's my time.' She started singing and dancing. She dressed up for a while, then got out the tea things. She did not know what to do with them, and made 'baked potatoes' and 'sugar'. She got very excited, saying to herself, 'No, I mustn't get excited,' and got more excited. Similarly with a doll, she said fiercely, 'I want to poke its eyes out,' then checked herself and started loving it. She said the room reminded her of things in her past but then said, 'No, I don't want to think about those things.' She made excuses not to tidy up at the end of the session and it became a battle. She kept trying to provoke me to anger. It felt like being with two people, which was quite uncomfortable and frightening.

Although her worker was feeling Alice's projected anger she was able to contain it, that is, experience it but not act on it. The value of the whole session became apparent when Alice went back to her group and was fine for the rest of the day. Alice's anger was expected to increase and staff spent time planning how to cope. As well as seeing Alice in the playroom, her worker worked with her every day in the residential unit, as part of the care team. All playroom workers met as a group with their training supervisor for an hour or more every week so that they could share feelings, understand what was happening and respond appropriately.

'All the perfumes of Arabia will not sweeten this little hand'

Jenny aged nine comes to a joint therapeutic play session with one other child and her teacher-therapist for an hour a week in a primary school unit. Her distress is experienced and contained at the slow pace which is all she can manage:

Jenny's physical and sexual abuse over a long time came to light a year ago. She is a classic victim, isolated and bullied at school, although an excellent reader. At first she spent most of her time playing with the dolls, lifting the girl doll's skirt and belting it, giving it the beatings she used to receive. The baby was sent to bed without supper for being naughty. After the beatings Jenny would get the girl doll and bath it, washing it, her 'dirty' self, clean. She did this again and again. Her mother says that at home when Jenny is upset she fills the sink or bath with bubble bath and washes herself clean. One day Jenny seized a telephone in the playroom calling, 'Is that the WPC [woman police officer]? I want you to come here because I am beating my children and I think I might kill them.' I role played back on the other telephone, offering help. Then Jenny decided she would paint. (I usually ask the child if I may write down what they say about the painting and pin it to it.) Jenny painted a large patch painting with black cloud of 'a Viking ship on a stormy sea – all the people have been blown off – they're going to die – their families are upset that their sons are dying of cancer'.

Another painting was her 'aunt's house' which was red and black with a black roof, with a small yellow sun and a garden of black and brown flowers 'knocked off'. This sad painting was followed by a crude patch painting of a figure outlined in red with red arms, brown hair, purple body, and a huge protruding purple patch 'pocket' (penis?), all on two pin legs on a black line. In the top corner was a small yellow circle. Jenny said, 'Joe my dad, he's working, that's why he's got that suit on – his pocket is inside out – he's standing on tar – it helps him push his car more easily – it's night, the moon is shining.' She sounds like Madge Bray's doll with her 'head full of muddles'. I write down Jenny's comments for her which is as much as she can take. If I try further reflecting she abruptly changes activity. She now enjoys the 'nurturing' start to the session when we sit together on the floor cushions and sing or share a story. Today she is painting stripes, pressing so hard with the brush that you can see the scratch marks in the paper. I expect her to be a victim for some time to come.

Both Alice and Jenny showed signs of internal muddle and confusion. Feelings of being 'a mess' are often an early theme in therapy. Art therapist Carol Sagar (1990: 92, 97, 113) explains why messy play is helpful:

Using art and play materials, because of their tactile, physical nature which relates directly to sensation and emotional feeling, is arguably the most useful therapy for children who have been sexually abused . . . as they can work with their feelings and experience them directly in the handling of materials used in the therapies. The process and results express clearly the confusion and damage which abused children suffer and reflect how they find ways in their work to bring about repair, change and growth from within. . . . Often the way in which most satisfaction seems to be found in using art materials is by making a messy mixture which is then spread on any surface. Messy packages may be formed and given to the therapist to keep. Containers and packages of the mixture may have to be kept for a long time until the child emerges from the compulsive need to handle and examine the internal chaotic feelings where 'good' and 'bad' are indistinguishable. The messy package may represent the secret which the child has had to hold, often over a long time, which is now passed into the therapist's keeping. At some point later the package and the containers of mess will be asked for by the child who may decide that they can be disposed of – usually thrown away – or who may not yet be ready to let go of them. Later the child may begin to use the materials to represent and express present phantasies and the current relationship with external reality. . . . A 12-year-old girl made a very large painting within the outline made by drawing round her body whose insides were represented by thick black paint. The painting was rolled up so that the paint, when dry, made it impossible to unroll the paper. This was trusted to the care of the therapist for some time before being undone.

Philip's 'useless house'

Play therapy was a part of the work in a residential special school for children with learning difficulties and emotional problems. The therapist, a teacher trained in art therapy, worked within the symbolism of play:

I began seeing Phillip two years ago when he was nine years old. He was referred for play therapy because he was aggressive towards other children and could not talk about his feelings. His life had been one of confusion and chaos. He was one of five children. There was a question whether his grandfather had sexually abused his younger sister, and Phillip's father had left the family home a year before. Mother had a new partner whom Phillip resented. On top of this he had been sent to our school because of his educational needs, so I suspected he felt sent away (punished?), perhaps even responsible for events at home. My initial aim was to help him express his feelings through art and play, and come to terms with the loss of his natural father. Phillip used clay models of dad and himself to express deep anger at dad's departure. Just before our summer break he seemed calmer and happier than he had for some time. He put the clay dad away in the cupboard and said goodbye to him.

However, the holiday brought disaster. Phillip's sister was taken into care and his grandfather imprisoned. The new 'dad' had sexually abused Phillip's 14-year-old aunt and been banished from home awaiting prosecution. Phillip returned to school in a chaotic state. For several weeks he was unable to 'use' anything and could only dash around the room shouting and screaming, hide under tables and chairs, and try to destroy materials. This left me feeling exhausted and useless, and I felt our good work had been undone. It was after this period of chaos, however, that the most important sessions began. Phillip was flitting anxiously from one activity to another, unable to sustain anything. I said to him, 'I know you had a terrible holiday and you must be feeling very hurt and upset.' He nodded. I suggested that at the moment it must be hard for him to say how he feels and that it might help if he could use the dolls and the doll's house. He said that he couldn't. However, when I told him that we had only five minutes left, he fetched the house and pulled it apart. The whole house began to collapse and he said, 'This is a useless house, it's just like a house in [the town where he lived].' I said, 'Is this your house?' and he said 'Yes.'

In our next session he went straight to the broken house. He began to pull the furniture apart and then spent a long time trying to mend it, refusing my offers of help. He took the grandfather doll and put him in a bed. He then took several other dolls, pulled their legs apart and put them on the bed too. He hurled the grandmother doll to the floor and was very angry with her. He also pulled the feet off the girl doll (his attempt to stop her going away perhaps). He put the beds on the roof balancing over the edge of the building. He put the toilet in the bedroom. The whole scene was one of danger and chaos. He took a doll and said it was Spider Woman and made her try and fix things. I said, 'Can Spider Woman do anything right now?' He replied, 'She wants to but she can't.' Again I was left feeling helpless. He then brought in Spider Baby (himself?) who also tried to sort things out but couldn't. I said, 'Do you think that if Spider Woman and Spider Baby work together they can do anything?' He tried this with the dolls but said, 'No, they can't do it.' I asked if there was anyone who could help. He said 'Super Man can do it . . . but he isn't here right now.' As we left he said, 'I'll need to use this again next time, I have so much to do.'

The following week he used the sand tray and dolls. He threw the family into the sand saying, 'This is quicksand.' I asked how they got there and he said, 'The first dad did it.' He took the dolls and buried them, then rescued them. He did this again and again. He then took the man doll and threw him into the sand with the rest of the family. I asked who this was and he said, 'It's the bad dad.' I asked if this was the real dad. He said, 'Yes it is.' I asked who put him in the quicksand and he said, 'I did.' I said, 'You feel it is the real dad's fault and you are very angry with him.' He said, 'Yes.' He took out the boy doll and the woman doll (Phillip and myself/mother?), washed them and put them in a jar of clean water. They were naked and upside down (quite a disturbing sight). He took the second dad figure and the girl doll, washed them, wrapped them up and put them in the top of the jar. He put the jar on top of the cupboard 'where no one can touch them'. As we left he said, 'They'll have to stay there till next time!' In fact those figures stayed up there for many weeks. He occasionally went to check they were still there and to top up the water.

It is only recently that he has been able to remove the figures from the jar and he still felt very angry with them, throwing them into the sand tray and saying, 'They stink.' As he did this I gently removed the boy doll from the pile, washed him, wrapped him in a paper towel and said to Phillip that I would look after this boy doll because I thought he was a very special doll. He seemed delighted and almost unbelieving. Since that time, myself, a teacher or a member of the care staff has taken care of the little 'boy'; Phillip chooses who. He has made the boy some clothes, a bed and blankets and he is at present building a model house. These actions reveal that despite all he has developed some self-worth. Play therapy has not cured all his problems, but he is less aggressive, he is able to cry (something he did not do before), he will allow himself to be comforted by a trusted adult. He talks, however tentatively, to those caring adults around him about how he feels about what is happening at home. I believe that our time together has given him a consistency that was so lacking in his young life and an opportunity to express his innermost fears and feelings in a safe way. I hope that this space and the materials will be available to him for as long as he needs.

Phillip's therapist's approach indicates a willingness to be receptive to how he is feeling and to what he might have a need to express, even when its meaning is unclear. She survives the period of chaos and feeling useless, offering real 'containment'. There are echoes of Axline in the account of the quicksand. In a crucial intervention, using the symbolism of play, she intervenes positively to take care of the boy doll. This taking care then becomes shared with other carers in the school, providing a wider therapeutic environment.

From play therapy to filial therapy in foster care and adoption

Foster carers and adoptive parents need to be involved and supported in providing the wider therapeutic environment which the most emotionally damaged children need. Filial play therapy can help carers in developing understanding of their child's feelings and in learning the attunement skills which promote attachment. Carers are taught how to lead non-directive play sessions, initially in a playroom supervised by a play therapist, later on their own at home but still with some supervision and support. Two case studies illustrate the process.

After longstanding concerns about serious neglect, Hannah aged five was removed from her mother's care. A year later in foster care she was soiling, smearing and showing sexualized behaviour. Her social worker referred her for play therapy, which her therapist describes:

I began long-term weekly non-directive play therapy with Hannah four years ago. I let her know that I was aware things had happened to her that may have left her feeling sad, angry, scared and confused and that she may also have some worries about what is going to happen in the future. Initially she was very talkative and seemed younger than her years. I had to transport her to play therapy sessions and she readily came along with me, appearing quite independent. She repeatedly told me about some of her experiences in what seemed like a rehearsed way, which was something others found irritating and attention seeking. It gradually became clear that her apparent independence masked a deep-seated insecurity and her repeated accounts of past abuse were attempts to have her experience acknowledged and understood. At first her fear was evident in her anxiety about what lay behind closed doors or of particular play objects such as a witch puppet, a large pencil resembling a stick, and a punchbag, all of which had to be taken out of the room. She also needed reassuring that the shadowy paintings of people on the walls were not real. She was often quite controlling with me as she sought to create safety for herself. Her imaginative play was limited. At first she would exclude me, not letting me even watch her, or she would set me up as a role model which she would imitate. She played out scenarios full of danger. Houses were unsafe, windows broken, things stolen, children were hurt and adults stabbed. Ambulances and police came to the rescue.

As she began to name her fears and became more familiar with the predictability of therapy and with me she became more confident and less controlling. She was able to talk about some of the frightening things that had happened. Her need for nurture was apparent in some regressive play in which she drank out of a baby's bottle and sucked her thumb while listening to bedtime stories. Her play often included babies being cared for by a safe mother figure. Also she appeared to use being ill as a way of obtaining nurture and assuring herself she would be looked after. Over time her play and conversations became less about the past and more about missing her mother and her fears about her planned adoption and having a new mum. She wanted to continue therapy during the transition and this was agreed in order to offer some continuity and to help her manage her feelings.

From the start I had reviewed Hannah's progress with her foster carer, social worker and teacher after every eight sessions. As the adoption neared I hoped to involve her adoptive mother Jane in filial therapy to help her understand Hannah better and feel more confident as a parent, helping strengthen their relationship and attachment. Filial therapy teaches the same skills of attunement and reflection which a mother uses in bonding with her infant. I continued individual therapy sessions for six months and then trained Hannah's adoptive mother Jane (first through modelling and later by observing her sessions and giving feedback) to carry out filial play sessions at home. I no longer had direct contact with Hannah but offered supervision and support to Jane through regular meetings. Jane told me about Hannah's play themes of repairing and fixing, mastery of fears and trauma, creating safety and belonging. Hannah often cast Jane as a monster and herself as a fairy being chased by the monster that was sometimes armed with a knife. Over a number of weeks Hannah directed Jane to become more scary as she in turn became confident to fight back until the monster was defeated. A year later filial play sessions were less frequent, with Hannah choosing not to play or not mentioning the time at all. Jane and I both felt that she was now settled and no longer needing particular play times. Jane was confident about generalizing the skills she had learnt to everyday life, as I had hoped. I ended work at this point on the understanding that Jane could contact me again if she needed.

Liam, taken into care at age four following domestic violence and gross neglect, and now age eight, had been making progress in his foster placement, his fourth. However, he had begun soiling and was functioning at a much younger level. His school was struggling with the complexity of his needs. His foster carer was keen to engage him in filial therapy. A play therapist trained her in the basic skills. The foster carer observed six play therapist's sessions with Liam before beginning 30 minutes play sessions herself. Follow-up discussions between foster carer and play therapist took place after each session when Liam was not present. The therapist writes:

Early play therapy sessions were dominated by chaos and disintegration. Liam would act out gruesome scenes in the play tent. For example, he would not allow the 'lion' any food and then punch it and kill it with a knife. He stabbed and killed what he called 'the wicked witch' and referred to dead skin, eyeballs, a mouth and a tongue. He made scary noises, and laughed when the doll screamed. He would draw or build people with body parts missing, an indication of his fragmented sense of self. He was alert to any noises outside the playroom. One moment his play would be calm and relaxed and the next, without any apparent trigger, it would change to violent aggression. On one occasion he jumped towards me saying, 'Put your hands up or I will cut your throat out' as he swung a long plastic tube above his head, just missing me. One session had to be stopped because he lost total control. So many things were connecting at a traumatic level that developing a coherent narrative was impossible. Setting clear limits helped him cope better. His false independence and underlying fear meant he was very control-ling. At times I felt quite overwhelmed and clinical supervision was important in helping me understand and deal with my feelings. The foster carer expressed some relief that there was now someone else who was supporting Liam. She said that observing the sessions gave her valuable insight into his traumatic past and how it was continuing to affect him. When she began sessions with Liam herself, the follow-up times with me gave her an opportunity to discuss the play in detail as well as to offload her own feelings.

As Liam's sense of safety with his foster carer grew, he gradually became calmer, less controlling and his sessions more free-flowing, although there is always a sense of impending danger and he worries what would happen to him if his foster carer died. Sensory experiences, such as completely immersing his hands in paint and glue, helped give him early experiences he had missed. He used jigsaw pieces of teddy bears, described as upside down, invisible, having no head, no face and no legs, to express feelings of being sad, all mixed up and lost. His anger is becoming more focused on his birth family, especially after letter-box contact; he fears his father might kill his mother and might also seek him out. At first he was afraid to leave the house but now he has the con-fidence to play in the street with friends. He is less controlling although it recurs when he is feeling insecure. He is now able to compromise, show some empathy to others and accept affection. He is more able to talk to his foster carer about his fears of his father and his worries about his mother. He can think about the future with more hope and asks about taking his foster carer's last name. However, his sense of security is quite fragile and he continues to need a therapeutic environment at home and at school. When therapy in the playroom ends, as it will soon, the foster carer will continue with special play times, on the same day, same time and same place each week, for as long as Liam needs it. Once these are going well I will offer only occasional follow-up sessions with his foster carer.

The hope is that in due course the attunement of the carer and her enjoyment of their child will be generalized to everyday life, enabling the carer to provide the emotional containment within which the child can recover and grow.

Conclusion

We have seen how children who have experienced continual trauma and loss from early in their lives, without a sense of someone holding them in mind, have fragmented inner worlds of chaos, muddle and mess. The task is to provide a framework of safety within which they can be helped to start to connect these fragments into a more integrated sense of self, gradually developing a coherent narrative of their life, and with it some sense of hopefulness. As we have seen from therapy sessions, this is not an easy or straightforward process. Complicated and strong emotions are likely to be aroused not only in the child but also in the adults. Adult networks are vital in providing a coherent and connected external world within which the child is safely held so that emotional work can take place. These networks are only too liable to mirror the child's projected chaos and conflict, so that much thought is needed in maintaining connectedness and providing thinking spaces where people meet, not to plan but to reflect on what is happening and make sense of it (Hay *et al.* 1995; Cant 2005). How these emotions can be managed and connections maintained in daily living are the subject of the next chapter.

Acknowledgements

Case examples from Mary Cowan, Anita Edwards, Christine Froude, Sarah Hemsby, Pam King, Rose Larter, Pauline Little, Christopher Richards, Julia Selley, Sarah Smith, Mary Stone and Jackie Whitelock.

Chapter 9

Therapeutic play in daily living with abused and traumatized children

Within the deprived, abused and traumatized child who longs to be loved and cared for is an angry fearful child who will attack any attempt to provide that care. They are insecurely attached, an attachment which 'is sometimes fiercer than ordinary good attachment' (Hunter 2001: 118), since the rebuff they received in past attachment seeking only increased their fear and alarm, which then heightens attachment seeking, if of a defensive kind. Their attachment means that they feel unworthy of care and they will act to confirm this view of themselves. Further, they may have identified with and internalized aspects of the inadequate parent, for example, in identification with an abusing parent (Lanyado 1999). 'Underneath the neediness and fear of rejection are often other more malignant feelings' (Hunter 2001: 107).

The child may have lost touch with these feelings, hiding them within a compliant 'false self', but under stress they will erupt destructively, which is why so many placements break down. The child does not feel not held within their skin but experiences 'falling to pieces' or 'falling forever' (Winnicott 1965). Feelings cannot be held on to and thought about but have to be got rid of on to other people, often in massive blame and projective anger, or sometimes in a delinquent merger with other children. Violent panics and disruption are the 'hallmark of unintegration' (Dockar-Drysdale 1990: 131). Without a sense of self and agency the child cannot take responsibility for their own actions, often literally not able to remember, even moments later, for example, deliberately breaking the window.

The task of looking after these children requires more than providing good child care; there is repair work to be done. Caring for these children involves being able to think about the meaning of their apparently incomprehensible behaviour. It means being able to withstand the child's attacks and still come back with undiminished concern. It means noticing and responding not only when the child is vociferously angry or distressed but when they are depressed or mentally distanced, by 'reaching out', carefully managing the timing and intensity of approach, to bring the child back into contact with the world (Alvarez 1992). It is about providing emotional containment in daily living and not only in therapeutic sessions. This is a difficult task but an essential one, for without such help the child may eventually end up in prison or in the mental health system.

Providing primary experience in daily living

What the child needs is to go back 'to the point of breakdown' and to receive a version of the missed good nurturing experience they should have had in infancy, what Dockar-Drysdale (1968, 1990) describes as 'primary experience' (see Chapter 1). 'First, as Anna Freud says, build the house; first, as Klein says, introject the good breast; first, as Bion says, you have to have an adequate container; first, as Bowlby says, have a secure base' (Alvarez 1992: 117). The child needs sensitive and responsive care, with attention to reliability and continuity in managing the events of daily life, from waking and dressing, to play and school or work, food and mealtimes, travel and other in-between times, bathtimes and bedtimes. We need to provide complete experiences with attention to the child's experience of their beginnings and endings. Provision of good sensual experiences – warmth, comfort, food, good touch – helps restore a child's blunted senses. The whole task is too great for one worker or carer, although their contribution may be significant. Provision for each child needs to be contained and managed through a network of external and mutual support and help for the child's carers. This therapeutic work can take place in any setting – local authority children's home, foster or adoptive home, and it is not the exclusive preserve of 'therapeutic communities', although the model which they provide may be useful. Although the broad pattern of work is planned, much day-to-day work is spontaneous and 'opportunity led' (Ward 2007), seizing the moment for a helpful response rather than an unthought possibly angry reaction. The following example shows how this task can be done by a staff team as a whole:

Eight-year-old Nicolas was a stocky unattractive boy who was difficult to warm to. He was placed in a local authority children's home after his foster placement, his fourteenth move, had broken down after his violent sexual assault on a four year old. He had previously been living with his father who had a history of violence, although he had spent his early years with his mother, mainly in different women's refuges. He idolized his father and said he wanted to be with him. (Father was therefore given regular contact.) On his arrival in the children's home he stood in the doorway and urinated at the staff there to greet him. He spat, kicked, head-butted and screamed his way through the day, interspersed with idyllic behaviour and profuse apologies to those around whom he had hurt. His mood swings were extreme and, as one worker put it, 'When he "goes" he's quite frightening – like that child in *The Exorcist*.'

While initially fearful for the safety of other children, staff became excited at the prospect of working with such open disturbance in a structured, shared and open way, involving a team approach as well as individual supervisions. We decided that come what may we would try to hang on to him. We saw him as an 'archipelago' child and understood that he too found his panic states very frightening. We gave him a clear message that aggression towards others was not acceptable and that we would stop him, by holding him physically if necessary. When he panicked we made sure we never left him alone, held him if necessary, and communicated with him throughout.

We felt that we needed to do things for him as he showed no control over everyday matters. He would run a bath and deliberately let it over-flow; he would lose his toothbrush every day and not clean his teeth when a new one was produced; he would pour half a bottle of ketchup over his dinner and then slurp his food up with his fingers. Staff started to run his bath for him, clean his teeth for him and ask him if he had wiped his bottom when he had been to the toilet, giving him undivided attention. Someone was with him during all his waking hours, doing things with him and for him. His whole day was organized for him, trying to make things uncompetitive and achievable, encouraging his interest in art, swimming and growing things. We bought boxing gloves and a punchbag in the hope that he could channel his aggression. We gave him a Wendy house, sleeping bag and tent so that he could hide himself away in his bedroom. We sat beside him on the floor (due to his destroy-ing all his furniture) reading him bedside stories and singing lullabies at bedtime.

He is now inwardly and outwardly a much happier child. His violent outbursts have diminished greatly. His replacement furniture in his room remains undamaged and he is starting to put down roots. His knowledge and interest in growing things was a way of helping him relate to other children who had until then seen him as a 'nut case'. His healthy response to one of the staff the other night was 'I'm not going to let her wind me up you know' and he promptly had a bath and came out managing himself well.

A baby cannot put feelings and phantasies into words but expresses them through the body. 'In the early months omnipotent phantasies tend to predominate, so that angry baby may want his urine to be so scaldingly power-ful it blows the bad mother away until, in phantasy, he comes to believe his urine really is like that' (Farnfield 1997b). This gives us a clue to understand-ing Nicolas's urinating at staff on arrival. A thinking team made possible the good experiences which Nicolas received. Eventually, he was able to hold on to enough good feelings to be able to start to think. Working at understand-ing the meaning of a child's play, or inability to play, helps us think about ways of reaching them, as a therapeutic care worker describes:

Ezra came to us at age six after three foster placements had broken down. He had been abused within a paedophile ring and often talks of cameras in the walls. He told us that he often spent all night locked in a dark room with his sister. His chaotic state meant I often went home in utter confusion, an indication of his own feelings perhaps. He has been given a very highly structured routine, as you would with a baby. He can become suddenly violent and unaware of who or where he is, showing no sign of physical pain, and he needs to be held. He is obsessive about anything with a plug or batteries, risking putting himself in danger. He spends his pocket money on batteries and extension cables, spending ages looking at them, talking about them and putting the batteries into and out of toys, but not using them. He wants to switch the cooker on and off, and has spent hours switching lights on and off. This and his desire to look inside things reminds me of a toddler. I wonder if the switching on and off is something that gives him a sense of control, which cannot be said for anything else that has happened in his life. He is knowledgeable about how things work and what makes them go. While of course we have to keep him safe, I am wondering if there is any way this obsessive behaviour could be used to help him feel more in control and raise his self-esteem. Exploring this together the staff team won-dered about Ezra's 'dicing with death'. Ezra's own life experience like a battery was used and thrown away. Is he torn between wanting to die and wanting to live? They noticed that his batteries can be recharged and hold energy which is not used. Are they a magical way of staving off feelings – or of helping him feel alive and real? Where is the spark?

By recognizing that there is meaning in Ezra's activity, even if they do not yet fully understand it, there is hope of finding a means of further communica-tion. As with Nicolas, the team is containing the frightening feelings by together providing the safe highly structured care which is so essential to a child at an infantile 'pre-verbal' stage.

Symbolic primary experience

When the child starts to trust a little, to have an inkling of hope, they may seek a way to allow some basic infantile needs to be met. Dockar-Drysdale (1968, 1990) describes how this can be managed in a residential setting. It is rarely appropriate to allow a child to regress completely. Localizing it to a particular time and situation agreed with the child, and with a person chosen by the child, preserves the child's ability to maintain age-appropriate functioning elsewhere, and is comparable to what may happen in a therapy session. This kind of nurturing under the control of the child is very different from forced regression, better described as abuse. Management of 'individual provision' needs the careful support of the whole residential staff team, or of the household and its support network in foster care, both in protecting the boundary of the work and thinking about the meaning of likely envious splitting or angry rivalry provoked by the intensity of the child's attachment seeking. The child may see the worker as an all-providing 'mother' at all times which the worker is likely to find intrusive and even abusive. Alternatively the worker may find themself drawn into collusive splitting, becoming the 'good' mother and seeing everyone else as 'bad'. Separate therapy sessions with a play therapist or child psychotherapist who does not work alongside the child in daily living can make these issues more manageable and may be preferable. However, there was thoughtful support from the staff team for the following work by a therapeutic care worker at a residential therapeutic school:

Sandra came to the school a year ago and is now nine years old. She has been with foster parents following sexual abuse by her father and a good many of his friends, with her alcoholic mother's consent, from a very early age. Her contact with me started in various group situations within the school, mainly at getting up and going to bed times, in play activities, during outings and through a regular lunch-time bath. Relatively soon, Sandra started developing a dependency relationship with me, which the staff team formally acknowledged, allowing us a weekly half-hour session together. Consulting Sandra, I decided to use Sunday lunch-time, because I hoped that feeding her might provide a useful nurturing experience. As a location I chose, at her wish, a big play area with a settee, lots of beanbags and plenty of toys. Sandra chose Coke, chocolate ice cream and a bag of crisps for her 'lunch'. A pattern to the sessions soon emerged. Sandra brings her bed cover with her, takes her shoes off and snuggles under her cover on the settee. Then she asks me whether she can be my baby, and how old she is. Usually she wants to be a very small baby, no more than a few months old. Then she likes me to feed her her lunch, to which after a few sessions I added real baby food at her request, which she eats like a really messy baby. Often Sandra interrupts the feeding by hiding under her covers. I then have to pretend to have lost her and cry bitterly, until she moves so that I can 'find' her again. When we are reunited we both are relieved and happy. Then we often play hide and seek, which she enjoys very much, even though we usually know where the other is hiding. When her time is up, Sandra usually does not find it difficult to accept the end of her 'special thing' and to join the other children.

Foster carers and adoptive carers may find that the provision of a special time, such as they have learned to provide through filial play therapy (Ryan 2007) or theraplay (see Chapter 10), also serves to localize some aspects of the nurturing they provide. They are looking after such deprived and needy children whose attachment seeking, once the child risks trusting a little, may feel quite overwhelming, and may be at the expense of other members of the family. It needs to be part of a clear structure for the child's daily life.

Quite simple 'special provision' can be made to help a child 'go back' emotionally and fill in the gaps of missed primary experience. Sometimes a child asks for special food at bedtime which they will receive from the worker with whom they are building a relationship. Robert had been found concealing in his bedroom six yogurts which he had taken from the fridge. It was decided to make it possible for him to have something which he appeared to need, but in a way defined in terms of appropriate time and place. Robert received a pot of black cherry yogurt as his special provision five times a week for over a year. He 'saved all his yogurt pots and soon had a stack several feet high, a physical statement of what he had now stored up inside him in emotional and well as nutritional provision'. He had been helped not only to have but also to hold on to that crucial primary experience. A boy in the same therapeutic community asked for a special bed, as his worker describes:

One boy I worked with was Zak, 13 years old, untidy and easily led into delinquency because he lacked the ego strength to decide for himself to stay out of other people's trouble. Zak's clothes, possessions and room were always in turmoil. After many months of looking after Zak he suddenly asked me if he could make his bed into a boat. I had no real idea why this might be important for Zak other than as some sort of totally enclosing safe space for him so I said I thought that would be a great idea. We proceeded to construct a boat shape which would fit over his bed, using two sheets of hardboard bent to form a prow at one end, and with two pieces of 2 × 2 timber erected a mast at either end, Zak seemed pleased with our efforts. A few days later Zak called me shyly but excitedly into his bedroom to look. He had attached a long piece of string from the top of each mast running the whole length of his boat and over the string he had draped a blanket which now fell on either side of the bed like a tent. He was clearly pleased with it so I said, 'That looks brilliant Zak. You'll be safe in there.'

It was not necessary to know the full meaning of the boat for Zak but it was good enough to know that it meant something helpful. Through discussion with the consultant it became clear that the boat represented a secure container for Zak's 'stormy sea' which was evident from his chaotic room and possibly his life as well. I often thought of how his boat looked like one of those self-righting life-rafts, totally enclosed. I could speculate how much the enclosed boat represented some kind of womb-like structure, warm, dark and safe. Zak's boat was not a game. It was an important structure which was not taken apart when the bed was changed, nor was it ridiculed by anyone. Other children had beds built as nests, houses or castles, high up or at floor level, each according to the child's specifications. The culture was such that Zak felt able to ask for something which I suspect he would have been unable to in other places for fear of ridicule or because of a lack of understanding of the emotional importance to him of the provision of a boat. Zak continued to sleep in the boat for many months until he decided himself that he no longer wanted the tent on top. He then slept in his open-topped boat for many more months. Zak may have got the idea for a boat from family naval connections but it was not important to know this; what mattered was to know how to build it and that it needed to be built.

Zak's boat can be understood as a symbolic equation or realization (Dockar-Drysdale 1990), in that the symbolic provision is a version of a *real* 'primary experience'. As in Zak's case, bedtime is often an anxious time for children, representing both separation and for some a reminder of abuse.

Mike would often provoke staff and take two hours or more before he would settle down. One bedtime he asked his worker to hold his feet while he went to sleep. Initially uncertain, he agreed and wrapped Mike's feet gently in a duvet, looking after them on his lap. Mike confided how his dad would drag him out of bed by the ankles; he remembered that the bed had been small and he had curled up but he was still grabbed (see Alvarez's 1992 notion of children needing to put two things together to start to remember). His worker realized that this had been the prelude to the severe abuse which he knew the child had experienced. He felt that Mike was trying to find out whether things could be different. Mike asked to be tickled and he refused, feeling this was inappropriate and collusive, perhaps connected with exciting feelings which may have been part of the abuse. The solution was a shield of chairs around the foot of the bed. Eventually together they built a proper shield, within which Mike could feel safe to sleep.

Unintegrated children find group play situations difficult, quickly getting into conflicts or a delinquent merger with other children. With adult help to protect them from impingement they may play in the same general space as other children, in parallel play. This may take place in a household play space or in a nurture group in school (Boxall 2002), where the kinds of sensory play material provided – such as sand, water, paint, large boxes and blankets for curling up in – allows for the possibility of some more infantile experience. Some children may want to be tucked into their own 'nests' and read or sung to while others may be ready for a more symbolic provision. Dockar-Drysdale (1968: 152) describes a group of children playing with her in the garden. They were making nests out of twigs and grass, and came in turn to ask her for 'eggs' – small pieces of chocolate. One child wanted four eggs and another five, while a third asked for one egg. 'I just reflected what he said, giving him the one egg, and murmuring "Roy wants one egg". I thought to myself that this child – who was very greedy and loved chocolate above all things – nevertheless needed so much to be *the only one* that this symbolic experience became more essential than the chance to eat several pieces of chocolate.'

Symbolic communication through play in daily living

Symbolization, in Dockar-Drysdale's sequence, follows the child's good primary experience and his or her realization that this good thing has really happened. The child uses symbolization as a way of storing the good experience inside. Early forms are symbolic equations, as we have seen, in which the symbol is also the good experience. Symbolic communication, in which a child uses symbols to represent something else, is a developmentally later stage, although even some profoundly unintegrated children have pockets of integration and can make use of symbolization. 'Symbolization is the only way in which these deprived youngsters can communicate their desperate feelings, and if we can understand and make good use of the symbols we can bring them relief and understanding, which makes acting out no longer necessary' (Dockar-Drysdale 1990: 120). Where such communication takes place through play in the course of daily living, the carer's or worker's understanding and response can make the experience therapeutic, as shown in the following examples from therapeutic residential child care settings:

On returning after a weekend away, Derek's behaviour with adults seemed very omnipotent and controlling. Because of this I stayed physically present and mentally 'holding' him. He said he wanted to go to the indoor play area where he asked me to push him on a four-wheeled wooden trolley. This play felt quite controlling; he gave the instructions, I pushed him wherever he wanted to go. After a few minutes he asked me to crash the trolley. I would slow it down, tip it over and he pulled it on top of himself with his arms outstretched and eyes closed, looking like the victim of a fatal road crash. He then instructed me to be the rescue services. I would rush over making siren noises, rescue him from the wreckage and lie him stomach down on his righted trolley. We would then rush off to a corner which became the hospital, where I would take his pulse, put him to bed and be allowed to provide some concern and care. This game repeated itself probably four or five times in half an hour.

I was left with several thoughts about the meaning of his play. I thought he was acutely anxious about the transitions involved in leaving for the weekend and coming back again. His omnipotent mood seemed a direct defence against his own inner insecurity. The only way he could be safely cared for was within the game in the imaginary hospital; the need for real care was allowed in the transitional space between us. To have consciously interpreted the play by saying something like 'I think you are telling me how unsafe the weekend has felt to you' would have destroyed the play, which in turn would have made him unable to accept any form of care. I felt that in this case being involved in the play and the working through of his anxiety the play was far more beneficial than a verbal interpretation. Using his own symbols I was able to show continuing concern and to help him recover from the anxiety of the weekend. This piece of 'playing out' rather than 'acting out' where the boundaries of playing were partly contained in the physical environment show how the child's symbolic communication can be understood without the need to put it into words.

In this play, and in the following examples, it mattered that the worker was involved and playing too. As Winnicott (1971: 38) writes: 'Psychotherapy takes place in the overlap of two areas of playing, that of the patient and that of the psychotherapist. Psychotherapy has to do with two people playing together.' In the 'potential space' communication take place and something new can be created. Derek's fragile inner world could feel a little stronger.

The same worker describes another use of a non-directive 'enabling space', with an older child, again involving symbolic communication:

While working with Barry one day in his room he became very depressed about his future leaving plan. I think that after a period of deep dependence, he was beginning to recognize that he would separate from me and become independent, a recognition of transition in itself. I was sensitive and empathized with his depression, recognizing its importance, but made no attempt to help him out of it. While talking he started to doodle on a drawing pad. It started as an ominous black cloud, a symbol of his depression. Eventually it spiralled upward across the page and soon took the form of a flying bird, crane-like. It seemed that Barry was reaching a form of symbolic realization, tapping the creative resources that came from the potential space of the meeting of reality (his leaving) with fantasy (his symbolic expression). I think that the creation of a facilitating environment or enabling space in the here and now of the room enabled Barry to give form to his feelings. Shortly after finishing the drawing he was less depressed and was able to leave his room and function well for the rest of the day. This gave me a lead as to how to continue developing his creative potential, to allow a way of sublimating aspects of his disturbance.

Providing a potential space through play can sometimes enable a child to give birth to new feelings about the possibility of growth from deep dependence to some autonomy, to creating his own containing inner space. This birth was symbolically enacted in the following example (adapted from Whitwell 1998: 8–9):

When I first met Joe he was a small slight ten year old, of mixed race, full of fun and very lively. He looked younger, and would walk around holding my hand or be carried on my back. He developed an interest in dolphins and whales, in particular killer whales. At Christmas I gave Joe a cuddly killer whale which he took everywhere, becoming very important to him. At times of stress for Joe I would to talk to Whale who would tell me how Joe was feeling. Joe would use a special voice for Whale. Whenever my time off approached Whale became 'ill' and on my return would be at 'death's door', and it would take a good deal of care and time to enable Whale to recover. With our consultant Mrs Drysdale

I devised a way of helping Whale, and hence Joe, bridge the gap of my time away. When I was away Whale stopped eating so I suggested to Joe that I left a 'sugar shrimp' so that Whale would not go hungry. This seemed to make the gap more bearable and Whale thrived.

One day Joe told me that Whale's name was Winnie. The shrimp routine continued and Winnie used to swim happily in the sea while I was away. One night when I was putting Joe to bed he told me that Winnie was not feeling very well, which confused me as my time off was not due. I asked Joe what was wrong and he said he could not tell me but Winnie would whisper it – she was having a baby. Joe told me that Winnie would need a lot of looking after and that she would let us know when her baby was due. In discussion with Mrs Drysdale we decided I would need to follow Joe and Winnie's lead, and that it might be that in due course I would need to produce a baby whale. The pregnancy lasted some weeks and as fortune would have it I found a baby killer whale while out shopping. I had to have the baby whale close at hand at all times in readiness for the birth. Winnie had similar stresses and pains to those of most pregnant women, with morning sickness particularly evident. The day of the birth arrived and Joe sent me for hot water and towels as Winnie went into labour. As I returned Joe told me that Winnie needed covering with a towel which I did and that her brow needed mopping. When the baby cried that was my cue to bring the baby whale from beneath the towel. Mother and baby were fine and went for a swim in the sea. Father was always away swimming in a far off sea. Joe told me that Winnie was only going to have one baby, which was of great significance as Joe was a twin. Through this birth we were able to do a great deal of work around the issues of mothers, fathers, race and identity, and Joe's twinship, as well as the difficulties involved in looking after a baby. In this way Joe's feelings and fears were acted out symbolically through Winnie. We played out a drama in which Joe could experience (unconsciously) my struggle with fears and anxiety, and by doing so create a form of resolution and containment. This provided a process by which Joe was able to create a space to think, to take back into himself the confusion and dread, tolerating it in his own new containing inner space.

This work over a period of weeks involved the worker maintaining a continuing preoccupation with Joe, not simply empathizing with his pain but feeling it personally. His provision of symbolic food for the whale mother and his finding the baby whale who would be born mean that he carried Joe's anxiety and took an active part in the story, providing both containment and a helpful 'reaching out'. The play remained entirely that, communication staying within the symbolism of the birth of a healthy baby whale. It belonged to a pre-verbal period of infancy which was being reworked. An explicit interpretation would have been destructive. This was also the case in another therapeutic care worker's symbolic communication through play which also took place over a considerable span of time.

Play with eight-year-old Sarah took place in the normal course of the events of daily life. It was helped by the staff team's recognition that this work was important and needed support:

Among Sarah's main emotional preoccupations were her feelings about a mother figure and her need to belong. Her anxieties and needs were so great that she was driven to play make-believe games dealing with this theme day in and day out. She had two games that dealt with this theme; one was a dog/puppy game, the other was, not surprisingly, a mother and baby/child game. For months Sarah spent a great deal of time pretending to be a puppy or a dog. She had two basic versions of this game which she would play again and again. In one she would, for example, initiate a game by whispering to me, 'I am your puppy. You are the mummy dog. Carry me like a puppy.' We would then play being dogs with me looking after her. She preferred to play this game with me, but if I was not available she would also play it with other workers. In the second version Sarah played being a puppy who is given to somebody, again mainly and preferably to me, as a present. If we were in her bedroom, for example, she would wrap herself in a blanket and lie on the floor or in the washing basket. I then had to uncover her and pretend to be overjoyed at finding a little puppy there, while she would yelp in a rather endearing and helpless way. Often Sarah preceded these actions by telling me, 'Pretend you are a little girl and your mum gives you a puppy as a present.' In this variation the emphasis was on the fact that she was given to me as a present and from then on belonged to me. On most occasions the game therefore stopped once I had unwrapped 'my present' and had joyfully accepted her as my puppy.

Sarah's games revealed that she wanted to experience being a baby (puppy) belonging to somebody who would be pleased to have her and to look after her. The fact that she wanted to play these games so often indicates that her need for this experience was great, and indeed almost desperate. Considering that her mother had actually found it difficult to feel pleasure at Sarah's birth and be emotionally available, it is not difficult to understand Sarah's need. I think that she unconsciously used these games to work through and make up for the loss that she had experienced. The question remains why she so often chose to play out this theme as a dog rather than as a human being. Rustin and Rustin (1988: 251) point out how animals – real and imaginary – are used in many children's actual lives as projections of aspects of themselves and some of their central feelings. In pretending to be a puppy Sarah did exactly this. She projected her need to belong and be cherished and looked after on to the figure of a puppy. By playing at being this puppy herself she could take part in what happened to the puppy in the game. But at the same time, by projecting her needs into a 'puppy' she could distance herself from the feelings of loss that accompanied her need to play these games. Spending so much time being a dog also gave her a chance to get away from the anxieties and painful feelings that human interaction created for her. I think that the relatively simple life of a dog, as had her beloved dog at home, had a certain appeal and that in being a puppy she found relief from the anxieties of her internal world.

Occasionally Sarah's puppy games had more threatening themes. Once, playing that she was a puppy and I was the mummy dog, she told me to pretend that I thought that she was a murderer and run away from her not realizing she was my puppy. In this short game Sarah expressed symbolically the dilemma that she has faced since her birth. For her mother Sarah was not just a little baby – the puppy in the game – but somebody who threatened the life that she had established with her first-born child – the murderer in the game. Therefore Sarah's mother 'ran away' into depression, thus being unable to attend fully to her baby's needs, just as I had to run away from her in the game. By playing out painful feelings of abandonment, rejection and loss in a make-believe game Sarah had found the possibility of expressing them and coping with them without being overwhelmed by them, or indeed without becoming conscious of them. She also coped with them by projecting them on to me, so that I felt and contained them for her.

A similar opportunity for therapeutic communication presented itself through Sarah's fascination with certain fairy tales and stories. For example, she loved the stories of *Peter Pan* and *The Little Mermaid* which 'seemed to express symbolically some of her phantasies and emotional preoccupations and dilemmas'. Sarah wanted to hear these stories again and again; she would enact scenes or pretend to be one of the characters, and would ask numerous questions.

Workers in many settings tell children stories at bedtimes and other times, as well as giving them opportunities to look at and read books, or watch television and video. By becoming aware of the significance of the child's choice of story and working with the communication which this understanding makes possible, much spontaneous therapeutic work can take place.

From unintegration to integration

A final example demonstrates how an emotionally unintegrated adolescent boy, living in a residential therapeutic community for children, was able to achieve a sense of wholeness, an integrated self, through play within an overall therapeutic environment. What took place in play was shared with and had the support of managers, care staff and teachers. Discussion with a consultant outside the whole situation provided important support and objectivity in understanding what was happening. The child's 'therapeutic resource' describes the crucial contribution of communication through play (see also Bradley 1999):

We can use play to help the child express the horror of his original trauma, and to progress from that until he discovers his own creativity and eventually is able to establish his identity. I believe that in residential care, if we are able to provide the child with a suitable structure inside which he is able to initiate his own play, and the grown-up can respond to him in a sensitive way, then it may be possible to reach a level of communication which could not happen in any other setting.

When Tom arrived he was 15 but looked only 12. He could barely communicate and when you so much as said 'Hello' to him he shrank away as though you were going to hit him. Yet there was another side of Tom which would quickly spiral into excitement. He would 'merge' in with other boys' delinquency and only by physically separating him out from the person he was involved with would he quieten down. He could not distinguish between what was himself and what was other people. He lived in total merger with his environment and was deeply unhappy. Occasionally one would see bits of real ego functioning, but in between there lay chaos and despair. He attempted to prevent grown-ups from getting in touch with this part by using his quiet withdrawn self as a survival technique. We became very concerned and wondered if we would ever be able to help him. We could not discover what it was that he needed; all we could do was manage his life so that he did not get into serious trouble, that is, by making sure that somebody was looking after him most of the day. It did not seem possible to help him emotionally.

Tom's mother had been severely depressed during pregnancy and made several suicide attempts after he had been born. It was reported that she had sometimes locked Tom in a room on his own all day without food. She left Tom and his father when he was a few years old. Although the father had struggled to give Tom the care he needed, he became quiet and solitary and at seven years he was stealing from shops. The father eventually remarried and Tom found this particularly difficult to accept, even though the stepmother tried hard to relate to him. He became more and more delinquent and difficult to handle, running away from home, and then from the children's homes where he was placed. One evening, when I went to say goodnight to Tom in his bedroom, he asked me to read him a story, something he had always rejected when it was suggested before. I read him the story of *The Little Red Fox* who constantly found himself in trouble. He listened intently and after a while he began to play with a little toy car. I asked him if he had ever really played and he said, 'No.' I suggested that perhaps he would like a sand tray in his bedroom, so that he could play with it at bedtime or whenever he felt the need. He said he would like that very much and asked me if I would give him some animals to play with. He said specifically that he would like mothers and babies. I discussed what had happened with the rest of the team and the following day we provided him with the sand tray.

I bought him a selection of farm animals, a cow and a calf, a horse and a pony, hen and chicks, and some others. Tom was thrilled and immediately went into his room to play. He was quiet for the rest of the evening and when I went in to see him he was in the corner of his room, completely absorbed. I asked if I might join him and he nodded. He had split the sand into two sections, with a river in between. I noticed that the mother animals were on one side of the river and the babies on the other, neatly tucked into individual holes which he had made for them. I asked Tom what was happening. He told me that all the babies were going to run away as the mothers had left them alone and gone to play bingo. They were going to steal the mother hen's eggs and run away with them. At this point I felt I should intervene; it was clear that Tom was expressing something he was feeling but I did not know what. I asked Tom if I should go over to the other side of the river and bring the mothers back, as perhaps then the babies would feel safer and not need to run away. He said I could but he did not think they would return. I pretended to sail across the river in the boat he had made and tell the mother animals that their children were planning to run away as they were feeling so neglected. I brought all the mothers back just as Tom had lined the babies up ready to run away. I told him that the mothers were coming back, saying they would not leave their babies again. Tom immediately put the babies back in the holes with their mothers and said they would be all right.

By now it was late and I said that Tom should get into his bed too, now that he knew the babies would be safe. When he was in bed he asked me if I would make him a milky drink and a hot-water bottle, the first time he had done so. As I was tucking him up he told me he had planned to run away that night with another boy but now he had decided not to. I said I was glad that he had been able to tell me, and that perhaps he was beginning to feel safer with us. He settled down to sleep. I had not mentioned his sand play although it was now clear to me that this was what he had been acting out through the animals. It is quite likely that had I not been there and responded in the way I did, by being a 'concerned mother', he would not have been able to ask for the provision that he did. He symbolized what he was feeling and then was able to turn that into verbal communication.

After this breakthrough the sand tray came to be a focal part of Tom's treatment. I realized that we had been able to provide him with a means of communication. I arranged with the rest of the team that I would always be available to spend 15 minutes every evening playing with him, at the same time, just before he went to sleep. The sand tray became deeply important to Tom and when I was not there he would not use it, nor would he ever allow any of the other grown-ups to play with him, even though they all knew what was happening. As he came to depend on the time that I spent playing with him, so he was able to use the care and help offered to him in the unit. He seemed to be more at peace with himself and would often come to be looked after, developing aches and pains which needed attention. Eventually he felt secure enough with us to be able to show the more vulnerable unhappy side of himself. It became clear that he needed to be in a room on his own; up to that time he was sharing with another boy. Immediately he moved into his own room he was ill, so that he had to stay in bed for several days. During that time he was able to be helpless and dependent. At times he said he was too ill to eat, and had to be fed. He needed to be washed and his hot-water bottle had to be filled almost hourly! Much of the time he was ill he played with the sand tray. I kept to my regular time to play with him.

After four or five days Tom began to get back on his feet. When I went to play with him one evening I found that he had separated the animals into four groups, one in each of the four corners of the sand tray, the very small ones in one corner, slightly bigger ones in the next, and so on. The river was still in the middle. I asked what was happening. He told me that some of the animals were beginning to grow up and as they did they moved up a corner until they were properly grown, when they went into the river on their own, as they were by then big enough to look after themselves. This seemed to be the beginning of Tom's recovery. He seemed stronger inside and looked much more alive than he had done before. He was able to avoid other people's excitement by going off to his room to play with his sand tray, sometimes on his own accord and sometimes at the suggestion of a grown-up.

The sand tray became more symbolic. He bought a milkmaid who looked after sick animals. This seemed to represent myself, as after a day's illness I returned to be told that the milkmaid had been given the sack for having a day off without permission. Only after Tom had made a lot of heavy demands on me and needed much looking after was she reinstated. He made a small pen which he said was for the animals who got over-excited, so that they would feel safer and would not disturb the other animals. Daily I would notice that some of them had moved up a corner. At the same time Tom was developing a sense of his own identity and was beginning to relate more substantially to other people apart from myself.

After some time he became attached to the unit cat and spent a great deal of time cuddling it; it became his transitional object. He was much more creative than he had been before. He painted pictures and brought in plants. One afternoon we spent some time picking shrubbery for the sand tray, which Tom now called 'his real world'. At the same time he was also becoming much more real. Tom was almost at the state of integration when I had to leave the unit to work elsewhere in the community. He was able to survive this break without disintegration or acting out. He could verbally communicate his anxieties to other staff and was able to transfer his dependency from myself to them. After my departure he ceased to use the sand tray, eventually asking for it to be taken from his room. He no longer needed it. By now he was relating to other objects and was able to distinguish between what was himself and what was the outside world. He went to a unit for more integrated boys where he was able successfully to use the new experiences which were provided for him there. He had enough 'inner world' to be able to relate to the outside world.

If I had not been able to find a way of communicating with Tom through playing it might not have been possible to make a relationship with him. He made his first real contact with me through the sand tray, after which he was able to establish a primary bond and allow me to provide him with 'adaptations', the hot-water bottle and the milk. There followed a short period when he became totally dependent on me. During this time it was imperative that I was reliable and trustworthy, always keeping to the time I had arranged to play with him, never being late and never exceeding the boundary of 15 minutes. This way Tom knew exactly where he was. He was then able to separate out from me slowly and use the cat as his transitional object, the bridge between his inner world which his play experience had enriched and the external environment. Slowly he was able to become more creative and use the cultural opportunities of another unit. Through play Tom had moved from a state of non-being to being. After he became integrated he used his play as a space between himself and the outside world. Initially he communicated symbolically about his plans to run away. Later when I was leaving the unit he could talk about his anxieties and could describe how he was feeling to other people.

It is important that we are receptive when a child first tries to make contact with us. This can come in all sorts of strange ways which we may not even recognize. As long as we respond sensitively then it will allow him to feel that it is all right to carry on. 'If I had told Tom, when he attempted to make his first contact with me, that I did not have time to read him a story he might never have taken the risk again.'

Implications for residential foster and adoptive care

Winnicott (1971) wrote: 'It is in playing and only in playing that the individual child or adult is able to be creative, and it is only in being creative that the individual discovers the self.' We have seen how children in residential therapeutic care can have play experiences that help them develop emotionally towards a surer sense of self. This is possible where workers together think both about the meaning of a child's communication, about the difficult feelings aroused in the work, and about how they can together best provide physical and emotional holding and containment. The extensive literature on the work of therapeutic residential care (for example, Whitwell (2002)) is relevant to carers in other settings. Foster carers and adoptive parents are no strangers to difficult feelings, sometimes finding themselves locked in to parenting in a way they don't want to, with the child getting destructively under their skin, a projection of intolerable feelings (Ironside 2004). It is not surprising that placements break down. Like residential workers, these carers need to be seen as part of and partners in the treatment team rather than 'any port in a storm'. A major study of foster carers (Sinclair *et al.* 2005) showed that children with skilled and well-supported carers had fewer placement breakdowns and better outcomes. What mattered was carers' warmth, their persistence, their ability to set limits, their readiness to engage and do things (play) with the child, their ability to stay reflective, to interpret misbehaviour as communication and not get defensive, providing emotional containment. This was helped by the carers' ability to recognize and get help when needed, from a good network of extended family, school and other professionals providing continuing system of support (Wilson 2006). 'Unless all this links up, however, in an integrated environment, the emotionally disturbed child will fall through the gaps' (Whitwell 2002).

Acknowledgements

Case examples from Michelle Alfred, Christine Bradley, John Diamond, Margarete Lucas, Steve Lund, Caroline Owens, Simon Peacock and John Turberville.

Chapter 10

Play in therapeutic work with children moving to new families

Towards conceptualization and a coherent narrative

The aim of play therapy and therapeutic work with children is to help them develop a more integrated sense of self in which thinking and feeling can be connected, and in which their experience, however problematic, makes some kind of sense. Attachment theory makes clear that mental health requires a reflective capacity, the development of a coherent self-narrative, which consists of an account of their life that hangs together and makes sense, however difficult the child's experience was. At its simplest it is about the child finding a story which they can tell other people, and this may also involve finding a 'cover story' which will help the child get by. The achievement of a coherent narrative, however, happens at a more profound level, touching every level of the child's inner world. A child whose attachment is reasonably secure early in life develops a confidence that their good expectations of relationships with people who matter to them will be met. A separation, loss or other trauma may shake this confidence but the child has the capacity, given a containing relationship with an attachment figure or therapeutic worker, to mourn the loss or the bad experience, and to recover. This process involves putting feelings into words. Expression of feelings in symbolic play in the presence of someone who can think about the child's symbolic communication can be a significant stage in the healing process, and may be enough for the child to integrate the experience and move on with trust and hope, although in the long run they need a way to conceptualize their experience, to put it into place in their mind, whether or not it is actually put into words.

The process of developing a coherent narrative is more complex if the child's experience from infancy has been of more anxious, less emotionally containing and even damaging attachments. Continuing traumatic losses take their toll of the child's capacity to develop a 'reflective self-function' (Fonagy et al. 1994; Fonagy 2001) and an integrated sense of self. However, we have seen how given the emotional holding of a therapeutic environment, with containing relationships, the child's feelings can be expressed, survived, thought about and understood, with the child eventually in turn being able to become more of a container for their experience, although they may always be vulnerable to some degree. Becoming a container means being able to make sense of a sometimes apparently nonsensical story, of retaining the capacity to feel without either being overwhelmed by emotion or becoming too distanced, that is, they can think about feelings and manage, in due course, to talk about their present behaviour and their life experience (for example, in the Adult Attachment Interview) in a real and reflective way. Since part of this means thinking about painful experience as well as good experience, it can only happen usefully after a child has had enough good primary experience to sustain them, then symbolization of this good experience, followed by working through painful experience in symbolic ways. In Dockar-Drysdale's (1990: 99) words:

> These other processes, realization and symbolization, provide the essential stepping stones to what, after all, conceptualization really is, an economic method of storing experience and at the same time establishing the means of communicating experience.

So the last stage of therapeutic work with a child is about conceptualization, helping them to think in a concrete way about past and present experiences, and to consider the future. Dockar-Drysdale adds that 'conceptualization is only of value if it is retrospective – ideas must be the sequel to experience'.

Play in direct work and life story work with children moving to new families

The work of conceptualization may happen spontaneously and naturally, as child and worker reflect on the meaning of symbolic play or when the therapeutic relationship requires attention to real changes in the child's life. Once the child feels safe to begin to think and feel, and to connect the two, they are ready to start to make sense of what has happened in their lives. They cannot simply ignore the past and move on. The past must be 'understood, analyzed and accepted as a means to progressing' (Rose and Philpot 2005: 18). Distorted views of what happened, including self-blame, can be let go. Play-based work, using Clare Winnicott's (1968) notion of a 'third thing' to facilitate communication between child and worker, remains important (see Chapter 2). Work needs to be carried out in the context of a relationship with the child and not seen as an isolated task. It must go at the child's pace, with the child in control of what they are sharing, allowing for times for respite, such as when the child is in a crisis. Play techniques require creativity, imagination and empathy.

Planned life story work and direct work using more focused approaches may take place separately from therapeutic play. This may be *after* therapy has helped the child develop a capacity to connect feeling and thinking, or *in parallel* with therapeutic work. Ken Redgrave (1987: 122) believes that not all 'looked after' children need therapy before they can discuss and make sense of their experience:

> In undertaking therapy work with deprived and emotionally damaged children the emphasis, particularly in early stages of treatment, will be on the use of non-directed play (or other free forms of self-expression) but I am conscious of the fact that *most* of the children who are needing family placements or have been rehabilitated to their own families, or who have been adopted, are not in need of 'treatment' (e.g. psychotherapy) but are reasonably healthy kids who need to be able to talk and get things sorted out. I am also aware that many adult workers find it difficult to get the child and themselves exchanging ideas on some of these delicate areas. The 'games' I have spoken about have helped these conversations along.

It may be, however, that more 'looked after' children these days have experienced severe trauma, and are in need of treatment. Research showing that the provision of direct work was not related to children's progress in a new placement (Quinton *et al.* 1998) indicates that either this work was not at a high enough level or quite simply that it was not enough. We need to be clearer about what kind and level of treatment a child needs, which may be, for example, 'treatment foster care'. Claudia Jewett (1984: 129–130) summarizes the tasks involved in helping children to find identity and meaning in their lives:

> Because every major loss disrupts the development of self-esteem, the smooth progression of life, and the sense that events are predictable and meaningful, recovery from such a loss requires that damaged self-esteem be repaired, continuity be re-established, and a sense of meaning be restored. To recover fully from a loss a child must satisfy five needs:
>
> First, the child must understand that he was born to a father and mother; he must know who they were, why he was separated from one or both of them (without blaming himself for the separation), and what, if anything, he might do to return things to their previous condition. He must experience and share any strong feelings of anger, sadness, guilt or shame that he has been holding back.
>
> Second, the child must know what persons or families have cared for him if he has lived away from his birth parents. Who are the people in these places he has lived, why did he go to those places, why did he leave (or why will he be leaving), and what, if anything, might he have done to make things work out differently?
>
> Third, the child must say goodbye, directly or symbolically, to past caretakers (and, if a change of caretaker is forthcoming, he must say hello to the new caretaker).

Fourth, the child must receive permission from his caretakers to be happy, loved, successful and loving.

Fifth, the child must get ready to face the future with increasingly diminishing concern about the past.

Jewett's third task of saying goodbye to past caretakers needs to be understood in terms of our current understanding of attachment and loss, with its recognition that former ideas of 'a clean break' are a damaging denial of a child's past; the child will always carry some mental representation and memory of their family and fostering experience which forms part of their identity. It is not about necessarily ending contact or a saying an absolute goodbye, but more about being ready to make a new attachment based on a more optimistic inner working model.

A programme to prepare a child for a new family

Family placement worker teams may draw up a detailed programme for the intensive work of preparing a child for life in a new family, whether long-term foster care or adoption. A flexible approach is needed to address the needs of all members of the family, with regular meetings to assist open communication and expression of feeling. In planning each part of the work they must consider the child's specific need, what time scale and monitoring is needed, and who will carry out the work, as in the following condensed example of a programme to help a nine-year-old girl move from foster care to her adoptive family. The child's needs include the following:

1   *Good primary care experiences and play.* This covers all aspects of day-to-day care. Foster parents' pervading attitude should be one of care, giving a clear message of acceptance and value. Certain times of the day are particularly important: help in getting up and getting dressed, getting ready for and taking to school, food and mealtimes. Provide opportunities for play with an adult as well as with other children. Include messy and water play with no goal other than enjoyment. Give individual time at bathtime for play and conversation. Make bedtime calm and read a story. Good primary care to continue indefinitely, accepting expression of regressive behaviour. Foster parents to record significant play observations.
2   *Sensory experience.* This aims to renew and strengthen the five senses of touch, hearing, smell, seeing and taste, which may have become dulled through traumatic life experiences. Give a week to each sense, foster parents continuing each theme at home through the week.
3   *Who am I?* Introduce and help her to work through *My Life and Me* booklet, in sessions concurrent with sensory work, using a mirror, photographs or drawing one another. Notice what she likes and dislikes,

and what she is good at. Help develop a particular interest, such as dancing. Acknowledge and validate her feelings, perhaps using art materials or clay. Allow time for anger and grieving. Develop her self-awareness with different people and help her relate to new people without over-familiarity.

4   *Separation from birth mother.* Why did I get separated? Use small houses, roads, cars, puppets and play people to represent carers and other adults and the various moves and changes of circumstances. Use doll's house to re-enact or explore. Use picture flow chart to help her to see the sequence of moves and events. Dispel fantasies of returning ('lots of parents aren't good at bringing up children but are good at other things'). Consider candle ceremony in relation to carers and attachment figures. Foster parents to be involved and to carry out some of the work, as well as keeping an observation diary to monitor feelings expressed in play.

5   *Life story work.* Help her understand and live with the trauma of her life. Develop a fuller understanding of who she is, why she was separated, why her mother did not come, and what is going to happen to her. Use play people, life graph and map to give knowledge of family members. Use ecomap to show where father fits in the picture. Have photograph of and information on father. Explore how she feels about all this, including her fantasies, misconceptions and guilt. Fill in any gaps. Use sad, happy and angry faces to represent her feelings to adults. Use water play. Make a family tree. Help her make life story drawings. What positives has she received from her parents (life itself, needs met in the womb, colour of hair and eyes)? Pace the work according to her needs. Build up her life story book. Show birth certificate, photographs of birth, hospital, etc.

6   *Promoting attachment in a new family.* Help her know her worth and feel a sense of belonging in her adoptive family. What is happening to me? Will this adoptive family really stay with me? When I do something naughty will they send me away? How perfect do I need to be in order to be really accepted? I know I have opportunities but am I loved, really loved? Reflect on attention seeking, lack of concentration and behaviour/survival pattern. Give careful consideration to the promotion of attachment behaviours within *this family*. What are the unspoken expectations? Where are the satisfactions? What must change for parents and child to gel? Consider theraplay or filial therapy in relation to healing process and reparenting, courtship and commitment – claiming each other, warts and all.

Primary experience, nurture and sensory work

The task of treatment foster care, which needs in due course to be continued by adoptive parents, is to provide emotional containment for the child who has infantile needs for relating but lives within an older body. They need to become 'the steel box with a velvet lining', providing the child with repeated opportunities to experience dependency within secure boundaries (Archer and Burnell 2003; Hart and Luckock 2004), in a 'high nurture–high structure' approach – a kind of reparenting. Chapter 9 explains how to do this, drawing on the experience of therapeutic residential care in providing a primary experience, including nurture, good sensory experience and play, within an emotional holding environment.

Focused play approaches to facing painful feelings

In order to grow and develop, traumatized children must be able to face and cope with immensely painful feelings about the inadequacy of their early care. Chapter 8 shows how non-directive play therapy helps make these feelings more accessible and directed towards the appropriate object, rather than in self-destruction. As a child reaches this stage some play techniques make talking about feelings more possible. As we have seen, drawings of sad, angry, happy, scared and lonely faces, drawn on cards, or puppets, dolls and paper bag masks can be used in games (Jewett 1984). Redgrave uses a slider card, revealing one feeling at a time to talk about. He draws pictures of sad or angry children encased in a 'holding in' skin, contrasting this with feelings coming out, and asks the child which way it feels better. A water analogy shows children how they protect themselves. Coloured water, representing good feelings, is poured into a glass, representing the child, but most is spilled. The little remaining water in the glass is covered with cling film which protects it but means that no one can pour in any more. The technique can show how the child was not 'born bad' but started as an empty glass, waiting to be filled with good feelings which their parents were unable to do. Then the child can be helped to think what 'lids' they now use (Redgrave 2000; Ryan and Walker 2007).

Children need help to direct their justifiable anger appropriately. We can notice which part of the body – hands, feet or mouth – they use to express anger and then help them to yell, thump clay, tear newspaper, hit or stamp on a cushion, or throw soft balls at a target. The child might draw, paint or model the object of anger and then destroy or hit it with rolled up newspaper. A child can write a letter, not actually sent, or draw a picture of 'horrible stuff', then tear it up and put it in the bin; they can direct role play, or talk to a person imagined in an empty chair (Jewett 1984). Objects resembling real weapons should probably be avoided. Once anger is expressed and validated, other deep-seated feelings of hurt, sorrow or loneliness often start to emerge. Some family placement workers make use of a candle ceremony to express grief (Owen and Curtis 1988; Ryan and Walker 2007). The child may be helped to light candles, signifying loving and caring feelings, for each member of the family, and to express sorrow as a candle is moved away, still alight, representing loss of that person but showing that loving and caring feelings remain as a good memory. The child may need a cuddle or some physical comfort. This is a powerful ceremony and not to be used lightly. These techniques should only be used within the context of a caring and containing relationship, built up over time, and carried out by someone who is attuned to the child, who can judge whether or not a method is appropriate, and who can work creatively and sensitively.

Life story work – towards a coherent narrative

Research shows the importance of helping children become more informed about their lives. Children's discontinuous lives and multiple placements mean that their histories have often been lost. 'These children lack the sense that people know them, know about them in the ordinary continuous way that children in their own families take for granted', which makes their sense of self and self-esteem harder to maintain (Hunter 2001: 26). They feel a sense of 'discontinuity between past and present' and 'an inner feeling of holes' through never having been told 'some of the basic facts about their lives such as their birth date, their real name and why and when they came into care' (Harper 1996: 21). One child's life was described as 'like a badly constructed jigsaw' (Connor *et al.* 1985: 34). Confusion, guilt, blame and fantasies abound for these children. Life story work is helpful in giving children information about their origins and the reasons for key decisions made on their behalf, such as why they were removed from birth families, or had to move placements. It allows gaps and misperceptions to be identified and corrected, so that children develop a more realistic appraisal of their history (Luckock and Lefevre 2006). Much life story work has been criticized for being carried out as a routine procedure for 'looked after' children, without sensitivity to the timing, pacing and depth of the work, or to the child's level of cognitive understanding and their preferred ways of communicating, such as drawing, play or stories. Sometimes children say they do not understand or remember it (Thomas *et al.* 1999: 89). When done well it can 'help take the child on a therapeutic journey through parts of their life that pose most pain and conflict' (Ixer 1988: 26).

Edith Nicholls (2006: ix) argues that life story work must start 'from the very moment a child is separated from their family' and be a continuing and integral part of the care planning process, not something that takes place only when plans for permanence are being made. She suggests that a specialist fostering and adoption team carries out the work in parallel with the work of the child protection team. Such work needs to be done initially *for* rather than *by* the child, with the worker collecting information relevant to the child's identity development, catching and preserving aspects of a child's experience which might otherwise be overlooked or lost. This can be stored in memory books and boxes, photograph albums and family history books, to use with the child when the time is right.

Whether a child is on the verge of being looked after, in transition between placements or leaving care, it is often particularly helpful to the child to hear their story from their family, a process which a worker's presence can facilitate and contain. Where the child's story has been lost it is painstaking work to carry out the detective work needed to reconstruct their history. The tools are much the same tools as those used in the current popular occupation of researching family history – that is, searching through documentary records, visits to places where the child has lived or gone to school, interviewing and recording (and videoing) family members and others in the community to hear their stories. This may be a time to understand the complexity of a child's ethnic background (Rose and Philpot 2005). Where possible the child accompanies the worker. The aim in life story work is not to impose the worker's version of children's lives on them but to provide an opportunity for information to be shared and discussed so children can construct their own life narratives.

As the information is gathered, regular life story sessions with the child help with the process of internalizing what has been understood, integrating it into the child's inner world. It is the process of the work rather than the end product which yields most benefit to children, for it enables clarification of feelings about events and their causes (remembering both good and bad times) and the correction of possible misunderstandings – for example, about why a child was moved (Ryan and Walker 2007). Rose and Philpot (2005) suggest using wallpaper rolls which allow the child to collect material and write about their lives without ever turning over a page where it may be forgotten. Once the worker has gathered as complete information as possible about the child's life they can write down the child's story, in the third person, to have an account to draw on in the course of work. A final version is written with the child, in the first person if possible but sometimes it is only bearable for the child if told in the third person. The worker needs to stay with the truth but express it in ways which the child can bear to hear and to learn from. The aim is a narrative that avoids either idealization or denigration. Nicholls reminds us of the need to attend to carers' feelings of loss and grief when a child moves on, without which they become less able to provide the involvement that the next child needs. She emphasizes the importance of life story work being a shared responsibility, with foster carers and adoptive parents not only becoming the guardians of the child's memory books and boxes, family histories and photograph albums (with copies kept safely elsewhere) but also continuing the work into the future. A word of warning – computer disks and DVDs may contain a wealth of beautifully presented information but technology dates quickly, with the risk that the material may not be accessible in years to come. A paper-based version is also essential.

The worker needs the emotional capacity to tolerate and think about painful feelings and process them with the child, watching for clues about how and when to proceed, and respecting their defences, such as resistance to getting in touch with feelings at times, or a refusal to own parts of their history. This emotional 'holding' demands a great deal of the worker's own capacity to stay with painful areas and they may be surprised by how hard it can be, for example, to tell a child that they were born of rape, or were found in a dustbin, or as a baby were abused by their father. Our body language, such as not looking at them or turning away, tells the child that what happened was not acceptable or bearable. Certainly judging the timing of information is essential, but in the end we must believe in the child's right to 'be' and to have the information they need to make sense of their life. Ixer recommends that workers should undergo their own life story work first so that they are in touch with the confusion, anger and distress that may be evoked. Unconscious dynamics are inevitable. 'It is vital, therefore, that direct work takes place in a context where "thinking" time, i.e. reflecting on what is happening in the sessions', and its impact on the worker, 'is recognized as important and valuable' (Ruch 1998: 39). The worker requires support and supervision. Direct work with children should always take place within the context of work with others in the child's life, their families or carers and social workers. They may also be able to join in the work (Romaine 2007).

Who am I?

If the worker is new to the child, getting to know one another might start with a car journey or other shared activity, allowing the child to test the adult out to see if they feel safe. It is important to start with the here and now, rather than jump to the beginning of a child's life and painful memories (Holody and Maher 1996). Children may take the lead in suggesting what they might like to draw or write about, for example, an enjoyable day out or a special interest. They might list 'things I like' or draw or describe themselves (or have their outline drawn for them), or use King's *Talking Pictures*, Sunderland and Englehart's (1993) *Draw on your Emotions*, Farnfield's sentence completions or Barnardos's *All About Me* game. Workbooks such as BAAF's *My Life and Me* booklet (Camis 2001) are available. Interactive computer activities, such as *Where We Are At* (Barnardos), may appeal. Racial and cultural identity need to be explored. Black children or children of mixed parentage may find Maximé's (1987) workbooks helpful, as well as resources such as Chambers *et al.* (1996) on celebrating identity. If the worker is white, black colleagues may need to be involved as role models, as well as for advice, for example, on words used to describe physical appearance (Banks 1992; see also Chapter 3).

Where do I come from? Where am I going?

Play and games are used in life story work to link feelings to people and events but allowing a playfulness as well as sense of control for the child.

Illustrated genograms or family trees give a picture of family structure and relationships. An ecomap reveals who matters to the child and the strength of the child's present relationships. Picture flow charts of places lived and schools attended show how people fit into a child's life and how they are linked together, and it is usually not too hard for the child to say if each was a happy or a sad place (Cipolla *et al.* 1992; Farnfield 1997; Redgrave 2000; Ryan and Walker 2007). Trigger pictures, such as Alton and Firmin's (1987) *Moving Pictures*, help children to talk about past moves, as does Macliver and Thom's (1990) *Family Talk*. Owen and Curtis (1988) use 'brick-wall', the bricks and gaps representing the child's life and moves to a new family. In a *Moving Around* board game a road is divided into squares with houses along the way representing each move a child has made, whilst question cards help the child to think about why ('Do you know why mum and dad could not look after you?'). Redgrave (1987: 137) devised a board game *Marathon Walk*; road blocks represent particular difficulties (such as 'mother can't get a house') which they can discuss to see which can and which cannot be moved. He wanted 'to show the child that they could move forwards, towards a goal, even though when the game started we did not know what the end goal would be'. He also makes a game using Fahlberg's (1988) notion of three parent circles – birth, legal and substitute or 'now' parents – to help children to talk about their expectations of each.

Some people tell stories, sometimes telling the child's life story in the third person, or using symbolic stories, such as the story of the suitcase which became increasingly battered and got more and more labels stuck on it as it made more journeys. Published stories include Jacqueline Wilson's *Story of Tracy Beaker, The Suitcase Kid,* and *Dustbin Baby*, Seeney's *Morris and the Bundle of Worries* (with accompanying *My Book Of Worries*), van der Meers's *Joey*, and Orritt's *Dennis Duckling, Going into Care*, Kahn's *Tia's/ Tyler's Wishes*. Computer interactive materials from BAAF include Thom and Macliver's *Bruce's Story*, Betts *Speak Easy*, and Betts and Ahmed's *My Life Story*.

Play-based direct work with very young children moving to a new family

Play-based work is particularly necessary with very young children. Storytelling or enactment with dolls and puppets can help children to understand what has happened to them. They can also be used to introduce them to new families and involve them in the thinking about their future. Children as young as three can use a people and places chart, depicting people in their life and the building each belongs to. They can be helped to name and cut out figures representing different people, attaching them to big cut-out houses stuck on to a large coloured sheet. A visual time line – a string on which pictures, photographs and objects are pegged in time order – helps a young child build up a picture of their life.

Enid Hendry (1988: 4–5) describes how, as a family placement social worker, she prepared four-year-old Jamie and his two-year-old sister Jenny for their new family. The children were in a short-stay foster home, having come into care because of long-term neglect and abuse. At first neither could walk or talk but both progressed physically and Jamie was able to speak a little, but both remained withdrawn and showed little emotion. She wanted to involve them actively in understanding what had happened to them and what was planned next, and to help them to express some feelings. First she wrote out a simple script telling their story, making this into a book, illustrated with drawings. She hoped the foster parents would use this as a regular bedtime story. She visited the foster home with a collection of play materials, a teapot house with rooms inside, simple cardboard houses she had made, two cuddly hand puppets, cars and Playmobil figures of parents, children, babies, doctors and nurses. The children were at once eager to look inside the yellow teapot house where they found the figures. She told them she was going to tell them a true story about 'a little boy called Jamie and a little girl called Jenny'. She continues:

> I invited the children to choose a figure to be Jamie and one to be Jenny. Jenny observed quietly. Jamie got involved in choosing figures. I explained how 'Mummy Sue' and 'Daddy Jim' had lots of cross arguments, and how 'Mummy Sue' had gone away. 'Daddy Jim' had tried to look after them on his own. At this point Jamie took the figure that stood for 'Daddy Jim' and shut him in the teapot house, holding down the lid. I remarked that he had shut 'Daddy Jim' in the house but made no other comment. I continued explaining how they went to hospital – moving the figures about as I did so. Jamie said, 'Sore tail.' The foster mother, who was sitting quietly observing, said this was his expression for his sore penis, which had been severely ulcerated when he was admitted to hospital. It seemed clear that he was not only able to follow the story, but was connecting it with memories he had of what happened. Encouraged, I continued the story of their coming to the foster home. Jamie then insisted on introducing another figure into the story – an elderly female figure – a 'grandma'. The foster mother told me that the grandmother rang from time to time to inquire about the children, and was important to them. It was clear that 'grandma' had to be included in the story and in any future plans that were made for them.

She went over the story twice, using the same phrases, and then watched as Jamie played repeatedly shutting the daddy in the house, ignoring the mother figure. She then gave them their 'book about them', including photographs of the children and foster family, and adding mention of grandma and Jamie's sore tail. The book became extremely important to Jamie from then on, a symbol of continuity and his identity. (In retrospect, Hendry thought she should have made a book for each child.) On her next visit she told the story again and introduced the idea that the children needed a family that could look after them for a long time, as this family only looked after children for a short time. She continues:

> The prospective family had two children and a dog, so I made the family with play figures plus dog, and pretended to drive them along in a car saying that they could come and visit Jenny and Jamie. I had previously arranged with the current foster parents and the intended foster family a first visit to the foster home to meet the children, so shortly after I had enacted the visit with play figures the 'new family' arrived, complete with dog. The story was told again. The current foster parents helped Jamie to take photographs of the visitors, and helped him to put them in the book, thus symbolically giving him permission to include them in his life. Jenny quietly showed the visitors the yellow teapot house. The 'new' family were invited to have a drink, and they settled down to play with the children and look at their life story book.

This simple but beautifully effective piece of work enabled the children to move happily and laid the foundation for much further work with the children. It was successful because it was attuned to young children's need for a concrete representation of their experience. A similar approach might be helpful to children with learning disability. Telling the story in the third person gave the children enough emotional distance from it to hear what it was telling them. Through play the children were actively involved and contributing important changes, such as the role of the grandmother. Young children's limited concept of time was recognized in the prompt arrival of the new family after play had introduced them. Foster parents were involved at all stages. Above all, although the work was structured this was done so as to receive communication from as well as to give it to the children.

Facilitating attachment for children moving to new families

Facilitating attachment in children with a 'developmental trauma disorder' is the 'road to emotional recovery and behaviour change' (Hughes 2000). All attachment therapies emphasize attunement, mirroring the positive interactions that occur naturally when mothers are attuned to their infants, showing new parents how to use play to promote attachment and bonding. Filial play therapy (Ryan 2007) helps them use non-directive play and its skills of empathy, attunement and reflection (see Chapter 8). Theraplay (see p. 50) specifically emphasizes the reaching out needed to engage a distanced child. These are sides of the same coin. Non-directive filial play therapists at times may incorporate aspects of theraplay. For example, a child who had formed a good connection with adoptive parents hid away when distressed rather than seek comfort, leaving them feeling distanced and helpless. Using theraplay at these times was helpful 'as the girl was gently presented with enticing reasons to emerge from behind her protective shield', giving both child and parents more confidence in closeness. At other times symbolic play permitted a degree of 'safe distance' from painful experience, aiding its assimilation (Barnes 2007: 45). From providing regular special play times these skills can be generalized to opportunities arising in daily living. Webster Stratton's (2004) and other parenting programmes, such as the Parent–Child Game, parent mentoring and relationship play work similarly in facilitating a child's attachment to a new parent or carer. It is not just a matter of teaching skills. It is about providing mental spaces to think together about what is happening in daily living, about the difficult feelings aroused – there will be hate as well as love – so that they are more easily accepted and tolerated. When new parents experience emotional holding and containment they are better able to provide it for the children who become free to play and to 'surprise themselves'.

A case study of a theraplay approach

Family placement worker Tricia Cattell describes how she used a theraplay approach as part of her work to facilitate a child's attachment in a new adoptive family:

> Five-year-old Jade had moved to live with adoptive parents and their eight-year-old son. She was the youngest of several children, seriously neglected from infancy. As a toddler she would sleep anywhere, including the dog's bed. In her new family she was unable to play, just looking at a toy and then putting it down again. She could not accept cuddles, wanting to be alone and in control as she had always been, carrying all her possessions around in a bag. Yet anxiety made her constantly interrupt when other people spoke to her adoptive mother, causing her embarrassment and really getting under her skin. Like so many adoptive parents, she was distressed that her love and care did not seem to be

enough and found it helpful to hear how a child traumatized in infancy has a damaged brain which needs repair. Jade's family placement worker hoped that the nurture and unthreatening physical contact of theraplay might help Jade make an attachment to her new mother. The boundary of play was provided by a rug with cushions. Initially sessions were short, about seven minutes, and never more than 20 minutes. There was a prepared programme so that as soon as one game palled another started. Each game was very brief. In one Jade and her mother sat facing each other with a cushion on their lap, and blew a cotton wool ball to each other. In another the mother used handcream to gently massage Jade's hand and then press it on paper to make a hand print. A silly game with mother putting a soft toy on her head, letting it fall and getting Jade to catch it, created laughter, as well as reminding the parent not to aim too high. Playing 'Row, Row Your Boat', the mother held Jade's elbows, a closer contact than holding hands. Another game was punching a newspaper sheet held by the mother but having to wait for a trigger word in a list. Other games included mirroring actions, bubble and balloon play, and face painting. Listening and eye contact were part of most games, and the mother needed to be encouraged to use exaggerated expressions to gain Jade's attention. Each session would end with the mother feeding Jade or giving her a drink. The adoptive mother struggled with the idea of such 'baby' play and was surprised when her own son wanted to play too. His enjoyment helped her realize its value and she persevered. After weekly sessions over two months Jade was allowing real contact, and went on to do well in her new family.

Conclusion

Much as we would like to, we cannot wave a magic wand and take away a child's hurt. What we try to do is restore the child's capacity for growth and development. At times this may look like going backwards rather than moving forwards. As a child becomes more in touch with painful experiences and feelings, rather than bury them or defend against them, they may become more difficult to live with rather than easier. It takes time and much good new experience for a child to develop trust that they are loved and cared for and to really feel that they are worthy of that love and care. Living with painful feelings can be harder than pretending they do not exist. It becomes possible through the experience of finding that someone else is able to bear these feelings with them. In the process something more joyful and creative happens, which is the healing power of play. As children find themselves and learn to live with what they find the future becomes more hopeful. For certain it will not be a smooth path. There will be setbacks and doubts, and old fears may reappear for a while. Courage and hope make possible the risk of growth.

Recommended reading

Axline, V. (1989) *Play Therapy*, Edinburgh: Churchill Livingstone.
Bowlby, J. (1988) *A Secure Base: Clinical Applications of Attachment Theory*, London: Routledge.
Brazelton, T. and Cramer, B. (1991) *The Earliest Relationship*, London: Karnac.
Byng Hall, J. (1995) *Re-Writing Family Scripts*, New York: Guilford Press.
Cattanach, A. (1992) *Play Therapy with Abused Children*, London: Jessica Kingsley Publishers.
Copley, B. and Forryan, B. (1987/1997) *Therapeutic Work with Children and Young People*, London: Robert Royce/Cassell.
Crittenden, P.M. (2000) *The Organization of Attachment Relationships: Maturation, Culture and Change*, Cambridge: Cambridge University Press.
Erikson, E. (1965) *Childhood and Society*, London: Hogarth Press.
Fonagy, P. (2001) *Psychoanalysis and Attachment Theory*, London: Karnac.
Fonagy, P. *et al.* (1994) 'The theory and practice of resilience', *Journal of Child Psychology and Psychiatry*, 35, 2: 231–257.
Greenhalgh, P. (1994) *Emotional Growth and Learning*, London: Routledge.
Hardwick, A. and Woodhead, J. (1999) *Loving, Hating and Survival: A Handbook for All who Work with Troubled Children and Young People*, London: Ashgate/Arena.
Hawkins, P. and Shoet, R. (2006) *Supervision in the Helping Professions*, 2nd edn, Maidenhead: Open University Press.
Hinshelwood, R. and Skogstad, W. (2000) *Observing Organisations: Anxiety, Defence and Culture in Health Care*, London: Routledge.
Holmes, J. (1996) *Attachment, Intimacy and Autonomy*, London: Routledge.
Hunter, M. (2001) *Lost and Found: Psychotherapy with Young People in Care*, London: Routledge.
Jennings, S. (1999) *Introduction to Developmental Playtherapy*, London: Jessica Kingsley Publishers.
Lanyado, M. and Horne, A. (1999) *The Handbook of Child and Adolescent Psychotherapy: Psychoanalytic Approaches*, London: Routledge.
Lanyado, M. (2004) *The Presence of the Therapist*, London: Routledge.
Klein, M. (1986) *The Selected Melanie Klein*, J. Mitchell (ed.), Harmondsworth: Penguin.
McMahon, L. and Ward, A. (2001) *Helping Families in Family Centres: Working at Therapeutic Practice*, London: Jessica Kingsley Publishers.

Obholzer, A. and Roberts, V. (1994) *The Unconscious at Work*, London: Routledge.

Redgrave, K. (2000) *Care-Therapy for Children*, Poole: Continuum.

Ryan, V. and Wilson, K. (1996/2000) *Case Studies in Non-Directive Play Therapy*, Baillière Tindall/Jessica Kingsley Publishers.

Trowell, J. and Bower, M. (eds) (1995) *The Emotional Needs of Young Children and their Families*, London: Routledge.

Ward, A. and McMahon, L. (eds) (1998) *Intuition Is Not Enough: Matching Learning with Practice in Therapeutic Child Care*, London: Routledge.

Waddell, M. (1998/2000) *Inside Lives: Psychoanalysis and the Development of the Personality*, London: Duckworth.

Wilson, K. and Ryan, V. (2005) *Play Therapy: A Non-directive Approach for Children and Adolescents*, 2nd edn, London: Baillière Tindall/Elsevier.

Winnicott, D.W. (1965) *The Maturational Processes and the Facilitating Environment*, London: Hogarth Press.

Winnicott, D.W. (1971) *Playing and Reality*, London: Tavistock.

Useful journals

British Journal of Play Therapy
Clinical Child Psychology and Psychiatry
Journal of Child Psychotherapy
Journal of Social Work Practice
Play Therapy, Newsletter of the British Association of Play Therapists

Bibliography

Ahmed, S., Cheetham, J. and Small, J. (eds) (1986) *Social Work with Black Children and their Families*, London: Batsford/BAAF.

Aldgate, J. and Simmonds, J. (eds) (1988) *Direct Work with Children*, London: Batsford/BAAF.

Aldgate, J., Jones, D., Rose, W. and Jeffrey, C. (2005) *The Developing World of the Child*, London: Jessica Kingsley Publishers.

Alton, H. and Firmin, C. (1987) *Moving Pictures*, London: BAAF.

Alvarez, A. (1992) *Live Company: Psychoanalytic Psychotherapy with Autistic, Borderline, Deprived and Abused Children*, London: Tavistock/Routledge.

Andreou, C. (1999) 'Some intercultural issues in the therapeutic process', in M. Lanyado and A. Horne, *The Handbook of Child and Adolescent Therapy*, London: Routledge.

Archer, C. and Burnell, A. (2003) *Trauma, Attachment and Family Permanence*, London: Jessica Kingsley Publishers.

Axline, V. (1964a) *Dibs: In Search of Self*, New York: Ballantine and Harmondsworth: Penguin.

Axline, V. (1964b) 'Recognition and reflection of feelings', in M. Haworth, *Child Psychotherapy*, New York: Basic Books.

Axline, V. (1989) *Play Therapy*, Boston: Houghton Mifflin and Edinburgh: Churchill Livingstone.

Ayres, J. (1985) *Sensory Integration and the Child*, Los Angeles: Western Psychological Services.

Bailey-Smith, Y. (2001) 'A systemic approach to black families: experience in family service units', in L. McMahon and A. Ward, *Helping Families in Family Centres: Working at Therapeutic Practice*, London: Jessica Kingsley Publishers.

Banks, E. and Mumford, S. (1988) 'Meeting the needs of workers', in J. Aldgate and J. Simmonds, *Direct Work with Children*, London: Batsford/BAAF.

Banks, N. (1992) 'Techniques for direct identity work with black children', *Adoption and Fostering*, 16, 3: 19–25.

Banks, S. (2000) *Ethics and Values for Social Work*, Basingstoke: Macmillan.

Bannister, A. (1989) 'Healing action – action methods with children who have been sexually abused', in H. Blagg *et al.* (eds), *Child Sexual Abuse: Listening Hearing and Validating the Experiences of Children*, London: Longman.

Bannister, A. (2003) *Creative Therapies with Traumatized Children*. London: Jessica Kingsley Publishers.

Bannister, A. and Print, B. (1988) *A Model for Assessment Interviews in Suspected Cases of Child Sexual Abuse*, NSPCC Occasional Paper 4, London: NSPCC.

Barn, R. (ed.) (1999) *Working with Black Children and Adolescents in Need*, London: BAAF.

Barnes, A. (2007) 'Integrative work with children in long-term placements', *British Journal of Play Therapy*, 3: 40–51.

Barnett, L. (1995) 'What is good day care?', in J. Trowell and M. Bower, *The Emotional Needs of Young Children and their Families: Using Psychoanalytic Ideas in the Community*, London: Routledge.

Bateson, G. (1973) 'A theory of play and fantasy', in G. Bateson, *Steps Towards an Ecology of Mind*, London: Paladin.

Bentovim, A. (1977) 'The role of play in psycho-therapeutic work with children and their families', in B. Tizard and D. Harvey (eds), *The Biology of Play*, London: Heinemann.

Bentovim, A., Elton, A., Hildebrand, J., Tranter, M. and Vizard, E. (1988) *Child Sexual Abuse within the Family: Assessment and Treatment*, London: John Wright.

Bettelheim, B. (1976) *The Uses of Enchantment: The Meaning and Importance of Fairy Tales*, Harmondsworth: Penguin.

Bifulco A., Moran, P., Jacobs, C., Bunn, A. and Schimmenti, A. (submitted 2007) 'Insecure attachment style, childhood experience and disorder in high-risk young people'.

Binney, V. (1991) 'Relationship play therapy – improving mother–child attachments in 4–6 year olds with serious relationship difficulties', lecture to Oxford ACPP Conference on the Application of Attachment Theory and Ethology to Clinical Problems, 18 March.

Binney, N., McKnight, I. and Broughton, S. (1994) 'Relationship play therapy for attachment disturbances in 4–7 year old children', The Clinical Application of Ethology and Attachment Theory, *ACPP Occasional Paper*, 9.

Bion, W. R. (1962) *Learning from Experience*, London: Heinemann.

Black, D. (1990) 'Averting a crisis', *Social Work Today*, 15 March: 11.

Blagg, H., Hughes, J. A. and Wattam, C. (eds) (1989) *Child Sexual Abuse: Listening Hearing and Validating the Experiences of Children*, London: Longman.

Bluebond-Langer, M. (1978) *The Private Worlds of Dying Children*, Chichester: Princeton University Press.

Blunden, P. (1988) 'Diagnostic interview using family tasks', *NAPOT Newsletter*, Spring.

Boston, M. and Szur, R. (eds) (1983) *Psychotherapy with Severely Deprived Children*, London: Routledge and Kegan Paul.

Bowen, B. (1996) 'Externalising anger', *Context*, 26: 30–33.

Bowen, B. (1997) 'Stories in the context of family therapy', in K. Dwivedi, *The Therapeutic Use of Stories*, London: Routledge.

Bowen, B. and Nimmo, G. (1986) 'Going over the bridge – a practical use of metaphor and analogy', *Journal of Family Therapy*, 8, 4: 327–337.

Bowlby, J. (1969, 1982, 1973, 1980) *Attachment and Loss*: vol. 1 *Attachment*; vol. 2 *Separation, Anxiety and Anger*; vol. 3 *Loss, Sadness and Depression*, London: Tavistock, Hogarth Press and Harmondsworth: Penguin.

Bowlby J. (1988) *A Secure Base: Clinical Applications of Attachment Theory*, London: Routledge.

Boxall, M. (2002) *Nurture Groups in Schools: Principles and Practice*, London: Paul Chapman.

Bradley, C. (1999) 'Making sense of symbolic communication', in A. Hardwick and J. Woodhead, *Loving, Hating and Survival*, London: Arena/Ashgate.

Bratton, S., Ray, D., Rhine, T. and Jones, L. (2005). 'The efficacy of play therapy with children: a meta-analytic review of treatment outcomes', *Professional Psychology: Research and Practice*, 36, 4: 376–390.

Bray, M. (1988) *Monsters and Rainbows*, Everyman Programme, BBC video.

Bray, M. (1989) *Susie and the Wise Hedgehog Go to Court*, London: Hawkesmere.

Bray, M. (1991) *Poppies on the Rubbish Heap – Sexual Abuse: the Child's Voice*, Edinburgh: Canongate.

Brazelton, T. and Cramer, B. (1991) *The Earliest Relationship*, London: Karnac.

Bretherton, I., Ridgeway, D. and Cassidy, J. (1990) 'Assessing internal working models of the attachment relationship', in M. Greenberg, D. Cichetti and E. Cummings (eds), *Attachment in the Pre-school Years*, Chicago: University of Chicago Press.

Brodzinsky, D., Singer, L. and Brabb, A. (1984) 'Children's understanding of adoption', quoted in A. Burnell (1990) 'Explaining adoption to children who have been adopted', Post Adoption Centre Discussion Paper 3, January.

Brummer, N. (1986) 'White social workers, black children: issues of identity', in S. Ahmed, J. Cheetham and J. Small (eds), *Social Work with Black Children and their Families*, London: Batsford/BAAF.

Bruner, J. (ed.) (1966) *Studies in Cognitive Growth*, New York: Wiley.

Bruner, J. (1983) 'The functions of play', address to the Pre-school Playgroups Association Conference at Llandudno, in *Contact*, December.

Bruner, J. S., Jolly, A. and Sylva, K. (eds) (1976) *Play: Its Role in Development and Evolution*, Harmondsworth: Penguin.

Bundy, A., Lane, S., Fisher, A. and Murray, E., Lane, S. (2002) *Sensory Integration: Theory and Practice*, Philadelphia: FA Davis.

Burnell, A. (1990) 'Explaining adoption to children who have been adopted: how do we find the right words?' Post Adoption Centre Discussion Paper 3, January.

Byng-Hall, J. (1995) *Re-Writing Family Scripts: Improvisation and Systems Change*, New York: Guilford Press.

Cairns, K. (2006) *Attachment, Trauma and Resilience: Therapeutic Caring for Children*, London: BAAF.

Calam, R. *et al.* (2006) *In My Shoes*, computer package (www.childandfamily training.org.uk).

Camis, J. (2001) *My Life and Me*, London: BAAF.

Canham, H. and Emanuel, L. (2000) 'Tied together feelings – group psychotherapy with latency children: the process of forming a cohesive group', *Journal of Child Psychotherapy*, 26, 2: 281–302.

Cant, D. (2002) ' "Joined-up psychotherapy": the place of individual psychotherapy in residential provision for children', *Journal of Child Psychotherapy*, 28, 3: 267–281.

Cant, D. (2005) ' "Only connect" – a sexually abused girl's rediscovery of memory and meaning as she works from the transition from a therapeutic community to a foster family', *Journal of Child Psychotherapy*, 31, 1: 6–23.

Carroll, J. (1998) *Introduction to Therapeutic Play*, Oxford: Blackwell.

Carroll, J. (2002) 'Play therapy: the children's views', *Child and Family Social Work*, 7: 177–187.

Case, C. and Dalley, T. (eds) (1990) *Working with Children in Art Therapy*, London: Routledge.

Cattanach, A. (1992) *Play Therapy with Abused Children*, London: Jessica Kingsley Publishers.

Cattanach, A. (1997) *Children's Stories in Play Therapy*, London: Jessica Kingsley Publishers.

Catholic Children's Society (1983) *Finding Out about Me*, Purley: CCS.

Chambers, C., Funge, S., Harris, G. and Williams, C. (1996) *Celebrating Identity: A Resource Manual for Practitioners with Black and Mixed Parentage Children*, Stoke-on-Trent: Trentham Books.

Chodorow, J. (1991) *Dance Therapy and Depth Psychology: The Moving Imagination*, London: Routledge.

Cipolla, J., McGown, D. and Yanulis, M. (1992) *Communicating through Play*, London: BAAF.

Cockerill, H. (1992) *Communication Through Play: Non-directive Communication Therapy 'Special Times'*, London: Cheyne Centre.

Cockett, M. and Tripp, J. (1994) 'Children living in re-ordered families', *Social Policy Research Findings*, 45.

Cohen, D. (1987) *The Development of Play*, London: Croom Helm.

Connor, T., Sclare, I., Dunbar, D. and Elliffe, J. (1985) 'Making a life story book', *Adoption and Fostering*, 9, 2: 32–46.

Copley, B. and Forryan, B. (1987/1997) *Therapeutic Work with Young Children*, Edinburgh: Robert Royce/London: Cassell.

Couper, D. (2000) 'The impact of the sexually abused child's pain on the worker and the team', *Journal of Social Work Practice*, 14, 1: 9–16.

Crittenden, P.M. (2000) *The Organization of Attachment Relationships: Maturation, Culture and Change*, Cambridge: Cambridge University Press.

Crittenden, P.M. 'Care Index' (www.patcrittenden.com).

Crompton, M. (1980) *Respecting Children: Social Work with Young People*, London: Arnold.

Crowe, B. (1974) *Playgroup Activities*, London: Pre-school Playgroups Association.

Crowe, B. (1980) *Living with a Toddler*, London: George Allen and Unwin.

Crowe, B. (1983) *Play Is A Feeling*, London: George Allen and Unwin.

Dale, F. (1983) 'The body as bondage: work with two children with physical handicaps', *Journal of Child Psychotherapy*, 9, 1.

Dare, C. and Lindsey, C. (1979) 'Children in family therapy', *Journal of Family Therapy*, 1: 253–269.

Dartington, T., Henry, G. and Menzies-Lyth, I. (1976) *The Psychological Welfare of Young Children Making Long Stays in Hospital*, London: Tavistock Institute.

Daws, D. and Boston, M. (eds) (1977) *The Child Psychotherapist and Problems of Young People*, London: Wildwood House.

Dearling, A. and Armstrong, H. (1994) *The New Youth Games Book*, London: Russell House.

Deco, S. (1990) 'A family centre: a structural family therapy approach', in C. Case and T. Dalley (eds), *Working with Children in Art Therapy*, London: Routledge.

DOH (2003) *The National Service Framework for Children and Young People and Maternity Services – Standard for Hospital Services*, London: HMSO.

Dockar-Drysdale, B. (1968) *Therapy in Child Care*, London: Longman.

Dockar-Drysdale, B. (1990) *The Provision of Primary Experience: Winnicottian Work with Children and Adolescents*, London: Free Association Books.

Dockar-Drysdale, B. (1993) *Therapy and Consultation in Child Care*, London: Free Association Books.

Donaldson, M. (1978) *Children's Minds*, London: Fontana.

Dorfman, E. (1951) 'Play therapy', in C. Rogers, *Client-Centred Therapy*, Boston: Houghton Mifflin.

Douglas, G., Murch, M., Robinson, M. and Scanlon, L. (2001) 'Children's perspectives and experience of the divorce process', *Family Law*, 31: 373–377.

Doyle, C. (1987) 'Helping the child victims of sexual abuse through play', *Practice*, 1, 1: 27–38.

Doyle, C. (1990) *Working with Abused Children*, London: Macmillan.

Dunn, J. and Kendrick, C. (1982) *Siblings: Love, Envy and Understanding*, Oxford: Blackwell.

Dwivedi, N. (ed.) (1993) *Groupwork with Children and Adolescents*, London: Jessica Kingsley Publishers.

Dwivedi, N. (ed.) (1997) *The Therapeutic Use of Stories*, London: Routledge.

Dwivedi, N. and Varma, V. (1996) *Meeting the Needs of Ethnic Minority Children*, London: Jessica Kingsley Publishers.

Dyke, S. (1984) 'Letting go: a psychotherapist's view of endings', *Maladjustment and Therapeutic Education*, 2, 1: 52–63.

Dyregrov, A. (1991) *Grief in Children: A Handbook for Adults*, London: Jessica Kingsley Publishers.

Eaker, B. (1986) 'Unlocking the family secret in family play therapy', *Child and Adolescent Social Work*, 3, 4: 235–253.

Eichenbaum, L. and Orbach, S. (1983) *Understanding Women*, Harmondsworth: Penguin.

Erikson, E. H. (1965) *Childhood and Society*, New York: Norton/Harmondsworth: Penguin.

Erikson, E. H. (1976) 'Play and actuality', in J. Bruner, A. Jolly and K. Sylva, *Play – Its Role in Development and Evolution*, Harmondsworth: Penguin.

Fahlberg, V. (1988) *Fitting the Pieces Together*, London: Batsford/BAAF.

Farnfield, S. (1997a) *'Can you tell me?' Some Useful Approaches to Eliciting Children's Views* and *Guide to Using 'Can You Tell Me?'*, Reading, University of Reading.

Farnfield, S. (1997b) *Phantasy and Symbol Formation: An Introduction to the Work of Melanie Klein*, Reading: University of Reading.

Farnfield, S. (2001) 'Assessment and implications for intervention using an attachment perspective', in L. McMahon and A. Ward, *Helping Families in Family Centres: Working at Therapeutic Practice*, London: Jessica Kingsley Publishers.

Ferenczi, S. (1984) 'Confusion of tongues between adults and the child', in J. Masson *Freud: The Assault on Truth*, London: Faber.

Ferguson, H. (2005) 'Working with violence, the emotions and the psycho-social dynamics of child protection: reflections on the Victoria Climbié case', *Social Work Education*, 24, 7: 781–795.

Feynman, R. P. (1985) *Surely You're Joking, Mr Feynman*, London and New York: Norton.

Fonagy, P. (1996) 'Attachment and theory of mind: overlapping constructs?', address to ACPP, London, 26 June.

Fonagy, P. (2001) *Psychoanalysis and Attachment Theory*, London: Karnac.

Fonagy, P., Steele, H., Steele, M., Higgitt, A. and Target, M. (1994) 'The theory and practice of resilience', *Journal of Child Psychology and Psychiatry*, 35, 2: 231–257.

Forehand, R. and McMahon, R. (1981) *Helping the Non-Compliant Child: A Clinician's Guide to Parent Training*, New York: Guilford Press.

Fraiberg, S. (1959) *The Magic Years*, New York: Scribners.

Fraiberg, S. (1980) *Clinical Studies in Infant Mental Health*, London: Tavistock.

Freud, A. (1936) *The Ego and the Mechanisms of Defence*, London: Hogarth Press.

Freud, A. (1965) *Normality and Pathology in Childhood*, Harmondsworth: Penguin.

Fundudis, T. (1989) 'Children's memory and the assessment of possible sexual abuse – annotation', *Journal of Child Psychology and Psychiatry*, 30, 3: 337–346.

Gardner, D. (1981) 'Mutual story-telling technique', in C. Schaefer (ed.), *The Therapeutic Use of Child's Play*, New York: Jason Aronson.

Garvey, C. (1977) *Play*, London: Fontana.

Garwood, F. (1989) *Children in Conciliation*, Edinburgh: Scottish Association of Family Conciliation Services.

George, C., Kaplan, N. and Main, M. (1985) *Adult Attachment Interview*, Berkeley: University of California.

Gerhardt, S. (2004) *Why Love Matters: How Affection Shapes a Baby's Brain*, London: Routledge.

Gersie, A. (1990) *Storymaking in Education and Therapy*, London: Jessica Kingsley Publishers.

Gersie, A. (1991) *Storymaking in Bereavement*, London: Jessica Kingsley Publishers.

Gibran, Kahlil (1972) *The Prophet*, London: Heinemann.

Gil, E. (1991) *The Healing Power of Play – Working with Abused Children*, New York: Guilford Press.

Gil, E. (1994) *Play in Family Therapy*, New York: Guilford Press.

Gil, E. (2000) *Cultural Competence in Play Therapy*, New York: Guilford Press.

Gillespie, A. (1986) 'Art therapy at the Family Makers project', *Adoption and Fostering*, 10: 1.

Glaser, D. and Frosh, S. (1988) *Child Sexual Abuse*, Basingstoke: Macmillan/BASW.

Goddard Blythe, S. (2004) *The Well Balanced Child: Movement and Early Learning*, Stroud: Hawthorn Press.

Golding, W. (1954) *Lord of the Flies*, London: Faber and Faber.

Goldschmeid, E. (1986) *Infants at Work: Babies of 6–9 Months Exploring Everyday Objects*, video/DVD and leaflet, London: National Children's Bureau.

Goldschmeid, E. (1992) *Heuristic Play with Objects: Children of 12–20 Months Exploring Everyday Objects*, video/DVD and leaflet, London: National Children's Bureau.

Gordon, R. (1986) 'Working with children of separating parents', *Marriage Guidance*, Summer: 24–27.

Gunaratnam, Y., Bremner, L., Pollack, L. and Weir, G. (1998) 'Anti-discrimination, emotions and professional practice', *European Journal of Palliative Care*, 5, 4: 122–124.

Hardwick, A. and Woodhead, J. (1999) *Loving, Hating and Survival: A Handbook for All who Work with Troubled Children and Young People*. London: Ashgate/Arena.

Harold, G. and Murch, M. (2005) 'Interparental conflict and children's adaptations to separation and divorce', *Children and Family Law Quarterly*, 17: 2.

Harper, J. (1996) 'Recapturing the past: alternative methods of life story work in adoption and fostering', *Adoption and Fostering*, 20, 3: 21–28.

Harris Hendricks, J., Black, D. and Kaplan, T. (1993) *When Father Kills Mother: Guiding Children Through Trauma and Grief*, London: Routledge.

Hart, A. and Luckock, B. (2004) *Developing Adoption Support and Therapy*, London: Jessica Kingsley Publishers.

Harvey, S. (1984) 'Training the hospital play specialist', *Early Child Development and Care*, 17: 277–290.

Harvey, S. (1987) 'Value of hospitalized children's artwork', *Journal of National Association of Hospital Play Staff*, 2: 3–8.

Harvey, S. and Hales-Tooke, A. (1972) *Play in Hospital*, London: Faber.

Hawkins, P. and Shoet, R. (2006) *Supervision in the Helping Professions*, Maidenhead: Open University Press.

Haworth, M. (ed.) (1964) *Child Psychotherapy*, New York, Basic Books.

Hay, J., Leheup, R. and Almudevar, M. (1995) 'Family therapy with "invisible families"', *British Journal of Social Work*, 68: 125–133.

Hemmings, P. (1989) 'The game which helps children come to terms with death', *Barnados Today*, 5.

Hemmings, P. (1990) 'Dealing with death', *Community Care*, 809: 16–17.

Hemmings, P. (1992) 'Direct work techniques with bereaved children: a thematic approach', in C. Kaplan (ed.), *Bereaved Children*, London: ACAMH.

Hemmings, P. (1995) 'Social work intervention with bereaved children', *Journal of Social Work Practice*, 9, 2: 109–130.

Hendry, E. (1988) 'Play-based work with very young children', *Journal of Social Work Practice*, 3, 2: 1–9.

Hinshelwood, R. and Skogstad, W. (2000) *Observing Organisations: Anxiety, Defence and Culture in Health Care*, London: Routledge.

Hodges, J., Steele, M., Hillman, S. and Henderson, K. (2003) 'Mental representations and defences in severely maltreated children', in R. Emde, D. Wolf and D. Oppenheim, (eds), *Revealing the Inner Worlds of Young Children: The MacArthur Story Stem Battery and Parent-Child Narratives*, New York: Oxford University Press.

Hogan, S. and Pennells, M. (1997) 'Separation, loss and bereavement', in N. Dwivedi (ed.), *The Therapeutic Use of Stories*, London: Routledge

Holody, R. and Maher, S. (1996) 'Using lifebooks with children in family foster care: a here-and-now process model', *Child Welfare*, 75, 4: 321–397.

Holmes, J. (1996) *Attachment, Intimacy and Autonomy*, London: Routledge

Hopkins, J. (1992) 'Parent–infant psychotherapy', *Journal of Child Psychotherapy*, 18, 1: 5–17.

Howard, J. and Shepherd, G. (1987) *Conciliation, Children and Divorce – A Family Systems Approach*, London: Batsford.

Hoxter, S. (1977) 'Play and communication', in M. Boston and D. Daws (eds), *The Child Psychotherapist and Problems of Young People*, London: Wildwood House.

Hoxter, S. (1983) 'Some feelings aroused in working with severely deprived children', in M. Boston and R. Szur, *Psychotherapy with Severely Deprived Children*, London: Routledge and Kegan Paul.

Hughes, D. (2000) *Facilitating Developmental Attachment: The Road to Emotional*

Recovery and Behavioral Change in Foster and Adopted Children, Washington: Jason Aronson.

Huizinga, J. (1949) *Homo Ludens: A Study of the Play Element in Culture*, London: Routledge and Kegan Paul.

Hunter, M. (1986) 'The monster and the ballet dancer', *Journal of Child Psychotherapy*, 12: 2.

Hunter, M. (1991) 'Psychotherapy with two children in local authority care', in R. Szur and S. Miller, *Extending Horizons*, London: Karnac.

Hunter, M. (1993) 'Emotional needs of children in care: an overview', *ACPP Review and Newsletter*, 15, 5: 214–218.

Hunter, M. (2001) *Lost and Found: Psychotherapy with Young People in Care*, London: Routledge.

Hutton, D. (2004a) 'Storytelling and its application in on-directive play therapy', *British Journal of Play Therapy*, 1, 1: 5–15.

Hutton, D. (2004b) 'Filial therapy: shifting the balance', *Clinical Child Psychology and Psychiatry*, 9, 2: 261–270.

Ironside, L. (2004) 'Living a provisional existence: thinking about foster carers and the emotional containment of children placed in their care', *Adoption and Fostering*, 28: 4.

Isaacs, S. (1933) *Social Development in Young Children*, London: Routledge and Kegan Paul.

Ixer, G. (1988) 'Life story books can damage your health', *Social Work Today*, 18 August: 26.

Jäger, J. and Ryan, V. (2007) 'Evaluating clinical practice: using play based techniques to elicit children's views of therapy', *Clinical Child Psychology and Psychiatry*, 12, 2: 1–14.

James, B. (1989) *Treating Traumatized Children*, Toronto: Lexington.

Jaques, P. (1987) *Understanding Children's Problems*, London: George Allen and Unwin.

Jefferies, B. and Gillespie, A. (1981) 'Art therapy with the emotionally frozen', *Adoption and Fostering*, 106, 4: 9–15.

Jenkins, A. (1989) 'NEWPIN – a lifeline', BBC Horizon programme, 19 June.

Jennings, S. (1992) *Dramatherapy Theory and Practice*, London: Routledge.

Jennings, S. (1993) *Play Therapy with Children: A Practitioner's Guide*, Oxford: Blackwell.

Jennings, S. (1999) *Introduction to Developmental Playtherapy*, London: Jessica Kingsley Publishers.

Jernberg, A. and Booth, P. (1999) *Theraplay: Helping Parents and Children Build Better Relationships through Attachment-based play*, San Francisco: Jossey-Bass.

Jewett, C. (1994) *Helping Children Cope with Separation and Loss*, London: Batsford/ BAAF.

Josefi, O. and Ryan, V. (2004) 'Non-directive play therapy for young children with autism: a case study', *Clinical Child Psychology and Psychiatry*, 9, 1: 75–87.

Judd, D. (1989) *Give Sorrow Words: Working with a Dying Child*, London, Free Association Books.

Jung, C. (1964) *Man and His Symbols*, London: Picador.

Kalff, D. (1980) *Sand Play: A Psychotherapeutic Approach to the Psyche*, Boston: Sigo.

Kanter, J. (2004) *Face to Face with Children: The Life and Work of Clare Winnicott*, London: Karnac.

Kegerreis, S. (1995) 'Getting better makes it worse: obstacles to improvement in children with emotional and behavioural difficulties', in J. Trowell and M. Bower (eds), *The Emotional Needs of Young Children and their Families*, London: Routledge.

Kerr, A., Gregory, E., Howard, S. and Hudson, F. (1990) *On Behalf of the Child – The Work of the Guardian Ad Litem*, Birmingham: BASW, Venture Press.

King, P. (1988) *Talking Pictures*, London: BAAF.

King, R. (1988) 'Hospital play specialist on a bone marrow unit', *Journal of the National Association of Hospital Play Staff*, 4: 11–13.

Klass, D., Silverman, P. and Nickman, S. (eds) (1996) *Continuing Bonds: New Understandings of Grief*, Washington: Taylor and Francis.

Klein, M. (1937) *The Psychoanalysis of Children*, London: Hogarth Press.

Klein, M. (1986) 'The psychoanalytic play technique', in J. Mitchell, *The Selected Melanie Klein*, Harmondsworth: Penguin.

Krasner, S. M. and Beinart, H. (1989) 'The Monday group: a brief intervention with the siblings of infants who died from sudden infant death syndrome (SIDS)', *Association of Child Psychology and Psychiatry Newsletter*, 11, 4: 11–17.

Kroll, B. (1994) *Chasing Rainbows: Children, Divorce and Loss*, Lyme Regis: Russell House.

Kubler-Ross, E. (1970) *On Death and Dying*, London: Tavistock.

Landreth, G. (2002) *Play Therapy: The Art of the Relationship*, 2nd edn, New York: Routledge.

Lansdown, R. (1988) 'Helping children cope with needles', *Journal of the National Association of Hospital Play Staff*, 3: 13–16.

Lansdown, R. (1996) *Children in hospital: a guide for family and careers*, Oxford: Oxford University Press.

Lansdown, R. and Goldman, A. (1988) 'The psychological care of children with malignant disease', *Journal of Child Psychology and Psychiatry*, 29, 5: 555–567.

Lanyado, M. (1991) 'On creating a psychotherapeutic space', *Journal of Social Work Practice*, 5, 1: 31–40.

Lanyado, M. (1999a) 'The treatment of traumatisation in children', in M. Lanyado and A. Horne, *The Handbook of Child and Adolescent Psychotherapy: Psychoanalytic Approaches*, London: Routledge.

Lanyado, M. (1999b) 'Holding on and letting go: some thoughts about the process of ending therapy', *Journal of Child Psychotherapy*, 25, 3: 357–518.

Lanyado, M. (2004) *The Presence of the Therapist*, London: Routledge.

Lanyado, M. and Horne, A. (1999) *The Handbook of Child and Adolescent Psychotherapy: Psychoanalytic Approaches*, London: Routledge.

Lanyado, M. and Horne, A. (2006) *A Question of Technique: Independent Psychoanalytic Approaches with Children and Adolescents*, London: Routledge.

Lilley, R. (2001) 'Case studies of opportunity led work in the public arena', in L. McMahon and A. Ward, *Helping Families in Family Centres: Working at Therapeutic Practice*, London: Jessica Kingsley Publishers.

Lindquist, I. (1977) *Therapy through Play*, London: Arlington Books.

Longhorn, F. (1988) *A Sensory Curriculum for Very Special People*, London: Souvenir Press.

Lowenfeld, M. (1979) *The World Technique*, London: George Allen and Unwin.

Lucas, M. (1992) 'Special things: the management of an individual provision within a group care setting for emotionally disturbed children', *Therapeutic Communities*, 13, 4: 209–219.

Lucas, M. (1993) 'Understanding and working with the symbolic communications of an eight-year-old girl in a residential setting', MA dissertation in therapeutic child care, University of Reading.

Luckock, B. and Lefevre, M. (2006) *Knowledge Review: Teaching Learning and Assessing Communication Skills with Children in Social Work Education*, London: Social Care Institute of Excellence.

Luckock, B. and Lefevre, M. (2008) *Direct Work with Children*, London: BAAF.

Lund, M. (1984) 'Research on divorce and children', *Family Law*, 14: 198–201.

McConkey, R. (1986) 'Changing beliefs about play and handicapped children', in P. K. Smith, *Children's Play*, London: Gordon and Breach.

McFerran, A. (1989) 'Rescue at hand for children of the marital storm', *Guardian*, 29 March.

Maclean, M. (2004) 'Together and apart: children and parents experiencing separation', *Findings*, 314, Joseph Rowntree Foundation.

Macliver, C. and Thom, M. (1990) *Family Talk*, London: BAAF.

McMahon, L. (1993) 'Autonomy through play', *Special Children*, November/December: 21–24.

McMahon, L. (1994) 'Responding to defences against anxiety in day care for young children', *Early Child Development and Care*, 97: 175–184.

McMahon, L. and Farnfield, S. (2004) 'Too close in or too far out: learning to hold the role of observer', *Journal of Social Work Practice*, 18, 2: 239–246.

McMahon, L. and Ward, A. (2001) *Helping Families in Family Centres: Working at Therapeutic Practice*, London: Jessica Kingsley Publishers.

Main, M., Kaplan, N. and Cassidy, J. (1985) 'Security in infancy, childhood and adulthood: a move to the level of representation', in I. Bretherton and G. Walters (eds), *Growing Points of Attachment Theory and Research*, Monograph of the Society for Research in Child Development 50, 1 and 2.

Main, M. and Soloman, J. (1990) 'Procedures for identifying infants as disorganized/disoriented during the Ainsworth Strange Situation', in M. Greenberg, D. Cichetti and E. Cummings (eds), *Attachment in the Pre-school Years*, Chicago: University of Chicago Press.

Marner, T. (1995) 'Therapeutic letters to, from and between children in family therapy', *Journal of Social Work Practice*, 9, 2: 169–176.

Martel, S. (ed.) (1981) *Direct Work with Children*, London: Bedford Square Press.

Masheder, M. (1989) *Let's Play Together – Cooperative Games*, London: Merlin Press.

Mattinson, J. (1975) *The Reflection Process in Casework Supervision*, London: Institute of Marital Studies.

Maximé, J. (1986) 'Some psychological models of black self concept', in S. Ahmed, J. Cheetham and J. Small (eds), *Social Work with Black Children and Their Families*, London: Batsford/BAAF.

Maximé, J. (1987) *Black Like Me*: workbooks 1 and 2, *Black Identity, Mixed Parentage*, Beckenham: Emani Publications.

Maximé, J. (1993) 'The therapeutic importance of racial identity in working with black children who hate', in V. Varma (ed.), *How and Why Children Hate*, London: Jessica Kingsley Publishers.

Meekums, B. (1988) *Back in Touch: Parent–Child Relationship Building through Dance*, videotape and training manual, Leeds: Leeds Family Service Unit.

Meekums, B. (2002) *Dance Movement Therapy: A Creative Psychotherapeutic Approach*, London: Sage.

Menzies-Lyth, I. (1988) *Containing Anxiety in Institutions*, vol. 1, London: Free Association Books.

Millar, S. (1968) *The Psychology of Play*, Harmondsworth: Penguin.

Miller, E. (1993) *From Dependence to Autonomy*, London: Free Association Books.

Mills, M. and Puckering C. (1995) 'Bringing about change in parent–child relationships', in J. Trowell and M. Bower, *The Emotional Needs of Young Children and their Families: Using Psychoanalytic Ideas in the Community*, London: Routledge.

Miller, L., Rustin, M., Rustin, M. and Shuttleworth, J. (eds) (1989) *Closely Observed Infants*, London: Duckworth.

Milner, D. (1983) *Children and Race: Ten Years On*, Harmondsworth: Penguin.

Minuchin, S. (1981) *Family Therapy Techniques*, Cambridge: Harvard University Press.

Mitchell, A. (1985) *Children in the Middle: Living through Divorce*, London: Tavistock.

Mitchell, J. (ed.) (1986) *The Selected Melanie Klein*, Harmondsworth: Penguin.

Moustakas, C. (1964) 'The therapeutic process', in M. Haworth, *Child Psychotherapy*, New York: Basic Books.

Muir, E., Speirs, A. and Tod, G. (1988) 'Family intervention and the facilitation of mourning in a four-year-old boy', *The Psychoanalytic Study of the Child*, 43: 367–383.

Murray, L. and Andrews, E. (2000) *The Social Baby: Understanding Babies' Communication from Birth*, London: Children's Project/ACER Press:.

Murray, L. and Cooper, P. (eds) (1997) *Post-partum Depression and Child Development*, New York: Guilford Press.

National Association of Hospital Play Staff, *Play Focus leaflets*, London: NAHSP.

New, R. (2000) 'Reggio Emilia: catalyst for change and conversation', *ERIC Digest*, 15.

Newson, E. and Hipgrave, T. (1982) *Getting Through to Your Handicapped Child*, Cambridge: Cambridge University Press.

Newson, J. and Newson, E. (1979) *Toys and Playthings in Development and Remediation*, London: George Allen and Unwin.

Newsom, E. (1992) 'The barefoot play therapist: adapting skills for a time of need', in D. Lane and A. Miller, *Child and Adolescent Psychotherapy: A Handbook*, Maidenhead: Open University Press.

Nicholls, E. (2006) *The New Life Work Model: Practice Guide*, Lyme Regis: Russell House.

Nind, M. and Hewett, D. (1996) *Access to Communication: Developing the Basics of Communication with People with Severe Learning Disability through Intensive Interaction*, London: David Fulton.

Nilman, I. and Lewin, C. (1989) 'Inhibited mourning in a latency age child', *British Journal of Psychotherapy*, 5, 4: 523–532.

Noble, E. (1967) *Play and the Sick Child*, London: Faber.

Nover, A. G. (1985) 'Mother–infant interactive play', *Journal of Child and Adolescent Social Work*, 2: 22–35.

Oaklander, V. (1978) *Windows to Our Children*, Utah: Real People Press.

Obholzer, A. and Roberts, V. (1994) *The Unconscious at Work*, London: Free Association Books.

O'Brien, A. and Loudon, P. (1985) 'Redressing the balance – involving children in family therapy', *Journal of Family Therapy*, 7: 81–98.

Opie, I. and Opie, P. (1969) *Children's Games in Street and Playground*, Oxford: Oxford University Press.

Owen, P. and Curtis, P. (1988) *Techniques for Working with Children*, Chorley: Owen and Curtis.

Parkinson, L. (1987) *Separation, Divorce and Families*, London: Macmillan.

Peake, A. (1989) *Working with Sexually Abused Children – A Resource Pack for Professionals*, London: The Children's Society.

Pearce, J. (1990) 'Case studies', *Journal of the National Association of Hospital Play Staff*, 8.

Peller, L. (1964) 'Developmental phases of play', in M. Haworth, *Child Psychotherapy*, New York: Basic Books.

Pennells, M. and Kitchener, S. (1990) 'Holding back the nightmares', *Social Work Today*, 1 March: 14–15.

Pennells, M. and Smith, S. (1999) *The Forgotten Mourners: Guidelines for Working with Bereaved Children*, London: Jessica Kingsley Publishers.

Perrin, S., Smith, P. and Yule, W. (2000) 'Practitioner review: the assessment and treatment of post-traumatic stress disorder in children and adolescents', *JCPP*, 41, 3: 277–289.

Piaget, J. (1951) *Play, Dreams and Imitation in Childhood*, London: Routledge and Kegan Paul.

Pinney, R. (1990) *Children's Hours*, Chichester: The Children's Hours Trust.

Pithers, D. (1990a) 'Expressing feelings', *Community Care*, 4 January.

Pithers, D. (1990b) 'Stranger than fiction', *Social Work Today*, 22, 6: 20–21.

Prescott, E. and Jones, E. (1975) *Assessment of Child Rearing Environments: An Ecological Approach*, Pasadena, CA: Pacific Oaks College.

Prestage, R. O. (1972) 'Life for Kim', in E. Holgate, *Communicating with Children*, Harlow: Longman.

Prevezer, W. (1990) 'Strategies for tuning in to autism', *Therapy Weekly*, 18 October.

Puckering, C., Evans, J., Maddox, H., Mills, M. and Cox, A. (1996) 'Taking control: a single case study of mellow parenting', *Clinical Child Psychology and Psychiatry*, 1, 4: 539–550.

Quinton, D. et al. (1998) *Joining New Families*, Chichester: Wiley.

Raphael, B. (1983) *An Anatomy of Bereavement*, London: Hutchinson.

Redgrave, K. (1987) *Child's Play – Direct Work with the Deprived Child*, Cheadle: Boys' and Girls' Welfare Society.

Redgrave, K. (2000) *Care-Therapy for Children*, Poole: Continuum.

Redl, F. (1966) *When We Deal with Children*, New York: Free Press.

Redl, F. and Wineman, D. (1965) *Controls from Within*, New York: Free Press.

Regan, S. and Young, J. (1990) 'Siblings in groups: children of separated/divorced parents', *Groupwork*, 3, 1: 22–35.

Richman, N., Stevenson, J. and Graham, P. (1982) *Pre-school to School: A Behavioural Study*, London: Academic Press.

Rivers, J. (2004) 'Enabling parents to become first therapists: a reflective study of parenting groups in a child and adolescent mental health service team', MA dissertation in therapeutic child care, Reading: University of Reading.

Robertson, J. (1970) *Young Children in Hospital*, London: Tavistock.

Robertson, J. and Robertson, J. (1976) *Young Children in Brief Separation*, London: Robertson Centre.

Robertson, J. and Robertson, J. (1989) *Separation and the Very Young*, London: Free Association Books.

Rogers, C. (ed.) (1951) *Client-Centred Therapy*, Boston: Houghton Mifflin.

Romaine, M. (2007) *Preparing Children for Permanence: A Guide to Understanding Direct Work for Social Workers, Foster Carers and Adoptive Parents*, London: BAAF.

Rose, M. (1990) *Healing Hurt Minds – The Peper Harrow Experience*, London: Tavistock Routledge.

Rose, R. and Philpot, T. (2005) *The Child's Own Story: Life Story Work with Traumatized Children*, London: Jessica Kingsley Publishers.

Ruch, G. (1998) 'Direct work with children – the practitioner's perspective', *Practice*, 10, 1: 35–44.

Rustin, M. and Rustin M. (1988) *Narratives of Love and Loss*, London: Verso.

Ryan, T. and Walker, R. (1985) *Making Life Story Books*, London: BAAF.

Ryan, T. and Walker, R. (2007) *Life Story Work: A Practical Guide to Helping Children Understand their Past*, London: BAAF.

Ryan, V. (2004) 'Adapting non-directive play therapy for children with attachment disorders', *Clinical Child Psychology and Psychiatry*, 9: 75–87.

Ryan, V. (2007) 'Helping children and new carers to form secure attachment relationships', *British Journal of Social Work*, 37: 643–657.

Ryan, V. and Wilson, K. (2000) *Case Studies in Non-directive Play Therapy*, London: Baillière Tindall.

Ryan, V. and Wilson, K. (2000) 'Conducting child assessments for court proceeding: the use of non-directive play therapy', *Clinical Child Psychology and Psychiatry*, 5, 2: 267–279.

Ryan, V. and Needham, N. (2001) 'Non-directive play therapy with children experiencing psychic trauma', *Clinical Child Psychology and Psychiatry*, 6, 3: 437–453.

Rye, N. (2004) 'A strange way to make a living', *Play Therapy*, 39: 16.

Rye, N. (2005) 'Filial therapy, parental separation and school refusal: a case study using an attachment perspective', *British Journal of Play Therapy*, 1, 3: 10–17.

Rye, N. (2006) 'A strange way to make a living', *Play Therapy*, 46, 14–15.

Rymaszewska, J. and Philpot, T. (2006) *Reaching the Vulnerable Child: Therapy with Traumatized Children*, London: Jessica Kingsley Publishers.

Sagar, C. (1990) 'Working with cases of child sexual abuse', in C. Case and T. Dalley (eds), *Working with Children in Art Therapy*, London: Routledge.

Sanders, J. (2006) 'Finding their feet: the development of infants' sense of self during heuristic play sessions in a children's centre', MA dissertation in therapeutic child care, Reading: University of Reading.

Satir, V. (1972) *People Making*, Palo Alto: Science and Behaviour Books.

Schore, A. (1994) *Affect Regulation and the Origin of the Self: The Neurobiology of Emotional Development*, Mahwah, NJ: Lawrence Erlbaum Associates, Inc.

Schore, A. (2003) *Affect Dysregulation and Disorders of the Self*, New York: Norton.

Seeney, J. (2007) *Morris and the Bundle of Worries, with My Book of Worries*, London: BAAF.

Sendak, M. (1963/7) *Where the Wild Things Are*, London: Bodley Head.

Shephard, M. (1989) *Music Is Child's Play*, London: Longman.

Sherborne, V. (1990) *Developmental Movement for Children: Mainstream, Special Needs and Pre-school*, Cambridge: Cambridge University Press.

Sheridan, M., Cockerill, H. and Sharma, A. (2007) *From Birth to Five Years – Children's Developmental Progress*, third edn, London: Routledge.

Silveira, W. R., Trafford G. and Musgrave, R. (1988) *Children Need Groups*, Aberdeen: University Press.

Sinason, V. (1988) 'Dolls and bears: from symbolic equation to symbol', *British Journal of Psychotherapy*, 4, 4: 349–363.

Sinason, V. (1990) 'The heart torn out of teddy', *Guardian*, 23 June.

Sinason, V. (1992) *Mental Handicap and the Human Condition: New Approaches from the Tavistock*, London: Free Association Books.

Sinclair, I., Wilson, K. and Gibbs, I. (2005) *Foster Placements: Why They Succeed and Why They Fail*, London: Jessica Kingsley Publishers.

Skynner, R. and Cleese, J. (1983) *Families and How to Survive Them*, London: Methuen.

Sluckin, A. (1989) 'The house-tree-person test', *Changes*, 6, 4: 128–131.

Smith, S. and Pennells, M. (eds) (1995) *Interventions with Bereaved Children*, London: Jessica Kingsley Publishers.

Stacey, P. (2002) 'How can you helpfully use relationships in social work with children and their families?', MA dissertation in therapeutic child care, Reading: University of Reading.

Stern, D. (1985) *The Interpersonal World of the Infant*, New York: Basic Books.

Stern, D. (1997) *The Motherhood Constellation*, New York: Basic Books.

Striker, S. and Kimmel, E. (1978) *The Anti-Colouring Book*, London: Hippo Books.

Stroebe, W. and Schut, H. (1999) 'The dual process model of coping with bereavement', *Death Studies*, 23: 197–224.

Sunderland, M. and Englehart, P. (1993) *Draw on Your Emotions*, Buckingham: Winslow Press.

Sylva, K. and Stein, A. (1990) 'Effects of hospitalization on children', *Association for Child Psychology and Psychiatry Newsletter*, 12, 1: 3–8.

Szur, R. and Miller, S. (eds) (1991) *Extending Horizons: Psychoanalytic Psychotherapy with Children, Adolescents and Families*, London: Karnac.

Thom, M. (1984) 'Working with children: the Violet Oaklander approach', *Adoption and Fostering*, 8, 3: 34–35.

Thomas, C., Beckford, V., Lowe, N. and Murch, M. (1999) *Adopted Children Speaking*, London: BAAF.

Thomas, L. (1999) 'Communicating with a black child: overcoming obstacles to difference', in P. Milner and B. Carolin (eds), *Time to Listen to Children*, London: Routledge.

Tod, R. (ed.) (1968) *Disturbed Children*, London: Longman.

Tomlinson, P. (2004) *Therapeutic Approaches in Work with Traumatized Children and Young People*, London: Jessica Kingsley Publishers.

Truax, C. B. and Carkhuff, R. R. (1967) *Towards Effective Counselling and Psychotherapy*, Chicago: Aldine.

Ulloa, M. (2006) ' "It's better just to go": an exploratory study of the anxieties and defences related to the quality of the attachment relationship in a pre-school setting', MA dissertation in therapeutic child care, Reading: University of Reading.

Valentine, C. W. (1956) *The Normal Child and some of his Abnormalities*, Harmondsworth: Penguin.

Van Fleet, R. (2005) *Filial Therapy: Strengthening Parent–Child Relationships Through Play*, 2nd edn, Sarasota, FL: Professional Resource Press.

Van Fleet, R. and Guerney, L. (2003) *Casebook of Filial Therapy*, Boiling Springs, PA: Play Therapy Press.

Waddell, M. (2000) *Inside Lives: Psychoanalysis and the Growth of the Personality*, London: Duckworth Press.

Walczak Y. and Burns, S. (1984) *Divorce: The Child's Point of View*, London: Harper and Row.

Wallerstein, J. and Kelly, J. B. (1980) *Surviving the Breakup*, London: Grant McIntyre.

Ward, A. (2001) 'Theory for practice in therapeutic family centres', in L. McMahon and A. Ward, *Helping Families in Family Centres*, London: Jessica Kingsley Publishers.

Ward, A. (2007) *Working in Group Care: Social Work and Social Care in Residential and Day Care Settings*, Bristol: The Policy Press.

Ward, A. and McMahon, L. (1998) *Intuition Is Not Enough: Matching Theory with Practice in Therapeutic Child Care*, London: Routledge.

Ward, B. (1995) *Good Grief: Exploring Feelings, Loss and Death with Under Elevens, a Holistic Approach*, London: Jessica Kingsley Publishers.

Waterhouse, S. (1987) *Time for Me – A Resource Book to Help Guardians Ad Litem*, Byfield: Daventry.

Waters, E., Weinfield, N. and Hamilton, C. (2000) 'The stability of attachment security from infancy to adolescence and early adulthood: general discussion', *Child Development*, 71, 3: 703–706.

Webster-Stratton, C. (1987) *Parents and Children: A 10 Program Videotape Parent Training Series with Manuals*, Eugene, OR: Castalia Press.

Weinstein, J. (1987) 'Working with sexually abused children – a response to the article by Celia Doyle', *Practice*, 3: 283–286.

Weller, B. and Oliver, G. (1980) *Helping Sick Children Play*, London: Baillière Tindall.

West, J. (1983) 'Play therapy with Rosy', *British Journal of Social Work*, 13, 6: 645–661.

West, J. (1984) 'Ending or beginning?', *Changes*, 2: 80–84.

West, J. (1996) *Child Centred Play Therapy*, 2nd edn, London: Arnold.

White, M. and Epston, D. (1989) *Literate Means to Therapeutic Ends*, Melbourne: Dulwich Centre Publications.

Whitwell, J. (1998) 'Management issues in milieu therapy: boundaries and parameters', *Therapeutic Communities*, 119, 2: 89–105.

Whitwell, J. (2002) 'Therapeutic child care', in K. White (ed.) Re-framing Children's Services, *NCVCCO Annual Review Journal*, 3 (www.johnwhitwell.co.uk).

Wickham, R. and West, J. (2002) *Therapeutic Work with Sexually Abused Children*, London: Sage.

Wilson, K. (2006) 'Can foster carers help children in resolving their emotional and behavioural difficulties?', *Journal of Child Psychology and Psychiatry*, 11, 4: 495–511.

Wilson, K. and Ryan, V. (2005) *Play Therapy: A Non-directive Approach for Children and Adolescents*, 2nd edn, London: Baillière Tindall/Elsevier.

Wilson, P. (2006) 'Trauma', address at Mulberry Bush School AGM, May.

Winnicott, C. (1964) *Child Care and Social Work*, Welwyn: Codicote Press.

Winnicott, C. (1968) 'Communicating with children', in R. J. N. Tod (ed.), *Disturbed Children*, London: Longman.

Winnicott, D. W. (1964) *The Child, the Family, and the Outside World*, Harmondsworth: Penguin.

Winnicott, D. W. (1965) *The Maturational Processes and the Facilitating Environment*, London: Hogarth Press.

Winnicott, D. W. (1971) *Playing and Reality*, London: Tavistock.

Winnicott, D. W. (1980) *The Piggle: An Account of the Psychoanalytic Treatment of a Little Girl*, Harmondsworth: Penguin.

Wood, A. (1988) 'King Tiger and the Roaring Tummies: a novel way of helping young children and their families change', *Journal of Family Therapy*, 10, 1: 49–63.

Worden, J. W. (1991) *Grief Counselling and Grief Therapy*, London: Tavistock.

Wright, J., Binney, V. and Smith, P. (1995) 'Security of attachment in 8–12 year-olds: a revised version of the Separation Anxiety Test, its psychometric properties and clinical interpretation, *Journal of Child Psychology and Psychiatry*, 36, 5: 757–774.

Wright, Y. (1991) 'Improving attachments through relationship building play', *NAPOT Newsletter*, Spring.

Index